DISCOVERING THE BEAUTY OF GOD

through FASTING AND PRAYER

RODICA VOLINTIRU

D0926282

DISCOVERING THE BEAUTY OF GOD

through FASTING AND PRAYER

RODICA VOLINTIRU

SUCCEED
PUBLISHING

Originally publish in Romania under the title:
"Cunoasterea frumusetii Lui Dumnezeu prin Post si Rugaciune"
Copyright @ 2013 by Succeed Publishing, Medgidia, Romania

Discovering the Beauty of God through Fasting and Prayer

Translated from the Romanian by: Alexandra Martin

Editor: Jason Chifan

Corrector: Rodica Volintiru

Cover: Albina Kettner

Photo cover: The author in Gethsemane Garden

Email: Roda4jesus@yahoo.ca

ISBN# 978-0-9937491-0-0

Printed in the USA
Printed by: Inner Workings, Grand Rapids, Michigan

TABLE OF CONTENTS

Testimonies About The Book

First, I want to thank God for touching many people's lives through this book.

I have seen the beauty of God in many aspects of my life. My prayer for you is that the Lord will open your spiritual eyes, that you can see His beauty and glory. I pray to God for a revival in every church because the more we seek God, the more we discover the beauty of God.

Shortly after my book was published in the Romanian language, I started receiving e-mails and phone calls with testimonies from the readers. I saw the beauty of God in these testimonies. I praise God for touching those hearts. Many of these hearts were broken and in need of healing.

I want to encourage you as you read this book, for surely the Lord will touch your heart no matter who you are.

I sent this book to a friend of mine in Canada, whose Romanian mother was a devout Orthodox believer and indifferent to Christianity. My friend prayed faithfully to God for her mother to become a Christian for about four years prior to receiving the book. After her mother received the book, it changed her life. Her speech and attitude were transformed, and God wiped away her fear and loneliness. She went into the streets and told everyone what she read in the book and how God changed her life. Her daughter led her in prayer to receive the Lord Jesus as Lord and Savior. Now every time she speaks with her daughter in Canada, they talk only about the Lord. What an answer to prayer!

Another person wrote to me because she was in the valley of depression. She was constantly weeping and had no desire to live any longer. After reading the book, she said, *"I'm on the mountain with the*

Lord and I don't want to get off." Glory to God because He used this book to bring hope, freedom and joy to this woman!

Someone else wrote to me with many questions about the Bible and Christianity. I sent her the book, and after reading it she told me that she received all the answers she was searching for. God helped her understand the importance of fasting and prayer in her life.

Another sister wrote to me after receiving the book from a friend. She had many traumas in her life and she became a very angry and rebellious person. When she first received the book, she threw it to the ground, and did not want to look at it. She was still in pain from her past, and carried many emotional wounds in her life. Two days after receiving the book, on her way to the train, she heard a voice saying, *"Take the book with you!"* Without hesitation, she knew it was God and put the book in her purse. On the train she began to read the book, then suddenly the Spirit of God came upon her and she began to cry and feel the presence of God. Later she contacted me and told me about the joy and peace she had received from Jesus. At the same time she was encouraged to fast with just water for 12 days. She fasted for the first time in 16 years. Today she is filled with joy and happiness and continues to seek God every day.

A man from Spain who recently received the Lord in his heart sent me a message. He desperately needed prayer because evil spirits were taunting him. I prayed for him and then he received a copy of the book. After reading the book and beginning to pray and fast, God delivered him from the tormenting spirits. Today he is on fire for God and has shared the book with many of his friends. Two of those friends have recently given their lives to Jesus after reading the book.

Another sister was on her way to getting a divorce because her husband abandoned her. But after reading the book, she fasted 3 days, and God restored her husband back to the family.

After reading the book, a woman from Moldova fasted 10 days with just water and had visions of heaven and visions of the throne of God. During this time, she received many revelations from God and His word, and now her face radiates with peace and contagious joy from God alone.

Also, a young lady told me that she really wanted to read the book but she could not because her mother was always reading it! Her mother had read the book five times already because through it she experienced God's life and joy.

Many people who have read the book have testified, explaining that they were touched by God and had begun to cry, weep and desire more of God in their lives.

One brother who ministered in the prisons took the book to jail and, to his astonishment, many people repented. Inmates were waiting in line to read the book.

A sister who helps the homeless in Italy decided to give the book to a young homeless man who was not a Christian. When he began to read the book, he began to weep, as the Holy Spirit began to move in his heart and he desired to go to church.

A very successful intelligent woman from Germany received the book and the Lord touched her heart. She said, *"This is what I want, a true and living God who speaks even today and heals and does miracles."*

Another sister from Spain, after reading the book, wanted to get more books to give to the sisters and brothers there. I sent her 40 books, and the Lord brought revival in the church as they began to fast and draw near to God. Some of those people who read the book said, *"I've never read such a practical book that touched me and blessed me."*

A lady in Sweden, after reading the book, decided to fast 40 days only with water and with some juice. She is a nurse and almost lost her job because she did not want to go to work in this time because all she wanted to do was spend more time with God. After fasting, her heart was changed and she had great victories in her life. After the fast, she was promoted at work, and even received compensation for the days she fasted. What a great God we serve!

We have received many testimonials from people who have started to fast for the first time more than 3 days. The Lord has answered their causes and we praise Him for the victory! A sister wrote to me saying that she had fasted for 21 days, but she did not yet receive the answer that she wanted from her fast. Instead, during the fast, she received joy from God as He changed her heart.

Another sister in Romania told me that she was lonely and very unhappy with her husband. One day her husband got angry and left her with three children. In her desperation she entered a three-day fast, and after the fast her husband returned home! She said,

"The Lord revealed to me my unforgiveness towards my husband, but now I praise the Lord for transforming my heart and healing my marriage."

A girl only 10 years old began to read the book after I gave it to her mother. She was asking questions about fasting and even asked her parents for permission to fast. God was even working in the heart of this child!

Daily I receive testimonies about what God is doing through this book. The Holy Spirit is powerfully using this book because it is the proper time for revival and awakening within the hearts of people.

The Lord told me to place on the cover of this book a picture from Israel when I had an encounter with God in the Garden of Gethsemane. The Lord showed me in a vision that from the book would come out rays of light like a laser, and those rays will enter the hearts of those who read the book. Then the Lord said to me, *"Many who read this book will be touched by God. But even more blessed is the one who applies this book into their lives; those lives will really be changed, blessed and transformed."*

Those who have tasted the beauty of the fasting and prayer, even through suffering many struggles, have said that they can hardly wait to fast another 7, 10, 21, or 40 days. Truly God will transform your life if you choose this path of humility, of prayer and of fasting.

So you, who have already started reading this book, get ready. The Lord is here and wants to talk to you. He wants to heal you. He wants to answer your questions. The Lord wants to release you and fill you with His love. Believe that He wants to give you power to be used in your home, your church and your nation. Daniel 11:32 says, *"Those who know God will do great exploits."*

When you get to know Him, you will be strengthened in your faith, and surely the Lord will raise you to another spiritual level of prayer. You will be filled with passion and love for Him and the lost.

You will experience His miracles.

Preface

I started writing this book because the Lord urged me to. Many other brothers and sisters in Christ had received similar promptings from the Lord for me to write this book. They encouraged me to put my testimony on paper, along with my experiences with the Lord. They urged me to write about the way He changed my life, how He called me in the ministry and how it's all about His glory.

The sole purpose for writing this book was for the glory of our Lord Jesus, who loved me so much that He has given Himself as sacrifice for me, as well as to strengthen and bless the readers of this book.

I give thanks to my husband Marian, who loves me and whom I enormously love. I am grateful for all his help, sacrificing many things so that this book could be published. I could not be involved to this extent in the ministry without his support.

I want to give a heartfelt thanks to my beautiful children Richard, Paul, Deborah and Grace because they were understanding and kind when I was busy or away. They are so special and set apart for God! I truly believe that God has great plans to use them as well. They encouraged and supported me in love, in fasting and in prayer.

I want to thank all the brothers and sisters throughout the world that supported us spiritually and financially.

I am thankful to God for my church, Westwood Community Church, Canada, and for the pastors that blessed and helped us, not only by prayer but financially as well.

I want the blessing of the Lord Jesus to be upon everyone.

It is wonderful that we are all members of the Body of Christ and that we can work together for God's glory and for the extension of His Kingdom.

The Cover Page: In The Garden Of Gethsemane

In 2005, by the grace of Jesus Christ I visited Israel with my church. I was so thirsty for a genuine encounter with Him, and my prayer was that He would reveal Himself to me during this trip.

I had many wonderful experiences there, but I want to tell you one that deeply marked my life. The cover image of this book pictures this very experience I had with Jesus in Israel.

The Bible tells us that Jesus went alone in the garden of Gethsemane to pray. There is a rock today where supposedly Jesus had cried on. A church was erected on it, named Basilica of Agony. When I visited the garden, I was astonished by what I saw. I asked my friend who was with me to take a picture of me near that rock. The moment I knelt and touched the rock, I felt a divine power which touched me so deeply that I felt as if I was transported to the time of Jesus' crucifixion. Suddenly I saw Jesus carrying His cross on His back. When I saw His suffering, I turned to Him and I asked Him, *"Lord, You are carrying my cross? I deserve it, I have sinned, and I have saddened You. Jesus, let me carry it!"*

I snuck under the cross so that we would both carry it.

At the same time, I would hear the crowds and the Pharisees shrieking and shouting, *"Crucify Him, crucify Him!"* I felt and I saw the hatred of the enemy against the Lord Jesus, which manifested through those people. Then I received the understanding of Christ's great suffering, because He knew the kind of death He would suffer. I felt His pain. The Lord allowed me in His kindness to partake in His sufferings.

Then Jesus, with teary eyes, but filled with perfect love, told me, *"My daughter, go and tell all people how much I love them, because they don't fully understand how great My love is for them, and how much I suffered for* them." After Jesus pointed to me and commissioned me, *"Go, tell all people about My love and My suffering for them."*

His voice was so sweet, so profound and so deep that it would drew me like a magnet. It was pure and powerful. Even today, this voice is alive in me.

Suddenly, the scene changed. I felt that I was brought into the glory of the heavenly Father, into a glory that cannot be expressed through words. An angel with a large scroll appeared before me. I wasn't capable of reading it. I was astonished by the splendors of the heavens and I was curious why the Lord had brought me there.

However, to my dissatisfaction, exactly when I tried to read the scroll to understand what it said, someone tapped my shoulder because it was time to get going with the group. I shouted *"No!"* but it was too late. It was exactly noon, and everyone was asked to leave.

In the meantime, I was weeping so much that the rock on which Lord Jesus cried on was wet with my tears. I can never forget all the suffering and love I experienced back then in the Garden of Gethsemane.

From that moment, my life was completely changed. The image of the cross and that of the Lord's sufferings remained vivid in my heart. I understood the Lord's mandate, that of bringing the news of His love and His suffering. My part is to intercede for the world.

The Lord gave me the grace of interceding with love and with tears for all those who are suffering and He has sent me to announce His love and power of the Cross.

These encounters with the Lord remain truly valuable for my soul.

My aim is to know Him and to discover His beauty, in communion with the Father, the Son and the Holy Spirit.

PART I

TESTIMONY OF A
CHANGED LIFE

"I want to know Christ, yes, to know the power of His resurrection and participation in His sufferings, becoming like Him in his death."
Philippians 3:10

"Let us acknowledge the LORD;
Let us press on to know Him.
As surely as the sun rises, He will appear.
He will come to us like the winter rains,
Like the spring rains that water the earth."
Hosea 6:9

"Now this is eternal life: that they know you,
The only true God, and Jesus Christ, whom you have sent."
John 17:3

The First Years Of My Life

I was born in a Christian family in a village near Bucharest, Romania. I am the eighth child out of ten children. When I was born, my mother was not ready for another child. Unknowingly, something happened in my mother's soul and she wanted me to be dead. She barely had time for me because she was too busy with gardening, the house chores and with my other siblings. I remember her putting me in a wide wooden tray and shoving me under the bed. From time to time, my older sisters would come to check on me to see if I was asleep. I was lying in the dark and in loneliness, deprived of my mother's love. It is understandable that this kind of start in life would leave a negative imprint on the years to come.

I also understood that my mother prayed that God would take me to heaven, in other words, for me to die soon. My mother opened doors for the enemy to harass me in life from a young age. I was dealing with rejection, insecurity, inferiority, lack of acceptance, and an expectation to die at a very young age. All these negative thoughts began to root in my early years. They began to stalk me from my childhood until my young adult years.

On one hand, I remember having a beautiful childhood, but on the other hand, my negative thoughts made me feel unprotected, unloved and unwanted.

On the outside, I was a talkative, bold girl, but on the inside, I was insecure, ashamed and shy. I was without vision in life and I wanted to die. Then, when my teenage years came, I felt completely unprepared to embrace life. My parents didn't properly teach me the things I needed to know by the time I reached my teen years.

Mothers, be careful what you think and speak about your children! You can either bring blessings or curses upon the lives of the young and you will either rejoice or cry, depending on what you decide today!

Parents, never be too busy to educate your children in the truths of the Bible and life, and how to discern good from evil. More than anything, they need to feel love and acceptance.

Children continuously need to be taught about certain lessons in life before they encounter them later on. If parents don't teach their children, society will and this could be very dangerous. Your children need to know and believe that *home* is where they find comfort, compassion and acceptance regardless of their mistakes or sins. Regarding this subject, God commands the following for the people of Israel through Moses:

> *"Love the Lord your God with all your heart and with all your soul and with all your strength. These commandments that I give you today are to be on your hearts. Impress them on your children. Talk about them when you sit at home and when you walk along the road, when you lie down and when you get up. Tie them as symbols on your hands and bind them on your foreheads. Write them on the doorframes of your houses and on your gates."* (Deuteronomy 6:5-9, NIV)

I am not sharing this story to judge my parents. My desire is to help mothers nurture and develop a loving friendship with their daughters. Through this, girls will no longer hide and fear their parents, but they will come boldly and fearlessly to discuss every problem, having the certainty that they will find acceptance, approval, love and sound advice.

Looking back at my life, I realize that my parents did not know how to teach me certain things that were necessary in life. Yet at the same time, I thank God for my parents and for the many positive things they exemplified. My mother and father were true examples in our family and in society. I remember my dad being gentle and kind, always showing peace and joy around him. He taught us the importance of reading the Bible and praying from childhood, laying a strong foundation in our relationship with God. Likewise, my mother would get up at four in the morning, starting her day with God and then working hard for her ten children. Regardless of her daily worries, she encouraged us to walk in the fear of God and always go to church. She suffered in silence as she would weep, pray and fast for each of her children. I thank God for such parents. They gave us everything they had and knew.

Even with everything that happened, I always loved my mother. She was an example of total surrender and dedication to God and her family. I was never upset or mad at her. I could never think badly of her. She was later proud of me because I was a fighter and hardworking. I never backed down, regardless of how difficult things were. My mother will always be the best mom for me because of her passionate and fervent prayers for me. Her prayers and tears helped break the evil power of her thoughtless words.

My father came to the Lord when he was only seven years old and was spared of many sins, hardships and adversity. He was a great preacher and a servant worthy of being followed. He left a legacy. His departure to the Lord in 2006 marked my entrance in the ministry to where God called me. It is as if the Lord chose me to carry on my father's ministry and God's love for the people, but in a different way.

I remember one time when my dad was a little upset. I do not remember the reason, but he raised his voice at my mother. She just told him, *"Oh my… the flesh, the flesh..."* meaning, *"You allowed your worldly flesh to lead you"*. I still remember up to this day how my father bowed his head, and without saying anything, went to the garden. He most certainly went to pray. Oh, how he would always give proof of self-control to leave and pray! Only now do I recognize and appreciate his inner man.

Even today, I am blessed to feel the effect of my parents' fasting and prayers for me. I praise the Lord for their prayers because all of their 10 children (my brothers and sisters) are Christian and are serving God faithfully. Blessed are the children that have Christian parents who fast and pray for them! Even if they leave home for a while, or run from God, the heavenly Father will bring them back because of His grace and because of the prayers of their parents!

THE ENEMY'S ATTACKS

As a teenager, I wanted like every other teenage girl, to love and to be loved. I felt a void that would burn in my heart, but I could not define it. It was the void only God's love could fill and satisfy. It is true that I went to church, read His Word, I prayed and worshiped the Lord, but there was still that aching feeling that longed for fulfillment. I wanted to be loved and appreciated. I wanted to discover my identity, so that I could in turn offer all my love to others. I was desperate, clueless, inexperienced, and naive. I had also been betrayed a few times, and I was raped and abused.

I will stop here with the details of those events. It is enough that I mention how guilty, dirty and sinful I felt after these experiences that I decided to end my life. To whom could I disclose my pain? I knew that if I told my parents they would not understand and they would judge and condemn me, making things worse. Left in a dead end, I tried to kill myself when I was about 16. I swallowed a handful of medicine and hoped to die. Before this, because I feared the Lord, I asked for His forgiveness. However, I thank the Lord that He did not allow anything bad to happen to me. I only felt some aches in my stomach, which went away after a couple of days.

> EVEN TODAY, I AM BLESSED TO FEEL THE EFFECT OF MY PARENTS' FASTING AND PRAYERS FOR ME.

I would later understand that God has given each of us a divine destiny that had to be fulfilled. That is why He did not allow me to die, because He wanted to use me for His glory. He watched over me, even though I did not understand it. I would always ask myself:

Why did I have to go through all these hardships?
Why did I have to go through this process of attacks, tests, sufferings and sin?
Why didn't God reveal Himself to me sooner?
Why did all this happen even though I went to church, prayed, read the Bible and loved God?

Through all of this, I felt that something had a controlling power over me, but I did not know who it was and why things were happening the way they were.

Every single day, countless people try to kill themselves due to various reasons. Oh, how I want to help them, to comfort them, to listen to their sorrow and sin, to weep with them, to encourage them and to give them hope! Oh, how I want them to fix their eyes upon the true Love, the real Source of Life, upon the One who is Love and doesn't judge. The One who doesn't abandon, but forgives, comforts, loves and accepts us. The One who restores our lives completely! His name is Jesus Christ, Lord of Lords and King of Kings!

Countless girls and women suffer the way I suffered. They have no peace, no love and no sense of fulfillment. Maybe you are in the same situation. If you are in this place, with love and tears in my eyes I tell you, my dear, that Jesus is the only one who loves you and only He can forgive you and change your life. Seek Jesus at all cost!

When we allow these negative thoughts to lead us, evil spirits can control our lives and our situation can worsen. That is what happened to me. The spirit of abandonment attracts other spirits:

- Of rejection;
- Of inferiority and timidity;
- Of shame;
- Of burden;
- Of condemnation;
- And other spirits.

All these influences seek to bring insecurity, confusion, doubt and fear in your life. After that, they want to bring bitterness because of the loneliness, rejection, and fear of men, and together with these, anger unleashes without control. In your inner self, you are defenseless and captive against many evil spirits. You repeatedly fall victim and your state only worsens. In this situation, even if you find a good spouse that loves you, there will still be pain in your heart and battles within yourself because only Jesus can take away all of these negative influences.

Most people in this condition fall prey to different addictions, such as alcoholism, sexual immorality, drug abuse, excessive purchasing, gossip and vengeance. Some are able to medicate the pain for a time, or hide it and pretend that everything is ok. But, when their mask wears off, the situation will always worsen. People fall into deep despair and loneliness, often leading to depression, and then the thought of suicide comes. What a sad life for the creation originally shaped by God's hands!

Why does it have to be this way, when we have such a loving Father? Maybe you ask yourself why He did not help you when you were mocked, beaten or abandoned. I know it is difficult to understand, but it is clear that God intervenes when we pray in faith, even though we feel like He is late.

My advice to you: do not hide your sin and seek a godly mentor, someone who will lead you to Christ and will encourage and strengthen you. Take your life with God seriously, because the enemy is ruthless, he comes to steal, kill and destroy. Once he has permission to enter the open door, he will not leave easily. We must combat the enemy through prayer and fasting, with true repentance and a serious decision to obey God and to seek His face above all things.

RESCUE FROM THE ACCIDENT

The events that marked my youth are plenty. I will recount some of them because they are linked to the plan God has always had for my life.

One day, my sisters-in-law and I were driving a Jeep to the market to sell our merchandise. That morning the fog was very thick and it was still dark outside. A carriage suddenly appeared in front of our car. That was all I could see before I pulled the steering wheel to the left. I do not know how we managed to steer clear, but slowly the car slid towards the left in a ditch and it tumbled. We saw *God's hand* at work holding our car. For one moment, I felt as if I were under the car because all the sacks were over me. I burst out crying, not knowing what to believe. I did not understand why I was alive and why the accident didn't kill me. Again, I wanted to die, I thought I would be happier if everything ended there. At the same time, I wept tears of joy because I clearly saw God's hand at work, allowing me to dodge that horse and avoid injury. It was dark and foggy and it was very unlikely that someone would find us in that ditch. However, God made a way for some workers who were passing by to find us. They came and helped us bring the car up from the ditch. There were no casualties and injuries, not even the car was damaged. We returned home to wash our car because it was filthy and then we set out again. Miraculously we sold more merchandise at the market that day than on any other day. How great is our God!

God has a purpose for you and me:

> *"For I know the plans I have for you," declares the Lord, "plans to prosper you and not to harm you, plans to give you hope and a future. You will seek Me and find Me when you seek Me with all your heart. I will be found by you," declares the Lord, "and will bring you back from captivity. I will gather you from all the nations and places where I have banished you," declares the Lord, "and will bring you back to the place from which I carried you into exile." (Jeremiah 29:11, 13, 14, NIV)*

TURNING POINT: MY SUICIDE ATTEMPT

The time had come for God to change the course of my life, and the enemy who wanted to hinder God's plan led me to a state of pain and disappointment. I had no joy of living, especially because the enemy tortured me and I had no freedom. One day, when my father found out some negative news about me, he entered my room, and filled with bitterness and anger, he beat me. That is when I said, *"I've had it! Why is my father guilty of my sin? Why does he have to suffer so much because of me? Especially him, who is such a great man of God and a beautiful example to me!"*

I thought there is no point in living. I felt like I was the most sinful and guilty person on the face of earth, and I could not stand the heavy yoke that tortured me. These moods set me to find my father's razor blade. I locked myself in a room and I cut my wrist. The blood was pouring on the carpet and I almost fainted. One of my sisters figured out that something was wrong with me. I do not know how she got in the room, because I locked both the window and the door, but when she saw me, she called my father, entered the room and wrapped something around my wrist in order to stop the bleeding.

I failed yet again... I pitied my mother and father who showed great love towards me! They would come and ask me gently and lovingly about how I felt and they would encourage me to pray. With all these, there were great battles inside of me: unrest, confusion and chaos. I would weep and pray: *"My Lord, how am I going to be saved from my inner turmoil? Who can fill my heart's void?"*

I want to emphasize that my sins were no longer torturing me, because I asked God for forgiveness and I knew and believed that I was forgiven. The problem was that I desperately tried to get rid of *that something* that was inside of me, yet I did not know what it was. I felt only unrest and sadness, moods that would not go away even if I went to church, prayed or read the Bible. I was caught in the enemy's snare, who wanted to destroy me, but the prayers of my parents, their tears and fasting brought me back to life, to freedom together with Christ.

I want to encourage you: young and old, children or parents, it is never too late to come to the Lord! No sin is too great or heavy for the Lord to forgive and cleanse. No stronghold of the enemy in your mind or heart is too strong for the power of love and His blood shed at Calvary.

I remember what my father told me once, *"I will fast for you until the Lord will change you, even if I get a stomach disease."* His suffering (even though he did not know all my pain and sins) crushed me and tormented me. I would ask myself, *"What can I do to make my mother and father happy?"* I saw myself bound, they did not know about my struggles or how to help me, other than fasting and praying, which later worked with power and brought change into my life.

Thus, the time has come for me to seek the Lord more and more. It was not anything new in my life, because I read the Bible and prayed every morning and every night. I never missed the Sunday morning service. There were times when I promised Jesus that I would serve Him, but I never had an actual encounter with Him - with the Holy Spirit - in the way I would experience in the years to come.

When you truly encounter God's presence, your life will be radically changed.

A DIVINE SIGN

I once felt that I should fast for 3 days with no food and water. My parents used to fast two days a week and I followed their example. In one of those days of fasting, I was extremely upset because it didn't seem like God was answering my prayers. I remember it was time for lunch. The entire family went to eat and I entered my room to pray. I wept with desperation and I begged God to answer me. In those moments, there was an earthquake (and it was felt throughout Romania). Oh, the joy overflowed in me! I went to our balcony and saw how the trees were bending and the people were agitated. I wept tears of joy because God answered my prayers through an earthquake, showing me that He took heed of my struggles and that He will intervene in my life. All the people around me were surprised by my peace and joy, but nobody knew the source of my mood.

I started praising God and thanking Him, but my life did not change immediately after that. When I look back to that event about 25 years ago, I realize that it was a sign from God for me, and a hope for my future. God heard my prayer! He cared about me! He truly had a plan for my life! This sign sparked an excitement in my heart for God, but it would take many years for me to really encounter the deep and healing love of God in my life.

In the meantime, good and bad things happened, but everything that happened drew me closer to God. I was more and more desperate and hungry for Truth, for the amazing God to whom I prayed, but One of whom I didn't truly know.

The Change Of Direction

In 1993, my sister from Canada invited me to go there and help her since she was pregnant and did not feel well. I did not want to go, because I started my pursuit of God and I saw flickers of light and hope in my life, but I left it in God's hand. To my surprise, I received the Visitor VISA and I left for Canada from Romania on September 23, 1993, at 29 years old.

My sister, Estera, is a gift from God, and I am extremely thankful to God to have her as a sister. She was really close to me and God ordained her to keep me in her prayers. There was a time when I was struggling with sin and confusion, and was searching for answers. I knew she suffered and wept for me. I am certain that her prayers and tears, together with those of my parents, helped change my life. Someone once said, *"The most hopeless man is the one whom nobody prays for."*

I want to thank my sister Estera and her husband Milan for all their help and support in our lives and in the ministry.

A new chapter of my life started here, one that radically changed me. Words cannot express my thanksgiving to God for what He had done. It is true that my coming to Canada was a grace, a favour and a privilege from God. God already had a mighty plan for me for His glory. Because of my suffering, loneliness, crushing, guilt and condemnation, I felt unworthy of anything and anyone. I was insecure, and didn't think too highly of myself because I never forgot the things I went through. I think God wanted to get me to that place, to be a soft piece of clay, crushed by His hands, so that He may shape me. Blessed be the Lord!

I encourage all of you that go through suffering, be it from your own sins or from life's problems and difficulties. God loves a contrite, broken spirit!

"For this is what the high and exalted One says— He who lives forever, whose name is Holy: "I live in a high and holy place, but also with the one who is contrite and lowly in spirit, to revive the spirit of the lowly and to revive the heart of the contrite." (Isaiah 57:15)

"My sacrifice, O God, is a broken spirit; a broken and contrite heart you, God, will not despise." (Psalm 51:17)

God can mightily use people who have walked through times of brokenness and testing.

Our flesh and pride are our greatest obstacles for the Holy Spirit's work in our lives. If you choose the way of the cross, no matter how difficult it may be, if you do not give up trusting in God's goodness for you and you do not forget His mighty purpose for your life, then He will elevate you, bless you, fill you and use you for His glory. Jesus is not too busy to answer you. Trust in Him, seek Him with all your heart and you will see Him, and if He seems slow or delayed, wait for Him. (*Habakkuk 2:3*)

THE TIME OF LOVE

As soon as I arrived at the airport in Vancouver, my sister, together with other brothers and sisters in Christ welcomed me. Among them, I saw a wonderful man who handed me a flower bouquet. As soon as I saw him, I felt something peculiar, as if I had met him before. I felt as if he belonged with me, that we had something in common, something invisible. I can say I fell in love at first sight, because inside of me was a desire to love and be loved especially after all those years of loneliness, abuse, pain, shame, burden and guilt.

However, to my disappointment, this man was a refugee who did not take any interest in me. He was a handsome man and all the girls flocked around him. A chain of suffering started. I was alone, I did not know anyone, I did not know the language, and I worked night shifts, cleaning houses with my sister. I would think of him every second; he was in my mind and heart. I would sometimes call him.

All this time I was praying for him, wanting him to be closer to God. Later, the Lord showed me that it has to be the same in our relationship with God: loving Jesus and always thinking about Him. Without genuinely loving Him, we cannot keep Him in our thoughts.

My love grew deeper for this man even though he would not pursue me. This is how our attitude towards the Lord should be: the more He seems silent, the more we should desire to seek Him and to long after Him and be in love with Him.

Nevertheless, after a year, the Lord united us, and Marian and I got married! Even though we had no Canadian citizenships, and no money, we had our love for God and each other. I cannot fully express the joy the Lord brought in my life when I was thirty years old. I finally had a home where I was protected against temptation, suffering and loneliness. This is how a new chapter began.

THE LORD PERFORMS MIRACLES

A short while after my arrival in Canada, before I got married, I caught a terrible cold. I had a fever, I was coughing and I had an intense pain in my throat. My tonsils were swollen and I could not swallow anything, it was difficult even to speak. Ever since my childhood I struggled with my tonsils, they were always swollen, I was in pain and I had trouble swallowing. Now because I was not a citizen, I didn't have proper medical insurance and I didn't go to the doctor. I remember lying in bed in great pain

> GOD CAN MIGHTILY USE PEOPLE WHO HAVE WALKED THROUGH TIMES OF BROKENNESS AND TESTING.

and the coughing would not stop. I have never heard of supernatural healings, of miracles, but I started praying in desperation, *"Lord, heal me!"* One night, I repeated this prayer until I started believing it. I think it was four in the morning, when I fell asleep. I do not remember anything supernatural happening, but when I woke up at 8 a.m. I had no pain, no fever and no coughs. Everything was normal! When I looked in the mirror, my tonsils were not swollen anymore.

I did not realize then that the Lord performed a great miracle. As years passed and I started knowing God more and more I realized that this was a divine intervention, the supernatural hand of the Creator who performed the healing surgery while I was asleep. For His glory, and His glory alone, I want to testify His greatness and goodness, shown before I even truly knew Him. Ever since that night, God not only healed my tonsils but He filled my body with His healing and I haven't been sick ever since – praise the Lord! Only when I was pregnant I felt sick, but it was due to the pregnancy. Even today I enjoy divine health and I praise my Mighty Doctor, *Jehovah-Rapha*[1].

THE SEARCH

Because I finally had a family of my own, my dream became real: I was married, I loved someone and I was loved. Then I started studying the Word of God more and more. We went to church and we had a prayer group coming over at our place every Saturday night. I needed more preparation for this kind of ministry, I needed a good coach, a spiritual mentor. How great it is to have an experienced mentor, one who knows how to answer many of your questions concerning life! How great it is to be open, to ask and to accept someone who teaches and counsels you!

I thank God that He prepared a friend who had more experience with God than me. She taught me many things, she counseled me, she guided me, especially praying for me, she wept with me, and she suffered together with me. She was an important pillar in my life at that time. Carmen was a great blessing for me and for my family for 10 years. I am certain that she will have great reward in heaven. I love her and I cannot forget her!

After a while, God took away my friend from me. God helped me grow through her, and now God wanted me to go directly to Him with my requests and He wanted all my love to be channeled only to Him. This does not mean we do not need mentors or spiritual parents. We do need them! We have to work together. However, in my case, the

---

[1] *Jehovah-Rapha* - One of the names God revealed Himself in the Scriptures. It means "I am the Lord that heals you" (Exodus 15:22-26)

Lord allowed my friend to move, not to depend on her, but to depend only on God.

I remember her words filled with value and wisdom. Before I was filled with the Spirit, she told me, *"If you only depend on your church, your prayer group, or on a beloved friend, you don't truly know Christ yet."*

I realized that my relationship with Christ was not very deep so, at that time, I really needed fellowship with my brothers and sisters in Christ. We had a prayer group every Saturday night at our place. That is where I began to grow in Christ and I even started praying aloud, although I had never done it before. In some denominations, the women are not allowed to pray in church, which is completely wrong. This is by no means His will! *I dare stand my ground on this matter before any leader.* The Lord urges us to pray continuously. There is great power in prayer, when we gather in fellowship and we intercede together for the people's causes. The lack of prayer in church points to spiritual weakness. Prayer is the most powerful weapon against the enemy. A prayer prayed only in our mind does not have

THE LEADERS SHOULD PRAY AT LEAST TWO HOURS A DAY IF THEY WANT TO SEE A CHANGE IN THEIR LIVES, CHURCH AND MISSION.

the same power as a prayer prayed aloud, guided by the Holy Spirit. Let us not forget that God created the entire Universe by speaking the Word.

> *"And God said, 'Let there be light,' and there was light… And God said, 'Let there be a vault between the waters to separate water from water.'" (Genesis 1:3, 6)*

No wonder why the spiritual lives of many Christians are weak and scrawny. This happens because they do not pray incessantly guided by the Holy Spirit at home and in church. If one does not pray at least one hour a day, he is weak and he can be easily knocked down by the hardships of life. The leaders should pray at least two hours a day if they want to see a change in their lives, church and mission.

Let us go back to prayer, remembering Paul's exhortation to *"pray continuously."*

As soon as I started praying like this, my life began to change. In these beginnings stages, I cannot tell you how nervous I felt when my turn would come to pray out loud in public, but by practicing it, through the Word and through the Spirit of the Lord, I was set free from my fear, my shame, and the intimidation of praying in public. Now prayer became a state of my soul and sometimes it is hard to stop!

Besides my perseverance in daily prayer and in Bible study, I would always listen to tapes, sermons and songs in order to renew my mind (*Romans 12:1*). The more I read and listened to the Word, the more I was hungry and thirsty after the most High God.

I slowly began to realize that although family life brought me great fulfillment, there was a void ever since my childhood. Something inside of me craved for the supernatural, after the living God. I began to realize who I was, why I was born, and who God really is. I started to understand His love and I craved after Him more and more. My prayers were filled with power and passion after Him.

Entering My Destiny

About that time, God allowed me to listen to the tapes of Pastor Joseph Ton. He is a great and wonderful pastor after God's heart and he is a pillar among Romanian Christians. I listened so many times to the tapes from the *"Spiritual Life"* teaching set. That is how my passionate pursuit of God started. It is as if the sun just started shining light in the world. I reached the conclusion that I knew many things about God, but I did not know Him personally. It is a big difference between having information regarding God and knowing Him personally and genuinely.

Dear reader, stand before the Lord and ask yourself if you truly know the Almighty God, the One we see on the Scriptures' pages. There is a great difference between knowing things *about* God and knowing *Him* personally.

1) I WANT TO KNOW GOD

In my desperation, I prayed to God for Him to reveal Himself to me as He is portrayed in the Bible:

- *Lord, I want to **KNOW** You, to know You in Your omnipotence, in Your beauty, in Your strength, in everything that You are, in all of Your attributes.*
- *Lord, I want to know Your Name, because I know that in Your Name there is mystery. How many names do You have, Lord?*
- *Lord, I want to know You like Abraham did, to walk with You like Enoch.*
- *Lord, I want to know You like Moses did, to climb the mountain and to ask You: "Show me Your glory!"*

- *Lord, I want to know You like Samuel, who as a child heard Your voice.*
- *Lord, I want to know You like David, who consulted with You when he went to battle and who together with You won against the lion, the bear and Goliath.*
- *I want to sing like David and I want to shout: "Blessed be the Lord! I have been saved from all my enemies."*
- *Lord, I want to know You like Joshua, Elijah, Elisha, Deborah, Esther, and others from the Old and New Testament who knew You.*
- *Lord, I want to make a difference in this world, because those who know You will do great deeds.*
- *Lord, I want to know Your heart and I want to know whom You truly are for me and for all the people.*
- *Lord, I want to know You and the power of Your resurrection and the partaking of Your sufferings and I want to be made conformable unto Your death...*

2) I WANT TO LOVE GOD

Then I came before the Lord with another desire, equally great and necessary:

Lord, I want to LOVE You, because You loved me first. You have saved me and You have forgiven me of my sins. I desire to love You with a burning, unstoppable love.

Lord Jesus, I want to be consumed by Your love and passion! I want to love You, like you commanded us; to love You with all our heart, with all our soul, with our entire mind, and with all our might and strength. Lord God, I know that You are love, that's why I want to experience that divine love, because human love is flimsy and conditional. How can You love a sinner like me and everyone else? I want to love You and the people around me more, regardless of what wrongdoing they might do to me.

Lord, I realize that neither my parents, nor friends, nor even my husband or children can give me what You have given me: an eternal love, unconditional, filled with fire that perpetually consumes me for You and for others. I desire, my Lord, to enter Your infinite ocean of love. Your Word says in Romans 5:5 that "Love has been poured out into our hearts through the Holy Spirit." I want to have faith, my Lord, I want to love You!

The New Testament talks about Mary who came to Jesus with an alabaster jar, which was the most expensive belonging she had. The jar was very expensive. It was the equivalent of a year's income. She broke it, she anointed Jesus' feet with myrrh and she wiped His feet with her hair so that the entire house smelt like perfume. *(John 12:1-8)*

In Mark 14:3, it says:

"...A woman came with an alabaster jar of very expensive perfume, made of pure nard. She broke the jar and poured the perfume on His head."

Verse 6 touched me deeply: *"She has done a beautiful thing to Me."* His Words convey a special love and power. They show the profound appreciation towards that woman. The Lord Jesus saw the woman's *sacrifice* and *love*. She showed Jesus an extravagant love and extreme obedience. As a reward, Jesus publicly elevated her:

"Truly I tell you, wherever the gospel is preached throughout the world, what she has done will also be told, in memory of her." (Mark 14:9, NIV)

Why did she need this kind of praise, when we know that the Gospel is about praising Jesus and what He has done, and not human deeds? Here we see the beauty of His unlimited depths of wisdom, love and praise for those who love Him. This act of radical love touched the heart of Jesus, because this woman risked her life, reputation, money, future and everything for His sake.

We see that her love spread a fragrance so wonderful in that room, a fragrance that can be felt even today. This very fragrance brought me to my knees before the Lord:

> *"Lord, I want to love You more, even more than Mary, I want to love You more than anyone in this world!*
>
> *I want to love You like no one has ever loved You, my Lord Jesus, because You are so wonderful, because You have forgiven me and You loved me and thought about me when You were on the cross...*
>
> *I want to love You, because You saved me from the pit of death, You took me out of the gutter and You put my feet on the Rock...*
>
> *I want to love You, because You deserve it, because You are the only One who I desire more than life: to fill me, to fulfill me and to feel Your love."*

Why did the Lord honor this woman so much? Jesus did not say such words not even about Peter, John or other apostles, even though they were the spiritual giants of the Bible. I understood that what this woman has done was an invaluable act of *worship* before the Lord. It was an attitude of real love, sacrifice and boldness. She gave everything she had to Jesus. She did this because she *loved* Him.

Today we can do many things: go on missions trips, preach the Gospel and give our money to the poor, but if we don't do these things out of love for the Lord, these things amount to nothing before Him (*1 Corinthians 13*). All these things are important, but He demands *love* in everything we do. In Ephesians 3:17, the Lord tells us that we must be *rooted* and *grounded* in love. I realized that without an intimate relationship with Christ, we cannot have love and our actions won't be out of sincere love. It was then when I understood for the first time this verse:

"Whoever does not love does not know God, because God is love." (1 John 4:8)

It became clear to me that the Lord is the One who put these desires to love Him inside of me. I understood the connection between *knowing* God and *loving* God. This is the first commandment, which after many years of faith, I treasure more and more. Only through love, we can know God, for He is love.

But how can I receive this love? How can I truly know and love Him?

Maybe you have had these questions or maybe you are still in the pursuit of this love, which is inherently

> I WANT YOU TO FORM YOUR CHARACTER IN ME.

connected to the true understanding of God. We can know God if we seek Christ. Meditating on His life and Word, we can understand the verse that says, *"Whoever sees Me sees Him Who sent Me" (John 12:45, AMP).* By seeking Christ, you find the Father. Once you reach this understanding and this divine love, your horizons will broaden to a place you never thought you'd reach or experience.

3) I WANT GOD TO FORM HIS CHARACTER IN ME

I asked/pleaded the Lord the following:

> *"Father, I want You to form Your character in me. I desire to have Your heart, Your humility and the fruit of the Holy Spirit in me."*

We will explore this more in the next chapter.

The Process Of Holiness

When I uttered these prayers, I did not fully understand what their fulfillment entailed, what it would cost me and how long the process would take.

It is important for you to know that you cannot be used by God and receive many of His gifts if your flesh is not crucified on the cross. If you do not die to yourself, what you build in 20 years can be ruined in 20 minutes!

I did not realize back then that I would go through necessary trials for my cleansing and through difficult circumstances so that God could form His character in me. This is how the molding process started in my prayers: to love Him, to know Him and to build His character in me. The third aspect was most difficult for me, and still is, because the process of holiness happens throughout our entire lives. God started breaking and cleansing me. I was tested in terms of love, patience, forgiveness, integrity, sincerity, fairness, patience, and acceptance of those who hurt me. God had a lot to clean in my life, and His work has not ceased.

There were moments when God's cleansing process made me shout, *"God, I can't take it anymore! It's too much!"* I was taking my stand as His righteous daughter, cleansed and set free, a daughter who started pursuing her intended destiny. However, it was a time for preparation, equipping, training so that I may be ready to answer to His divine calling. Remember: the higher the calling, the tougher the training and discipline.

> IF YOU DO NOT DIE TO YOURSELF, WHAT YOU BUILD IN 20 YEARS CAN BE RUINED IN 20 MINUTES!

He knows that you can overcome everything; otherwise He would not allow you to reach some extreme situations. If you give up and do not want to die to yourself, you will become more and more frustrated and disappointed because you are not in the place God has called you to be. If you do not want to pay the price for the heavenly prize, you will suffer the consequences of your disobedience, your stubbornness and wrong choices.

Accept His fiery furnace, because the gold is only purged through fire. Do not be scared, He watches over you so you will not stay a second longer than you have to. He wants you to be as pure as gold, highly valuable for His glory. In His furnace there is no room for impurities.

In the Kingdom of God and in His ministry, worldly flesh must not have a word to say. The Lord knows that our worldly flesh is the greatest obstacle when we work for Him. We cannot combine righteousness with sin, and that's why the Lord allows the pounding and the crushing, so that He alone will remain in us, He alone will work through us and He alone will receive His glory. All we need to do is to be empty vessels, fully surrendered to Him, so that He may pour something precious in us. Our heart's vessel has to be broken in order to smell His fragrance.

In my desperation, I told the Lord that I could not take it any longer. In that moment, I focused my attention to the radio and I heard someone preaching. A wonderful preacher said, *"Don't run away from life's circumstances, because through them, the Lord is forming His character in you."* Right then a heavenly ray of light scattered the darkness that surrounded me. The veil upon my eyes was torn and I saw the Light. Until then, I saw myself in a hole and everything seemed dark before me. I exclaimed:

> *Oh, now I understand, and I give You glory, my Lord! It is exactly what I asked from You three years ago to form Your character in me. Lord, if You have any tests and trials left for me, send them to me, Lord, pound me and crush me, Lord, cleanse me, Lord, because I want Your character in me, no longer I to live, but You to live in me.*

It is then when I finally understood Galatians 2:20:

> *"I have been crucified with Christ and I no longer live, but Christ lives in me. The life I now live in the body, I live by*

faith in the Son of God, who loved me and gave himself for me."

This is how I received peace and joy. I knew the Lord is in control, that He knows what He is doing and that He never fails. Even though it was difficult, I wanted to rest in Him, accepting His cleansing and the death of my flesh. Of course, there were hardships, obstacles and tests I had to pass for the Lord to elevate me to another step, for me to love and know Him more. Today, I thank Him for those hardships and trials!

After only a few years spent in Canada, there was a governmental audit concerning the taxes paid to the province. It is required for all people to declare their income and pay their taxes. Remember what the Bible teaches: it is right before the Lord to "give to Caesar what belongs to Caesar." However, in Romania we were taught to believe and the government was "stealing" from us, so we did not declare a couple of thousand dollars received in cash. Even some pastors and friends from Canada advised us not to declare them, since they believed that the government was corrupt as well, and that they were making us pay high taxes. However because God loves us and because He has plans for everyone, he wanted to save us from this unintegral sin. He allowed the fiery furnace to purge us from any kind of impurity.

When the Canadian government asked us if we had received any cash for income, what do you think we did? We lied. It was not easy for us to lie because we were convicted by the Holy Spirit for this sin. We knew that we had bit into the trap of the enemy.

Oh, how the enemy comes running to give us his solutions and lies, fooling us completely, telling us that we would get away with it! We often forget that he wants to steal everything, to kill and to destroy us! How foolish we were by accepting the enemy's help! How much credibility we gave him, making him our support and our help in times of need. Oh, how "good" was the evil to us!

Oh, but how wrong we are if we do not know the truth! When we are far from the truth, we run to the enemy for help. This "help" is actually a bait devised to kill us. Pay attention to this!

How far can a lie get? We deposited the cash in the bank and the authorities found out. Now you may ask why we didn't deposit the money in a different bank so that they wouldn't have caught us. This advice is another delusion of the enemy, even though it is sugarcoated. Can we fool God and the enemy? Through our actions, we open the door to the enemy and eventually we will pay for our actions.

Then I started talking to the Lord in a different manner. I came before Him with my good deeds, asking help to dodge the punishment. I reminded the Lord about the thousands of dollars we gave in His Name for His Kingdom and to the poor in several countries. Do you think we got away? No! In His loving kindness, God corrected us gently saying, *"These things have nothing to do with each other: for the money you gave in My Name you will be rewarded. However, it cannot cover your wrongdoings. You cannot pay money for your sins. They have to be confessed through a genuine repentance. I forgive you, but you must suffer the consequences."*

Gently, God told me, *"I want to cleanse you of all your impurities that block the fulfillment of My plan in your lives. The enemy cannot have anything to do with you, so that when you are in My ministry he won't derail you, tear you down or attract you towards sin. This is the fire of cleansing; accept it, because one day you will thank Me, even if you lose some money now. It is worth losing thousands of dollars to get an incorruptible character, so that the others might trust you."*

What mighty truth! I praised the Lord for His miraculous cleansing which has a higher purpose, for our future and good, only for His glory! We had to pay an additional $10,000 for taxes, penalties and interest above the $3,000 owing from that audit. It was not easy at all, but it was worth it. Blessed be the Lord!

Maybe you have not realized that certain financial practices in your business are sinful. Maybe you cheat or produce paperwork to fool the government. Maybe you lie so you won't have to pay taxes. Maybe you bribe others to make a deal or so that you won't have to pay fines, or have your business closed. Maybe you compromise everything in order to save your reputation, position or income.

Satan is so deceiving! He always cheats and manipulates. People let their guard down for the sake of money, but remember that the enemy hates us so much that he wants to destroy everything including our house, our family, our money, our health, our gifts, and our relationships. To do this, he baits us with what we like or need, and then we *always* have something to lose. He will not forgive us, not even our slightest mistake. If we accept using what belongs to him, we lose the joy of salvation and we no longer advance spiritually. We are bound and we cannot do everything God asks us to do. Why? It is because he has us in his grip and he controls us.

Maybe you try to get rid of your troubled conscience by doing good deeds, maybe even by giving money to people, but it will not help. With the risk of losing something, swallow on your pride, kneel and ask God to show you where you are making compromises. Then, repent and take the radical decision of not making the "pact with the devil" ever again. Stop embracing his strategies and lies because he will destroy you!

After that event, we were free and honest in our conduct. This constituted as a frontal attack against the enemy. We were ordained by God to attack the kingdom of darkness, not only to stand and dodge the enemy's attacks.

When your flesh rises, the Holy Spirit is saddened. However, in that moment you will hear the Holy Spirit's whisper saying, *"Be silent and patient, you have to die so that Christ may lift you, He will show you who you really are and will do you right."* The Word of God tells us that when we suffer, the Spirit of the Lord rests upon us. This suggests that our flesh and the Spirit of the Lord wrestle continuously. The moment you keep your mouth shut and endure it, you are a carrier of the cross: the flesh dies and the Spirit is free. He rests upon you and He works through you what the Father wills.

The moment we justify ourselves, we have ambition and we let the flesh be in control, the Spirit is saddened, and the flesh reigns over us. Why? Because this way we are doing exactly what the enemy wants us to do. That is why, whenever there is a problem or a confrontation, be careful what springs out of your heart: is it the fruit of the worldly flesh or the fruit of the Spirit? If the fruit of the Spirit is in your heart, blessed be the Lord! Strengthen yourself and go on further! However, if you have something in your heart that is worldly, humble yourself immediately, repent and ask for grace and freedom.

What Is Your Destiny?

In my life, I never heard someone teaching about purpose and destiny. I was never told that God created us here on earth with a purpose. The truth is that each and every one of us has a destiny set by God since the foundation of the world. In reality, many don't get to fulfill it because they were unaware like me because nobody had taught them how to align themselves to the will of God. All I knew in my life was to repent, to live a clean life and to live ready for the Rapture. Only later did I learn that between the moment of repentance and the Rapture there is a time of training and equipping to enter our ordained destiny.

Do you know your destiny? Why do you think God created you? Is it to be happy, to be comfortable, to go to church and to wait for the Rapture? There's so much more! The Lord wishes to work through us. Jesus completed His ministry on earth, now we are His hands and feet. He wants us to be workers together with Him, to snatch souls from hell, and to bring them into the Kingdom of God. We have all been given gifts, qualities and opportunities to fulfill His will and to work in His vineyard.

Ask God what your destiny is and ask Him to guide your steps towards it. Maybe you are already on your way, but you do not know it. Ask God to open your heart, to understand His will and calling.

Back when I did not know His plans for my life, I was focused on Him due to my desire to grow in His love, to know Him and have a genuine relationship with Him based on love. This was the best thing I did back then because it led to my spiritual growth, and my understanding of His calling.

Maybe you are young and energetic, motivated by the desire to go to missions trips, to preach and to work for the Lord. This is a desire after His heart, because in the body of Christ, all members have to work.

But pay attention to this: it is one thing to have a desire, passion and calling for ministry, and another thing to be ready and properly equipped for ministry. Why? Because on the battlefield, you will encounter all sorts of obstacles, problems, spirits and attacks. If you are not properly equipped for all of these, you will get hurt, discouraged and disappointed. You may give up and experience defeat. For a healthy growth and preparation, I advise you to keep in mind the following:

- Spend as much time as possible at the Lord's feet, in His Word, in obedience and in worship.
- Meditate day and night on His Word, until you receive divine revelation.
- Spend time around mature Christians, who experienced humility and God's forming process, so that you may learn as a disciple. If you do not learn how to respect and honor your authority, your elders and your guiding counselors, you will not advance in your spiritual life and you will not be respected.
- Always fast and pray. You have to be men and women of prayer and fasting, under the anointing of the Holy Spirit. Do you want hell to tremble before you, before Jesus Christ, who dwells in you? By fasting and praying, you will see the power of the Holy Spirit at work in your life.
- Start declaring God's promises upon your life and in the lives of others.
- Praise and worship the Lord at all times, praise Him continuously.
- Start giving tithes and offerings; do good deeds to everyone.
- Be responsible and faithful in every detail in your life.
- Sow peace, joy and love around you, knowing that you will reap what you have sown.

John the Baptist's message was one of repentance and preparation to enter God's Kingdom. Today, the Lord is seeking men like John the

Baptist, who would cry out, *"Prepare the way for the Lord, so that He may transform His bride!"*

What are the elements of preparation? His Word, prayer, fasting and worship. Fasting and prayer prepare us to be filled with the Holy Spirit, resembling Pentecost. Many people pray and expect to be filled, but it does not happen. A serious preparation in fasting and prayer will produce thirst and hunger after God. The Holy Spirit cannot wait to fill you up! The question is: do you desire the Holy Spirit more than anything else? Do you understand the necessity of being filled with Him or is it that you just want an experience? When the Lord fills a vessel that was emptied first, He pours His wholeness into it. The person becomes different in thinking, in speaking, in behavior and can be used completely by God for His great works.

THE BEGINNING OF A DISCIPLINED LIFE

My parents used to fast two days each and every week. When they fasted, they did not eat nor drink anything until 6pm. They never imposed on us the same thing. However, in the last years I spent at home, I would align together with them in fasting. I did not even want to eat, knowing they were fasting.

I knew that it was good to fast, and that the Lord was asking us to fast in his Word. Although I did not understand it then, fasting had positive effects in my life. When I started changing and fervently desiring God, I brought fasting to a higher level, which I will be discussing further on.

Moreover, I was thirsty after the Word of God, Christian literature, Christian music and sermons. Whenever I had spare time, I wanted to spend it only with the Lord in His presence. Since then, I no longer liked wasting time on useless conversations, on watching television or doing worldly things which served me nothing. Instead I found my treasure, I found true joy and I found the spring that gives life. I also had fewer friends because I devoted myself to seeking God. Many judged me, criticized

THE HOLY SPIRIT CANNOT WAIT TO FILL YOU UP!

me, and told me that I was too fanatic, too radical, and too spiritual. I still get hurt by certain comments, but blessed be the Lord that I do everything for His sake.

Once when I was praying, the Lord spoke to me through this Bible verse:

> *"Therefore this is what the Lord says: If you repent, I will restore you that you may serve Me; if you utter worthy, not worthless, words, you will be My spokesman."* (Jeremiah 15:19, NIV)

God brought this verse to my attention several times and I realized how serious God is towards His children. He does not want us to have a divided heart. He does not want us to have idols. Maybe you, my dear reader, will say you have no idols, but please, stop for a second and ask the Holy Spirit to show you clearly what your idol is.

What is an idol? It is anything or anyone who gets more attention, time and priority in your heart than God. These idols are hidden in your heart. They could be your reputation, your ego, your name, your rank, your pride, your spouse, your child, your car, your money, your house, the Internet, gaming, friends, different distractions, fear, your worries, even your sickness if you keep thinking about it all the time. The list could go on.

Be still and examine yourself. An idol can be something you do not yet have, but you desire so much that you beg, weep and pray continuously for it. The things you talk about all the time, or even dream about, could become your idol. In this case, God is not first in your life. If you still can't discern an idol in your life, ask yourself these questions:

- Where do I spend most of my time?
- What do I think about most the time?
- What do I talk about most the time?
- Who or what brings me the most joy?
- Where do I go to receive comfort or distraction?
- Who or what do I love the most?

Be honest when the Holy Spirit searches your heart, admit your wrongs, repent and turn wholeheartedly towards God who loves you so much. He commands us:

"Love the Lord your God with all your heart and with all your soul and with all your strength." (Deuteronomy 6:5, NIV)

"You shall have no other gods before Me. You shall not bow down to them or worship them; for I, the Lord your God, am a jealous God, punishing the children for the sin of the parents to the third and fourth generation of those who hate Me, but showing love to a thousand generations of those who love Me and keep My commandments." (Exodus 20:3, 5, 6, NIV)

The Lord wants us to love only Him and to not have a divided heart with the world around us. He advises us not to compromise because we will bear its consequences: we will get sick, we will get attacked, disappointed, frustrated and we will be ungrateful. The Lord did not tell us in vain:

"Enter through the narrow gate. For wide is the gate and broad is the road that leads to destruction, and many enter through it." (Matthew 7:13)

In my life, through spending time with the Lord on a daily basis, in the morning, evening and at night, in prayer, in fasting and worship, my hunger and thirst for Him grew. I felt the void in my heart starting to be filled. The more I tasted God, the more my hunger and thirst for Him grew. Like I said before, I didn't ask the Lord for anything worldly. My desire was to only know Him. I didn't want *information, theories, and theology about Him*, but a real encounter with the *One and only living God*, the God of the Bible. I also wanted to love Him more and to live the reality of His love, which He promises in the Scriptures.

The Encounter

"**F**inally I have found you!"

Since 1999, when I asked the Lord those 3 righteous prayers, I started seeking Him like never before. He drew me in like a magnet, like an irresistible force. I could not neglect my time spent with Him. It became a necessity. He was my soul's delight, my most important thing. That is why I fought to spend even more time with Him.

In the meantime, the Lord blessed us with two boys and two girls. Although I was very busy, I spent my spare time with the Lord. The more I sought Him, the more something divine and incomprehensible for me at that time, drew me closer to him, called me deeper and brought me unexplainable joy.

In 2003, even though I had a two-month old baby, I would spend time with the Lord every night after I put my children to sleep. The presence of God was my greatest delight. I was either alone or together with my husband, a brother and a sister in Christ. We stood at the feet of Jesus, listened to worship music, prayed, meditated on His Word and we recharged our spiritual "batteries." Oh, what great and unique times were those nights that we spent in the presence of the Lord waiting on Him, expecting passionately for Him to reveal Himself to us, to talk to us, to touch us and to comfort us.

On a February night in 2003, I was as usual spending time with the Lord, together with my husband and an elderly brother in Christ. I sensed in my spirit the heavens starting to move and the angels of the Lord getting ready. Some of them were ready to battle. A great moment in my life was about to happen: I sensed that the heavens were about to unite with the earth through the *fire of His divine Love*. The heavens and the angels of God were rejoicing because of the beautiful act that God was about to do within a hurt, broken, rejected, belittled, and worthless soul; a soul that had *decided not to relent until it found God*.

How brave it is for a finite soul to seek the infinite, true and almighty God! What audacity to ask for an audience with the King of Kings and Lord of Lords because of an urgent cause!

After years of desperation and prayer, God was persuaded by the love of a thirsty soul, and He showed up.

I was not looking for forgiveness because I had received it; I was not seeking financial help, health or anything else from Him. I sought Him and *only Him*, I wanted to know and love Him. At that time, I didn't realize that the Father desires this from us more than anything else.

He asked me:

- *Who comes to church only for Me?*
- *Who comes to Me without any demands?*
- *Who seeks only Me?*
- *Who worships in spirit and in truth?*

> *These are the people I am looking for. I fill them with My Spirit and with My love; I work through them, because I mean everything to them. Through love we are united, so there will be no hidden agenda. They won't look for My hand without looking at Me, they won't have My joy without seeing Me, they won't have My peace without My help, they won't have My prosperity without Me.*

Coming back to the story, I mentioned we were worshiping the Lord. We were singing, "*You are holy, You are holy, Hallelujah!*" and suddenly the heavens opened up. We felt the joy of heaven from the worship. The heavens opened up and I saw a fiery arrow coming towards me, like a mighty thunderbolt. With the speed of light, it was shot directly at my heart. In that divine, supernatural moment I was touched and filled with power. I started shouting like never before: "*Lord Jesus, I love You, I love You... You finally came to me! Finally, after I waited a long time, after I thirsted for You, You encountered me!*"

"FINALLY I HAVE FOUND YOU!"

That power entered in me and in my heart. Another power was manifesting through my mouth through shouting for joy, a power that was praising God like never before. It was a divine fire, which was consuming me for the Lord and for all the people. I was connected to heaven through that divine power which was continuously entering my body like a shock wave that cannot be put in words. That electrical flow, that power, that fire continuously entered my body, elevating me. I was kneeling with my hands raised and I was under the impression that I was touching the heavens. In those moments, there was nothing between heaven and earth: no clouds, no roof and no demonic realm. I was directly in contact with the Most High God through Jesus Christ, praising Him, rejoicing in the supernatural power of the Holy Spirit, in His overflowing love, in His presence, which I longed for many years.

I saw the glory of God, His might and love that burns, boils and consumes. I can say I saw the Lord with my eyes of faith, like Isaiah and John. I could experience unique, profoundly reverend moments because God is holy and He is a consuming fire. With the eyes of my heart I saw His nature and holiness. It was something divine, deep and profound, which cannot be put in words.

It is impossible to reproduce that experience, that real encounter with God. I wish those moments would never end because they were so magnificent, so sacred.

When that power entered me, my heart began to ache and I felt within my heart a physical burn. They were the flames of His love that were burning my chaff, a cleansing love, but at the same time filling me with heavenly, infinite, agape love that cannot be found on earth. It was the love that I had been craving for years. The reality of God was now in me; it wasn't far away! The Lord filled my void and quenched my thirst. It was the kind of fire that hurt and burnt, but

> IN THAT MOMENT I RECEIVED THE REVELATION OF LOVE, GREATNESS AND BEAUTY OF JESUS, AND I FELL IN LOVE WITH HIM.

at the same time was sweet and drew me in deeper. I didn't want the experience to end. There was a deep, indescribable *communion* between a broken, forgiven sinner, and a beautiful, infinitely loving God. I felt I had become one with Him. In other words, He entered in me and bound me to Him forever.

In that moment I received the *revelation* of love, greatness and beauty of Jesus, and I fell in love with Him.

Those flames I felt were the flames of the Holy Spirit. It was a baptism of the Holy Spirit in His divine love, because the first fruit of the Spirit is love. I can say it was a baptism with God's fiery passion. I started talking to Him:

> *Oh, what perfect, unique and perfected love I had found in You, my precious and beloved Lord.*
>
> *How did You, my limitless Lord, lower Yourself to reach me, a sinner?*
>
> *Where does all Your love come from? Where does this grace overflow from for all of us sinners?*
>
> *What kind of love do You have that You draw me like a magnet? Who are You, Lord? I cannot see You, but I feel You so close to me... even the air I breathe seems different; You are in the air... What is beyond my feelings? Is it You, the Holy and Almighty One, the One I have read so much about in the Bible? Is it really You, the One who created me, who gave me life and saved me from my pain? Is it you, the Supreme Love and perfected goodness that endures for all sinners?*
>
> *Why did You come to me?*
>
> *What plan do You have for me that you fill me with this much love? Lord, expand the territories of my heart and knowledge of You so that I may understand You, know You and truly love You. You are too wonderful, too holy, too mighty and too loving, I do not deserve You to lower Yourself to reach me.*

O, depth of richness and knowledge, who can contain You that cannot be encompassed?

You are giving me too much my Lord, the lover of my life. Do You really care about me?
Did you really see my desperation and longing after You?

Did You leave everything behind for me, my Lord?

Who am I to You? What is my worth in Your eyes?

Oh, how much I suffered! How much wasted time in my life! Why did you come so late? I have been searching and waiting for You for so long. Do You remember, Lord, how many nights I cried, staying up late and reading the Bible, weeping while telling You: Lord Jesus, if You happen to pass by my street, if You see my window with the lights turned on, know that I am waiting for You. Come, because I long for Your presence... I desire nothing else but to encounter You, my Lord, who gave Your life for me. I want to love You, but I can't love You more than I already do. I need Your love first.

Thank You for being gracious and that You came, Lord.

You remember, Lord, how many times I wept while singing:
  'Open my eyes; I want to see You, Jesus,
  To touch You with my hand, to tell You that I love You!
  Make my ears desire to dearly listen to You,
  Open my eyes; I want to see You, Jesus!'

Oh, open my spiritual eyes, to rejoice in Your splendor because You are so wonderful, so precious, so sweet, that words cannot even describe You... However, You have entered my heart and my heart knows how to convey Your message of divine love and words aren't needed anymore.

I can only weep tears of joy in the presence of Your divine beauty. Now the heaven was united through our loving bond, between the Most Gracious and Holy God and a redeemed sinner, whom You made a daughter of the King.
Thank You, Lord God, for Your unmerited grace. Only now can I say that I live and that I have a God in heaven who is in me and with me forever.

How can I praise and bless Your Name? How can I thank You best?

Oh, I know: I will come before You with thanksgiving and will bring the offering before all people. I will love You unceasingly and I will tell Your works and wonder, my God.

Now You are my sweet and precious Father who will never leave me alone ever again. I will always feel the breath of Your wonderful presence. I love you, my Lord, my strength!

These were a few of my thoughts and words, which were on my heart in those supernatural, divine moments. My body could no longer take that divine fire and supernatural power, so I prayed, *"Lord, please stop! I cannot take it anymore, it hurts and it is burning my heart!"* I felt the flames of His love consuming me for Him, but burning me at the same time (I was able to define that state only later). Therefore, the Lord withdrew *for a short while* from His surge and filling with power.

A NEW LIFE

From that moment on, everything changed in my life. That divine intervention, the anointing of the Holy Spirit and of His love, marked a new direction and trajectory for my life. I can say I *fell in love* with Lord Jesus, the Father and the Holy Spirit.

I started loving everything around me; I was singing and shouting for joy, it was the joy of encountering my beloved Lord. The Lord cleansed me and gave me a new set of eyes to see the people around me like He did. I loved the people around me without condition. I could no longer judge them because I saw the value God had put in them, even if it was covered by sin, lack of knowledge and disbelief. This love was paired with joy and sacrifice - true love sacrifices itself with joy. I experienced and I'm currently experiencing a radical change in my life, full of passion for God and for His Kingdom.

Ever since that encounter I became desperate for Him and only Him. All I wanted and all I sought was He and He alone, the God of the perfect Trinity. Since then, my thoughts, words, desires and actions have been only for Him and about Him. Sometimes, even my husband couldn't understand me because I no longer led the life I used to lead in the past. Even my children saw that my spare time was spent with the Lord in prayer, reading the Bible or listening to worship music and sermons. I encouraged them to do the same, praying to God that they would do it out of *passion* and not by force.

I now understood the difference between following God because of tradition, fear, culture or obligation, and following Him because I love Him. I know the time will come when many will be touched by the same love that changed me and then everything will be clear and wonderful. Many times even my friends don't understand me. The fire that is in me isn't there because of me, but because God Himself poured His love in me, through the Holy Spirit.

I realized that what I was longing for all these years was *His love*, but my mistake was that I sought it in the wrong places which only led me to suffer. But the Lord received His glory even from those experiences, because Romans 8:28 tells us, *"We know that in all things God works for the good of those who love Him, who have been called according to His purpose." (NIV)*

The pain, disappointment and desperation forced me to keep running the race and I finally found Him, my Prince of Peace, Lover of my soul and heart, the One who forgave me, accepted me, loved me and wiped my tears from my cheeks. Lord Jesus who washed my filthy clothes in His blood, who gave me His clothes of righteousness and praise, who put His covenant ring on my finger, who put on me the shoes of peace and safety and offered me a rich meal of His revelations from His Word. How great is our God!

ADVICE TO YOU FROM THE BOTTOM OF MY HEART

Maybe to some extend you can relate to some of my difficult situations. Maybe you are alone, desperate, disappointed and without hope. My advice to you is this: don't stop here! Don't give up! Help is on the way, right at your door. *"My God in His mercy and steadfast love will meet me" (Psalm 59:10, AMP)*. Continue your pursuit of the one true God, who is full of love, mercy, help, salvation, redemption and healing. He promises:

> *"You will seek Me and find Me when you seek Me with all your heart. I will be found by you," declares the Lord, "and will bring you back from captivity. I will gather you from all the nations and places where I have banished you," declares the Lord, "and will bring you back to the place from which I carried you into exile." (Jeremiah 29:13-14, NIV)*

Receive some heartfelt advice:

- Don't seek comfort from people; you will only get more disappointed.
- Don't remain alone and isolated, you will only be an easier target for the enemy to attack.
- Don't accept the enemy's lies regarding you or others. The enemy's voice whispers:

  - There is no forgiveness left for you
  - Nobody loves you
  - Everybody despises you
  - How can you even go out anymore?
  - What you did is worthy of death; your only hope is death
  - God is too far and too busy to listen to you
  - God doesn't care about you, look where you are
  - He doesn't listen to your prayers
  - There is no God; if He existed, He would help you

- Look at you, you are chained and there's nothing that could ever help you.

If any of these thoughts are running through your mind, *do not believe them* because these are the enemy's lies. He was and still is the father of lies. If you don't have a solid foundation to know who you are in Christ, and if you don't know about His wonderful promises for you, then it will be easy for you to accept the enemy's lies. Once the lies enter your mind, they will start controlling, attacking and bombarding your heart, rooting guilt, condemnation, disappointment, bitterness, unforgiveness, selfishness, isolation, disbelief, doubt, and fear in your life.

The Lord tells us in John 10:10, *"The thief comes only to steal and kill and destroy; I have come that they may have abundant life."*

These are the enemy's doings. He isn't happy until he steals *everything* from you: your integrity, your peace, your faith, your joy, and your kindness. The enemy will persuade you to satisfy your flesh, and will steer you towards sin that will only grow in your life, until it will control you.

For example, if you are an alcoholic or addicted to drugs, sex, spending money on useless things, you will only seem to be fulfilled through these. However, these momentary pleasures leave your soul empty and become addictions. You are stuck in the devil's snare, which is set on destroying your life, your health and your money. After such addictions like drug abuse, alcoholism or sexual immorality, other things like violence, anger, malice, disappointment, obsession and depression will follow.

The enemy wants to destroy your family, children and relationships so that you might isolate yourself. Many addicts end up in prison where they are completely discouraged and with slim chances of recovery or freedom. Satan's last blow is the desire of death, which seems like the only way out. The enemy deceives without shame and many attempt suicide without knowing that the endless fire of suffering is awaiting them.

God created us as free creatures. If you chose to live subdued in sin, the Lord is telling you: *"Come to Me!"* Even today He has the power to forgive, clean, set free, heal and renew.

If you find yourself in this situation, tell Him right now:

Lord Jesus, please forgive me for sinning and saddening You! Have mercy on me, a sinner! I believe in Your sacrifice at the cross, I believe that You died for me! I ask You today to enter my heart; I want You to be my Lord and Savior forever. Cleanse me from my sins, like You promised in the Bible: "...the blood of Jesus, his Son, purifies us from all sin." (1 John 1:7, NIV)

Lord, I declare today that You, and You alone are my Lord, Master and Savior!

I thank You that You forgave me, cleansed me and made me Your child! Fill me with Your Holy Spirit! I need You, guide me from now on, be with me, protect me from the enemy and may Your will be done in my life!

In the Name of Jesus Christ I pray! I thank You! Amen!"

The Time Of Revelation

After that wonderful night when the Lord bathed me in the beauty of His love, everything changed. Firstly, my prayer life took a new direction. As soon as I opened my mouth, the Spirit of the Lord prayed with power and interceded, and I could barely stop. I felt the power and the burn of His fiery love almost every time. I received filling after filling; I felt His continual presence. The desperation I had was great, and the Lord filled me abundantly by pouring His presence upon me in accordance to that desperation. The trials and hardships continued because the Lord still had to purify, equip and train me, but this time, the process didn't push me down. I saw it as an opportunity to be blessed and to grow spiritually. I collaborated with the Lord and I would tell Him, *"Lord, please cleanse all my impurities to make me pure gold and help me crucify my flesh for it is my enemy."*

A POWERFUL REVELATION FROM GOD'S WORD

At that time, after the Lord filled me, something melted inside of me and I started hearing God's voice. At first I didn't hear it constantly or clearly, but the experience manifested itself in different manners. At first He spoke to me through His Word, which became *Rhema*[2] (Living Word). It was like a fire shut up in my bones, burning as if God personally told me that verse. Each and every word was special to me; it became steadfast and remained there. The greatest proof was that all the Bible verses through which God spoke to me were full of life and power so that I immediately memorized them. They remained in my heart because I got them directly from God and they were specific for the situation I was in.

---

[2] **Rhema** is the Greek term translated as *the spoken word*. In contrast to *logos* (The inspired word of God), *rhema* is a particular word of revelation through which the Holy Spirit speaks to us personally.

After I prayed, I would stay quiet in order to hear God speak. I wanted a dialogue, not a monologue. One day I heard His voice that told me loud and clear:

> *"Read Luke 4:18!"* I read it immediately:
> *"The Spirit of the Lord is on Me, because He has anointed Me to proclaim good news to the poor. He has sent Me to proclaim freedom for the prisoners and recovery of sight for the blind, to set the oppressed free..."*

As soon as I started reading, the presence of the Lord descended and His fiery touch was upon me so I started weeping. I told Him, *"Lord, what are You telling me? This verse was speaking about Jesus. Why are You giving this to me? I don't understand, Father help me understand!"* I continued weeping in His divine presence. I heard Him tell me, *"This word is for you as well, my daughter!"*

This was the first Bible verse that the Lord spoke clearly to me. It was 2004. I received from the Lord a confirmation of this verse by the simple fact that in those exact days I read Isaiah 61: *"The Spirit of the Sovereign Lord is on Me, because the Lord has anointed Me to proclaim good news to the poor. He has sent Me to bind up the brokenhearted, to proclaim freedom for the captives and release from darkness for the prisoners..."*

It was difficult to understand what the Lord meant through this Bible verse, but I was certain of one thing: the Lord never says anything that doesn't meet a purpose or doesn't fulfill His Word. I started praying about this verse, declaring it by faith, so that it would become a reality for me. I knew God had a plan for me.

> *"The Lord said to me, 'You have seen correctly, for I am watching upon My word is fulfilled"* (Jer. 1:12, NIV).

Looking back, I am aware that God's beauty manifested itself through step-by-step preparation and awareness, so that I might enter the calling that He had for me since before I was born.

We cannot ask for something and expect to receive it or to reach the mountain's peak overnight. We need training (and by that I mean having your character formed and experiencing the Lord) in order to pass the tests which come our way and to reach what God has in store for us.

HOW CAN YOU HEAR THE VOICE OF GOD?

Here's an example from my life: I was cooking in the kitchen and suddenly I felt a wave of air in my ear, like the smooth wind or the flap of wings. I stopped immediately, not knowing what was happening. The Holy Spirit reminded me of the dove that once flew above Lord Jesus. I realized that the Holy Spirit, who came in the form of a dove, wanted to tell me something. It crossed my mind that in the old days people used pigeons to carry messages to other cities. I told myself, *"He came with a purpose, with a message from the Father, so that I can bring that request in prayer."* Why? Because this is how God works. He has plans for a country, a city, a person or a situation. He doesn't work without us because we were sent to be *"workers together with God."*

> *"For we are co-workers in God's service; you are God's field, God's building." (1 Corinthians 3:9, NIV)*

> *"As God's co-workers we urge you not to receive God's grace in vain." (2 Corinthians 6:1)*

He entrusted the earth to us, to rule it and govern it. That is why we have to receive our heavenly Father's commands. That through prayer and faith we can submit the earth into His rule. Together with His angels He accomplishes all His plans. Today God is searching for men and women, children and elders who surrender themselves completely to Him - people he can fill with the Holy Spirit. They can go before His presence and ask for His will to be done on earth as it is in heaven.

This revelation is powerful and necessary in order to understand our role here on earth, to know why we should pray, to see His will established here on earth, and to receive an answer to his prayers and supplications. Here is the secret:

"Then God said, "Let Us make mankind in Our image, in Our likeness, so that they may rule over the fish in the sea and the birds in the sky, over the livestock and all the wild animals, and over all the creatures that move along the ground." So God created mankind in His own image, in the image of God He created them; male and female He created them. God blessed them and said to them, "Be fruitful and increase in number; fill the earth and subdue it. Rule over the fish in the sea and the birds in the sky and over every living creature that moves on the ground." (Genesis 1:26-28, NIV)

"When I consider Your heavens, the work of Your fingers, the moon and the stars, which You have set in place, what is mankind that you are mindful of them, human beings that You care for them? You have made them a little lower than the angels and crowned them with glory and honor. You made them rulers over the works of your hands; you put everything under their feet: all flocks and herds, and the animals of the wild, the birds in the sky, and the fish in the sea, all that swim the paths of the seas." (Psalm 8:3-8, NIV)

What was God's initial plan? It was the plan of allowing the human creation to rule upon the earth and the rest of the creation. Yet He didn't cease His rights of ownership over the earth. Instead He entrusted man with the responsibility of administrating the earth. *When God said, "Let them rule," He still remained Sovereign.* He decided that He wouldn't intervene on earth to fulfill His plans and purposes by ignoring the mandate He gave to man. God put man on earth, not so that man could do anything he pleases, but so that through him, God could fulfill His will. God desires collaboration with man. How is this communication and collaboration possible? Through communion, prayer and His Word!

We see in the Scriptures that God always sought *a man* who would fulfill His plans. Since Adam's fall, God had already prepared a second Adam who would redeem the world and win back the dominion He once entrusted to man. God doesn't work on earth without man's collaboration. God used Noah to save the world from the Great Flood, He used Abraham for birthing the nation of Israel, He used Joseph for saving Israel from the drought, He used Moses to lead His people out of Egypt, and He used Joshua, Esther, Deborah and Mary. The Lord used them all for a specific purpose.

God is calling us *today* to be a channel through which He can pour divine answers to our prayers for our planet and for all the people around us. By this I want you to understand the importance and the necessity of prayer.

It is also essential to know our identity in Christ, to have true assurance and to understand our position from where we pray. We are God's children: adopted, redeemed, righteous, beloved, chosen and set to high places in Christ. We are a holy nation, His peculiar people, a royal priesthood, and God's righteous people. We are His seed and heaven's ambassadors. This is our position in Christ. We are co-workers with God.

When you know who you are, you have all the assurance, safety, faith and boldness to come before the throne of grace and mercy and pray to God. When you truly know who God is, who Jesus Christ is and who the Holy Spirit is, you have full certainty that your prayers are listened to, that they are not in vain, that the Lord takes heed to your supplications

WHEN GOD SAID, "LET THEM RULE," HE STILL REMAINED SOVEREIGN.

and that He will answer you. I mentioned some foundations of prayer, because we have to pray unceasingly and believe heaven is mobilized when we pray by faith.

Coming back to my experience, on hearing that wave of air near around my ears, I understood I had to pray. I kneeled and I asked myself, *"What should I pray for?"* At once I was exhorted by the Holy Spirit to pray for places I have never prayed for - for Africa. I felt the guidance of the Holy Spirit in the words I was uttering. The intercession was filled with power, divine anointing and passion. The prayer was "flowing" as if it was programmed. I simply surrendered myself. I obeyed and listened to Holy Spirit's exhortation, as He was the One praying through me because the Spirit knows the Father's plans. I know that only in eternity will I understand why I had to intercede in those moments, but then I had the certainty that I was fulfilling God's will, although I was taken by surprise. I was learning under the guidance of the Holy Spirit what it means to stay at the Spirit's disposal to pray and intercede.

Another time, I felt that same flap in my ears and recognized that it was a sign to pray. But I told God, *"Oh let me finish the meal first"* and I carried on cooking. In that moment, there was worship music in the background, and a song came on that touched me every time and made me weep. The Lord was pouring on me a spirit of prayer and intercession for others. Then I felt that I could no longer back out from God's calling for intercession. I turned off the stove and I started weeping, praying, and interceding with power, although I didn't know what for.

Then I was guided to intercede for my family's safety, my husband's protection at work, my children and my home. As I was battling in prayer, I felt an unwelcome presence in my house. As if it was standing on the steps of the house but couldn't approach me or come close to the place I was praying from. I couldn't stop, because the Holy Spirit was praying unceasingly through me.

I took the Sword of God, His Word and I started declaring Bible verses on protection, victory and praise. Then I rebuked with authority any of the enemy's plans and any evil spirits that could harm or bring something to my home. I prayed for their destruction in the Name of Jesus Christ and by the power of the blood of the Lamb. The battle was long and tough, but I interceded until I felt I had received deliverance and that unwelcome, horrible, burdening presence had left.

The Lord told me then, *"The enemy planned and will always plan to bring destruction, disaster, sickness, strife and problems in your family, but because you chose to listen to My voice to intercede, the enemy's plan not only failed, but was wiped out."* Blessed be His Name!

After that, I began to think about the numerous situations in which we are too busy or too indifferent to hear God's voice. How often have we not paid attention to His voice, or didn't believe it was Him, and then lost a battle, blessing and protection. When this happens, the enemy rejoices because he himself can freely bring disturbance, quarrel, gossip, pain and tension in to our families.

Lord, forgive us and help us stay awake, alert and watchful, knowing that our enemy, the devil, is prowling around like a roaring lion looking for someone to devour. Help us, Lord, be alert and pay attention to Your voice!

The enemy cannot wait to attack, destroy and kill us:

"The thief comes only to steal and kill and destroy; I have come that they may have life, and have it to the full." (John 10:10)

May everyone understand the benefits of prayer, so that we can raise a wall of protection around us and around other people. By praying, we put barriers in the enemy's way so that he won't enter our lives any longer or attack us. The devil doesn't fear our words or tears, but he fears the power of Jesus' Name, the power of His blood and the power of the Holy Spirit manifested in us. Knowing and using the power and authority we have been given, the enemy will flee from us. It is essential to ask the guidance of the Holy Spirit and to know how to pray with efficiency.

How changed would our lives, families, churches and countries be if we knew how to pay attention to God's voice, and to pray fervently, with faith, so that God's will would be done on earth as it is in heaven! What victorious life we would have based on Christ's victory on the cross, if we prayed unceasingly, like the Lord demands from us! In prayer we encounter God, because of Jesus' sacrifice. And by prayer we ask God to encounter the people we intercede for. We sacrifice ourselves when we intercede and we destroy the enemy's power.

OBSTACLES ON THE WAY

I was writing earlier about God's voice. How can we hear His voice?

Experience tells us that at first it is a struggle for a believer to hear God's voice, but once he deepens his relationship with God and comes before His throne, it is impossible not to hear it.

Maybe you have asked yourself how? Firstly, we have to know what God tells us on this matter and then we have to figure out how to practice it. God lowers Himself to the meek humble and broken man:

> *"Has not My hand made all these things, and so they came into being?" Declares the Lord. "These are the ones I look on with favor: those who are humble and contrite in spirit, and who tremble at My word." (Isaiah 66:2)*

> *"For this is what the high and exalted One says— He who lives forever, whose name is Holy: I live in a high and holy place, but also with the one who is contrite and lowly in spirit, to revive the spirit of the lowly and to revive the heart of the contrite." (Isaiah 57:15)*

The Lord has certain requirements. The most important is that we are right before Him, because we need a clean heart in order to commune with Him.

> *"Blessed are the pure in heart, for they will see God." (Matthew 5:8)*

We have to search our lives, hearts, intentions and attitudes by His Word, so that there is no obstacle hindering us from hearing God. The most obvious obstacles are sin and fear. Sin - whatever its nature - must be recognized and dealt with through repentance.

> *"If we confess our sins, he is faithful and just and will forgive us our sins and purify us from all unrighteousness." (1 John 1:9, NIV)*

BEING LED BY THE SPIRIT

After we cleanse ourselves in the light of His Word, through the Holy Spirit we must come with faith and joy before the Lord, who is described in John 10:3, 14, 15 as:

> *"The gatekeeper opens the gate for Him, and the sheep listen to His voice. He calls His own sheep by name and leads them out…I am the Good Shepherd; I know My sheep and My sheep know Me— just as the Father knows Me and I know the Father—and I lay down my life for the sheep."* *(John 10:3, 14, 15, NIV)*

Indeed, the sheep spend their time with their shepherd. They do not follow a stranger. The same applies to us: the more we spend time with Him, the easier it is to recognize His voice. His voice talks first and foremost through the Word of God:

> *"The Word became flesh and made His dwelling among us. We have seen His glory, the glory of the one and only Son, who came from the Father, full of grace and truth."* *(John 1:14, NIV)*

One way that God speaks to use is through the Bible. He reminded me His promises. Each and every time the enemy attacks us with doubt, we must search for confirmation in the Bible.

For example, many times God in His goodness told me, *"My daughter, I love you so much, you have value and I treasure you, I have plans for you!"* The Holy Spirit would confirm this to me, and with teary eyes I would be overjoyed that I am accepted, that the Most High God would reveal Himself and His love to me. I couldn't stop crying and my love for Him grew, I had an even greater desire to seek Him, serve Him and do everything for Him, because He loves me.

Then the Lord led me to His Word. For example, He told me to read Isaiah 54:10-11:

"'Though the mountains be shaken and the hills be removed, yet My unfailing love for you will not be shaken nor My covenant of peace be removed,' says the Lord, who has compassion on you. Afflicted city, lashed by storms and not comforted, I will rebuild you with stones of turquois...." (Isaiah 54:10-11, NIV)

When the Lord will make a way for you to understand, hear and listen to His urges and thoughts through the Holy Spirit, I guarantee you will become thirsty and hungry after Him. You will desire to understand Him, experience Him and you will do everything you can to always hear Him, to feel Him, listen to Him and obey Him radically. Until then, the struggle continues. But the Lord is waiting for you and He is more than willing to talk to you.

There are steps to be made and barriers to be removed so that everything will be easier. I cannot guarantee you won't struggle ever again or that you won't be confused, but you will be more mature and you will be able to discern certain things. You will search yourself, lest there should be any obstacles hindering you from hearing God. The fight may be tough and you will have to spend time in prayer and fasting, like Daniel. Still, with everything going on around, you will have peace and faith, knowing that He watches over you, that He is with you and that He will make your path straight.

When it is difficult and you have to make a major decision - like moving to another city, getting married or buying a house or a car - never make decisions alone! Pray and fast, talk to God about your need and wait upon His guidance. Circumstances play an important role in making decisions. You will probably feel it's not the right timing for buying a house or choosing your future spouse. If you notice there's no unity in your judgments, prayer is essential to clarify His will. Unity plays an important role, since Jesus said: *"... that they may be one as we are one"* (John 17:22, NIV). God is not the author of conflict, and He doesn't honor a decision that would later bring unrest. He can guide you through His Word. After you prayed to receive guidance, you simply have to trust His voice.

"To humans belong the plans of the heart, but from the Lord comes the proper answer of the tongue." (Proverbs 16:1, NIV)

"In their hearts humans plan their course, but the Lord establishes their steps." (Proverbs 16:9, NIV)

CONFIRMATION THAT THE LORD SPOKE TO ME

In 1999, with my husband and children (at that time we only had two children), we had planned a trip to Romania to visit our families. I had never met my in-laws and my husband's relatives. I prayed since 1998 that if God willed for us to go there, He would bring unity in making a decision and would help us find cheap tickets. In January, a friend of mine told me: *"There are cheap flights in June, but you have to buy the tickets now."* I called the agency and I bought them because it was the answer to my prayers. I felt it was God's will to go.

Then the Lord spoke to me from Genesis 28:15:

"I am with you and will watch over you wherever you go, and I will bring you back to this land. I will not leave you until I have done what I have promised you." (Genesis 28:15, NIV)

The verse suddenly became alive and brought life and faith in me. It was God's confirmation.

At that time there was a war waging in Yugoslavia and we didn't know what would happen until June. I told my husband that the Lord answered our prayers and we bought cheap tickets, this means it is His will to go. Why should I allow doubt to cause me unrest? Regardless of what could happen, I understood it's His will and I won't be scared of anything. We had confirmation from the Bible that He will bring us back safely and nothing will happen to us, because He is with us. We had to walk by faith because with all the unrest in Europe it was risky, and we were advised to insure our tickets. This was the big *test*, especially for my husband because he went to buy the tickets.

Should we the buy cancellation insurance for these tickets when we believed that God said we would go? He didn't buy the cancellation insurance, and he reminded himself of God's promises. June came around. We flew to Romania and returned home safely. I learned how important it is to receive a word from the Lord and to trust him, and to know that He is with us and will always watch over us wherever we go, and He will fulfill what he promises.

Many people run to prophets to receive direction. I don't mean to say it's a bad thing, but many times the Lord is telling us mysteries which we are not yet ready to understand. Maybe the Lord sets some conditions we don't like. Maybe we don't understand *the timing* for when He fulfills His plan and we are disappointed. Still, I want to challenge you to draw closer to God, to personally hear His voice.

The Lord wants to personally reveal Himself to us, He wants us to hear Him, but we are the problem. Maybe we have a hidden sin, which we haven't confessed. The Lord talks about this matter in Isaiah 59:1-2:

> *"Surely the arm of the Lord is not too short to save, nor His ear too dull to hear. But your iniquities have separated you from your God; your sins have hidden His face from you, so that He will not hear." (Isaiah 59:1-2, NIV)*

Our sin may be worldly desire, indifference or disbelief. We may be too preoccupied with life or there's so much noise in our lives that we never allow God to talk to us. When we go before God in prayer, don't rush. Pick the best time to pray, when you know nobody will disturb you.

> *"But when you pray, go into your room, close the door and pray to your Father, who is unseen. Then your Father, who sees what is done in secret, will reward you." (Matthew 6:6, NIV)*

So, decide on the appropriate time to pray, when you don't need to rush elsewhere, when you're not hungry or sleepy. You need quality time, just you and God.

Ask the Holy Spirit to enlighten you, search your heart and ask Him to pray through you the Father's will. You can structure your quiet time with the Lord like this:

- Worship Him, praise Him, adore Him;
- Confess your sins in the light of His truth;
- Thank Him for forgiving you;
- Intercede for others;
- Read and meditate upon the Word of God;
- Pair each prayer with His promises declaring His Word;
- Come before Him with faith, based on His promises;
- Believe and expect answers;
- Be still and wait upon the Lord;
- Communicate with Him and don't simply address a monologue;
- Continue by praising, worshiping and giving thanks;
- Write in your prayer journal.

"Lord, make me sensitive, polish me, teach me, and take me to places where I can understand your voice. I want to hear Your voice and recognize it, I want to listen to what You speak to me, concerning me and the others. Teach me, Lord, to wait in stillness for Your answer!"

Those of you who never experienced it, I want to tell you that it's going to be difficult in the beginning because there is a mess of thoughts and ideas running through your mind. They are not necessarily bad thoughts. If your mind and heart are filled with the Word of God, it will be easier to recognize Him. The wait can sometimes be short, sometimes long. God will speak to you through a Bible verse or maybe you will hear His voice in your speech. These moments will encourage you and it will bring you joy to know that God is speaking to you.

"This is what the Lord says: Stand at the crossroads and look; ask for the ancient paths, ask where the good way is, and walk in it, and you will find rest for your souls. But you said, 'We will not walk in it.'" (Jeremiah 6:16, NIV)

Other times, the Lord will show you something completely new. It may seem impossible, but I advise you to write in your prayer journal the words you receive from God, mentioning the date as well. If it is something big, ask the Lord for a confirmation.

It is possible to hear false voices that stem from your subconscious mind, knowledge and desires. If there is sin or idols in your life, the enemy can use it and hinder you, confuse you and instill fear into you. We mentioned earlier that an idol could be a need in our lives. If we focus and exalt our need over God in our prayers, we can make an idol out of it. In these cases, certain prophetic words or revelations can come to us distorted.

The more you persevere in your time spent with the Lord, the more He will teach you. It is said that in order to recognize counterfeit bills, you have to study the genuine ones. When you completely surrender to the Lord, you enroll in His school of teaching. You can't reach perfection in one stroke; that is reason why the Word of God and the revelations of the Holy Spirit for your specific situations must assure and strengthen you against the enemy's attacks. When we focus more in the truth of the Word of God, we will better recognize the enemy's voice or prophetic distortion.

Called For A Lifestyle Of Prayer And Fasting

In the spring of 2006, the Lord told me to fast for 3 days for a certain cause. I heard His urge with clarity. I fasted only with water; I didn't eat or drink at all (more details on fasting in the second part of the book). During the 3-day fast, the Lord told me, *"The next time you fast, it will be for 4 days."* Usually God told me when to fast a week in advance. After the 4-day fast for our children, He told me I would fast for 7 days for Africa. Blessed be the Lord for He uses me even today in Africa!

Once I started to fast every month, the Lord called me to fast for 10 days. While I was fasting, He spoke to me about my visit to Romania. This fast was on August 1st, 2006, and the Lord urged me to write these words, *"The year won't end and you will go to Romania, you will talk on the radio, in prisons and you will proclaim My Name; I will make a way for you to glorify Me because of what I've done in your life. I want you to proclaim My Word and My love."*

After I wrote everything down on paper, I couldn't help but tell the Lord, *"Who, Lord? Me? I don't think I heard it right, other voices are interfering! How? Why? Why should I go there?"* After we visited Romania in 1999, we didn't want to visit it any time soon. We intended to visit Romania later, when our children would be older, to show them where we grew up.

I sought confirmation in the Word of God. I was a little confused, but the Lord guided me to the verse I received with clarity from the Lord in Luke 4:18:

> *"The Spirit of the Lord is on Me, because he has anointed Me to proclaim good news to the poor. He has sent Me to*

proclaim freedom for the prisoners and recovery of sight for the blind, to set the oppressed free."

This verse now had a clear meaning and I wondered if it was God's timing to send me in the ministry.

But as time passed, I forgot these words even though I wrote them down. What I didn't know was that the Lord was preparing me for what was about to happen.

The next fast the Lord asked me to set apart 21 days in October to intercede for the child sacrifices on Halloween[3].

The Lord is faithful in His ways. When You are walking in His ways, He is right near you, even in the storm, in sickness and in destitution. He is always present. You need your eyes of faith to be open to see and believe Him.

When my time came for me to fast 21 days, it was extremely difficult. It was 1st of October and I couldn't enter my fasting period because I was struggling with myself. I questioned God: *How can I go on without eating so many days? To live only with water? ... O, Lord, it is too difficult... help Me, because You work in Me to will and to act.* It was difficult for me because I was cooking daily for my husband and children. Even more, I was also cooking for the guests that would come over on Sundays.

God, in His knowledge and strength and in His beautiful love, prepared me a book written in 1946 about the American Christians who fasted between 21 to 40 days only with water.[4] My sister worked as a early education teacher for children in a church at the time. Someone brought books and old tapes to donate to the church. When I heard about that, I went there to pick some books and Christian tapes and they were incredible resource for my growth. Reading about fasting, I knew the Lord guided every circumstance for my sake and I wondered how that person managed to donate that old, valuable book so valuable, not even found in libraries. I had read books on prayer and fasting before, but none encouraged me like this one.

---

[3] Halloween is widely known as a period in which the demonic manifestations targeting children gain amplitude. There are multiple testimonies stating that satanic cults kidnap children and use them in their sacrifices.

[4] Franklin Hall, *The Fasting Prayer*, 1947.

Again, I saw God's hand at work, fulfilling His plans for His glory alone. What do you think? As soon as I finished the book I entered my fasting period.

While reading about the great revivals in the United States from 1900 to 1940, I found out about the unique experiences and encounters the believers had while fasting between 21 to 40 days. I was encouraged and I had an ardent desire and faith regarding fasting.

For the first time in my life, I was fasting 21 days with only water. I didn't eat at all. The first days are always the toughest. For example, on the first days I felt weak and I had headaches because I used to drink coffee. But the good thing is that the body is detoxified. It's highly suggested to drink as much water as possible throughout the day (2-4 liters). I had great joy because I was motivated and especially because the Lord instructed me to fast. That's the reason why I had joy. After 2-3 days, the hunger went away. What is interesting to mention is that the transition itself was important: I no longer needed food from the world, but only required heavenly nutrition. I started developing a deeper hunger for the Most High God.

Before I was filled with the power of His love, my spiritual hunger was different and limited. But now I had a different hunger: not only did I desire to know and love Him, but I longed to enter His heart, to know Him and to fulfill His will.

You may ask, *"What do you mean by that?"* I wanted to be close to His heart so that I might hear His heartbeats beating for me and for others around me. I wanted to be one with Him through love, for His purposes on earth. I felt as if I could never fulfill His will until I understood and felt the suffering and pain which existed on earth and which required His divine intervention. When I reached my 10th day of fasting, I felt so well, so young, so lively, as if I were a child jumping in full health with no worries.

I thank the Lord for my husband who was an extraordinary support in this experience. He always took care of me, asking how I felt. Seeing that I did all the house chores alone he was encouraged. In fact, he even told me that I cooked better food than ever before. Yes, it might have been tastier because I cooked it with passion and joy!

Do you see how important our attitude is when we work? If we do everything in love and devotion, they will see it. It applies to every domain of our lives. The Lord urges us to, *"Whatever you do, work at it with all your heart, as working for the Lord, not for human masters."* *(Colossians 3:23)*. This devotion will be felt and others will sense a difference.

Still, it was difficult to fast. The days passed slowly, as if they would never end. But the Lord strengthened me and told me, *"Don't think about how many days you have left to fast, because it will drive you to despair. Think about today only and ask for My grace for today; do the same daily."*

I learned to focus only on the current day and at the same time I tried to spend more time in prayer. If our fasting is without prayer, there won't be great results. Fasting strengthens our prayers. The Spirit of the Lord came upon me with power and I would intercede and weep for the given cause. I prayed for all the children who were kidnapped and sacrificed for the enemy by the Satanists during Halloween.

> YOU CAN SPEAK GOD'S WORDS WITH AN EVIL SPIRIT.

Fasting is at the same time a moment for cleansing, devotion and seeking God's face. The Lord showed me even the tiniest impurities that were in my heart that displeased Him.

Here's an example. A friend of mine just dropped by. She didn't stay long because we had to go to church. She asked me if I had something to eat. I told her: *"I have some food in that cabinet, go and take what you want."* If you think about it nothing seems wrong, but the Holy Spirit softly rebuked me *"Why did you talk like that? Your tone and response wasn't filled with love, service and tenderness."*

"O, Lord, forgive me!" I prayed. The Holy Spirit is sensitive. I immediately realized I had to be more loving, sensitive and sweet. I asked my friend to forgive me, although she wasn't aware of my tone and I gave her what she needed. What did I learn here? The Lord wants us to always be guided by a spirit of love, kindness and devotion. But we sometimes talk in a harsher, colder manner to our loved ones. Even if they get used to our tone, we can sadden the Holy Spirit. I still need improvement in this area of my life.

A brother once told me, *"You can speak God's words with an evil spirit."* Lord, make us understand!

There were times when I felt in my spirit that the Lord was saddened when I listened to certain conversations or sermons. When we judge and criticize others, when we gossip, when we get angry, when we are obstinate and proud, we are of the flesh and not of the spirit. Extended fasting makes us more sensitive, it gives discernment and draws us closer to God so that we may see and feel like Him. I thank God for this grace; that I can minister, fast and pray for others. The wonder is that when we fast and pray for others, we receive a reward as well. The Lord changes us and we receive His blessings. When we help others, we actually help ourselves. Amazing grace!

During this fast, the Lord spoke to me and showed me some things. He let me know that I would be fasting for 40 days the following spring. How wonderful and wise is the Lord! He was preparing me, even if I didn't understand. I felt I had to obey and I made it in love and joy. This sacrifice is not easy and desirable if you look at it from the outside, but it's so wonderful once you taste its fruit! I discovered that fasting plays one of the most important roles in hearing God's voice and in spiritual growth. Fasting destroys obstacles standing between the Lord and us. It cancels other voices that confuse us and it aids us to properly hear God.

HOW PROPHECY WORKS

After you receive a prophetic word or a promise from God, a certain period of time must pass and there needs to be a process, a test, that equips you to be ready for it. Many receive prophetic words that seem impossible, but are exciting and can bring joy. Careful not to be proud, thinking that fulfillment is one step away. We sometimes want to fulfill it by our own natural abilities, but we end up disappointed and confused. This happens because we don't understand the *process* of equipping and preparation. We may take a shortcut, thinking we are smarter, but as soon as we face resistance and attacks, we fall. May the Lord help us understand the process and give Him praise. The process is for our own good.

Sometimes God only shows us the first step, because He knows our tendency to try to fulfill everything by our own strength. Time must pass for the fruit to be ripe. Look at Christ's birth for example: Mary was promised that her son would be the Saviour, but 30 years had to pass until that promise was fulfilled. Jesus had to be prepared, equipped, tested, filled and He had to obey before He set out to minister. If Jesus needed this process, we need it all the more.

It's easier to fast for yourself, for your problems or for your loved ones than for people you don't know. When God asks you to fast for a cause or a person you don't know or have any sympathy towards, it's a lot more difficult. This is when the Holy Spirit intervenes, who uses your emotions and makes you fast after His will. He will give you a desire and burden to pray and fast for those causes and for His will to be fulfilled.

Coming back to my experience on fasting, without knowing it, I was in the process of transformation, preparation, equipping, obedience and testing. This was before Christmas. Suddenly, the Lord told me to fast for another 7 days without telling me the cause. Maybe He wanted to tell me what for, but I didn't understand what He wanted to tell me. I obeyed and fasted. I could see a different identity forming inside of me, one in Christ, which I didn't have before. I saw how I was more and more desperate and hungry after Him. I felt how my flesh started being obedient and how the Holy Spirit was in control. He would reveal profound ideas and revelations from the Word and I could clearly see those three desires that I uttered before the Lord in 1999: to know Him, to love Him and to be transformed. Those three desires are continuously shaping me, because they are limitless. Holiness is an ongoing process.

Entering The Mission Field

After we begin to fast and pray, spend time with Him and talk to Him, we begin to develop a relationship with Him. It can take time! We ask Him questions and He answers, even if we don't always understand Him.

On the December 27, 2006, the Lord told me, *"Go check your journal and see what I spoke to you before."* I obeyed and I opened it exactly to August 1, 2006. I wept as I was reading because the Holy Spirit touched me, but at the same time I was confused. It was written, *"By the end of the year you will set out to Romania."*

Then I prayed: *"Where, Lord? How? Why should I go there? Was this You? There are three days left until the New Year - it's impossible. I have no reason and no desire to go. It's winter. It's snowing. I don't have money. Why did you speak to me, Father? If it wasn't You, who was it? I know from your Word that you allow a spirit of deceit upon those who are far from You or who have sinned. How did I sadden You? What did I do wrong? Lord, have mercy on me, a sinner. I don't understand anything anymore, but may Your will be done! I know Your Spirit was upon me when I wrote that word, that's the reason why I praise and glorify You. I thank You! I'm looking forward to seeing Your hand at work."*

After that entire struggle, I received peace, I was calm and I left all my troubles in God's hand. In those moments I felt an urge to call my family in Romania. I was reminded of the verse, *"In their hearts humans plan their course, but the Lord establishes their steps" (Proverbs 16:9, NIV).* I called Romania and my mother told me that my father was very sick and she asked me to pray for him. After our talk, I prayed to God. I asked what would happen to my father. As I was praying I heard it loud and clear, *"Your father will die in three days."* I doubted it so I asked again, *"Will he really die, Lord?"* I was sad but I meditated and I was curious to see how God will work and how He would fulfill His Word.

The next day I went with my family in the park and suddenly I saw a double rainbow. I shouted of joy, because I felt that His promises are

"Yes" and "Amen" in Him. I was reminded that God keeps His promises, and that this was another confirmation that I will go to Romania. Yes, sometimes God gives us these kinds of confirmations. We are confused and we cannot see or understand. What better confirmation could I receive? The God of the Universe has shown me a double rainbow as I was driving my car. I didn't need any other proof. The sky was cloudy, and suddenly there was a double rainbow and rays of sunlight.

Then, I dealt with another fight. *My father is really going to die?* I haven't seen him in seven years and at that time he was quite sick. I wanted so much to meet him, and for him to see how radically the Lord changed my life. His fasting and prayer, along with that of my mother, helped change my life, which has now been completely committed to the Lord. That's why I wanted to talk to him.

Exactly after three days, on the December 30th, 2006, before I spoke with to my mother, I kneeled before the Lord and I asked Him what I should tell her. As I was praying, the Lord in His faithfulness showed me a vision that I will remember for the rest of my life.

I saw my father in this vision, he was dressed in a bright, white, long garment. In this vision he was young and handsome as a 30-year old man. Next to him was an angel who put his hand on my father's shoulder and guided him to a huge golden gate. My father turned to my mother and said to her, *"Vaneta, don't cry because this place is so wonderful and you will come here after a short season!"* (Exactly 7 years later my mother went to the Lord, as I was writing this book). The angel led him to the gate and stopped for a while. I asked the Lord, *"What is behind the gate?"* The Lord, in His infinite grace and love, took me there to see what's behind the closed gate. No matter how hard I tried, I cannot explain in any human language the beauties I witnessed there. There are no words to express the absolute love, peace and joy that I felt and experienced in every fiber of my being. There was such a divine presence, that it cannot compare to anything on earth. I felt light and weightless. There was no pressure of time, space and gravitation. There was no pain. I felt absolute, infinite and pure love.

All of heaven was filled with divine love, like an infinite ocean. I felt absolute peace, which held me in a state of safety and divine reverence. There was a feeling of unspoken joy surrounding me, absolute happiness, which made me feel one with the heavenly atmosphere.

This atmosphere was in me, as if the entire splendor of heaven was in complete oneness with me. Time and gravity was no more because it has no relevance in eternity.

Oh, what splendor, what wondrous beauty is awaiting us! In that awestruck state, I told the Lord: *"Oh, how I want to stay here, Lord!"* I saw great light in the distance. I *knew* that the throne of God was there (everything is clear there, there is neither confusion nor fear). The heavenly atmosphere is indescribable and cannot compare to anything found on earth. That is why Apostle Paul said he couldn't say anything about what he had seen, because there is no proper way of comparison. Nevertheless, whoever tasted that glory, at least a grain of it, desires nothing found on earth. All the riches and splendors of the earth are nothing but a shadow compared to heaven's splendor. In that very state, all of a sudden my vision ended and I felt disappointed because I came back my reality.

The Lord didn't allow me to stay there for long because my time wasn't up yet. After this experience, I called my mother and she told me that my father was almost dead: he couldn't move, couldn't talk, couldn't hear and could barely breathe. Then, I realized that he was on his way. I told them about the vision, telling them that he will soon be with the Lord. After several hours, I received the news of his passing.

THE PROPHETIC WORD COMES INTO BEING

This is where the Lord's ministry came into existence.

After I received the news of my father's death, I was crying and telling my family to buy a funeral wreath from us for my father's grave. In those moments, I felt the Holy Spirit coming on me with power, wanting to tell me something. I started crying, telling Him, *"What should I understand of this? What do you want from me, Lord? What do I have to do?"*

He then told me: *"It's time for you to go to Romania."* I replied, *"Lord, help me understand and clear my doubt and confusion: why should I go there? Even though my father is dead, I don't feel like I need to go there."*

The Spirit reminded me of His promises and of all the things that the Lord has shown me lately. Before my father's passing, Marian, my husband, without knowing my struggles, told me: *"You weep, pray and fast may days. You have to go and give what you received."* I replied: *"Go where? If the Lord doesn't send me, I won't go anywhere."*

Now, guided by the Holy Spirit, my husband told me that my time had come, that I had to go to Romania to be a testimony for my relatives that were coming to my father's funeral.

God was telling me again, *"It's time for you to go."*

I had to step out of my comfort zone and that was not easy. I had to face the unknown, I had to accept God's will without conditions. I had to learn how to walk by faith. I still prayed and wept. After I called our pastor to come pray for me, he had the same words from God: *"It's time for you to go to Romania because the Lord has great plans for you. This is only the beginning of a great ministry. You are not going to Romania only for your father; this was only one reason for you to go there. The true purpose is awaiting you there: to fulfill God's plan that is starting to unfold."*

I was struggling because I had to leave the comfort of my training ground, of the spiritual equipping and I had to take action, fight, attack, talk and encourage. I had to confront shame, doubt, timidity and demonic powers. On top of that, I had to go without my husband, because he needed to stay home to take care of our four children.

After I calmed myself, I called an agency and I found a plane ticket the next day for a 2pm flight, on December 31st! I had only a few hours to pack my bags, but the Spirit of the Lord would remind me with joy and tenderness, *"I told you that the year won't end before you went to Romania."* Divine joy overflowed my entire being, and I couldn't help but shout for joy and praise Him, because His Words are true and were about to be fulfilled. Together with my sister, Estera, on the 31st of December 2006 we flew to Romania, the country the Lord decided for me to start His ministry of fasting, prayer, preaching, evangelism, serving, helping and encouraging.

Several months before, the Lord showed me in a vision that I would be flying with a *"swan."* I did not understand what the Lord wanted to tell me then, but I remembered the Bible teaches that we know in part and we prophesy in part. I searched on the Internet for the meaning of the swan, but I never understood its mystery until I the next time I set foot on an airplane. Before me was a small TV screen featuring a swan which was flying. KLM's logo is a swan, and then I understood that the Lord showed me which flight I would take. How mighty and considerate God is! A time of preparation, dedication, fasting and prayer is needed for us to know Him and understand His message for us.

You may wonder how you can have a deeper relationship with the Lord. God does not look at outward appearances. I am not better or more special than any other person. I have nothing I can brag about. What I wrote describing my personal experiences are meant to glorify God and to encourage other people. The secret of a profound relationship with God is this: time spent in communion with the Lord, in fasting and prayer, in complete surrender!

FIRST STEPS IN THE MINISTRY

When I arrived in Romania, the Lord began to unfold His plans for me. How great is our God! A pastor from Bucharest invited me to go and speak at a prison in Rahova. God touched all the women who were there. Someone invited me to speak at S.O.S Radio in Ploiesti, to share my testimony and what the Lord had done. I remember the director's wife, who saw me for the first time, told me, "*God sent you here!*" Then I went to certain families' homes to pray and encourage them. I experienced His healing, forgiveness and His transformation, and now it was time for me to share it to the others. There was a woman who searched for God for years and now she received Jesus as Lord and Saviour. Since then, her life changed completely. Glory to God who is gracious and loves us so much.

At that time, I received the passion, for a first time, to minister to the Romanian people. He put this burden, this task, and this love to intercede for Romania on my shoulders. Before that, I had prayed from time to time for Romania and for my relatives, but this time it was a passion coupled with sorrow and manifested with tears. I was consumed by it. I felt a divine love for the Romanians. It was clear that I was not the author of that feeling. It was not something that I searched for; it was not imposed by anyone. That love came directly from God's heart. This was His ministry alone, because it was humanly impossible to feel such love and pain for a country that you do not even live in.

After I returned to Canada, the Lord called me to fast for 7 days in February 2007. He then told me to start my first 40-day fast on April 1st, 2007. When I told my husband about it, he agreed that it was the Lord's doing and we understood that we were called to do His work.

I want to emphasize His beauty, which worked in my husband's life as well. The Lord gave me exactly what I needed in my husband, so that we may work together in His ministry. The Lord chose us from the beginning to be together. If I had a legalistic, religious husband, he certainly would not have allowed me to do God's work. My husband received the same desires and feelings when I received them from the Lord. Even if he didn't hear God's voice in that period, he still supported me, allowed me to fast, to attend conferences and prayer meetings. He understood that God had a plan for me, for both of us, since we are one.

What I want to underline is that I would not be able to serve the Lord if it were not for my husband's help and support. I owe it to him as well that I am in God's ministry today. That is why I respect, love and obey my husband. The fact that he understood God's plan and calling for our family mattered so much to me!

When the Lord called me to fast, it was difficult for him because he had some health problems with his stomach. When he acknowledged the seriousness of God's calling for our life concerning our Romanian brothers, he started fasting as well. He ate little at night because he had to go to work. He initially wanted to fast only a week. Seeing that I felt good only by drinking water, he was motivated to carry on fasting for an extra week. After the second week, he decided to fast another week with me. After that, he was encouraged to fast and pray even more, so that we together completed a 40-day fast.

Maybe you are in the same situation. Do not tell me you cannot fast. Everything is possible. You must want it, to be determined and have a serious motivation from the Lord (more details on fasting in the next chapter).

THE FORTY-DAY FAST

On the April 1, 2007, I started my 40-day fast. The Lord spoke to me, telling me to bring to the attention of the Romanians to God's call of fasting for revival, because He has a plan to bring revival in Romania that would affect all of Europe. I thought to myself:

> *"How? Who am I, Lord, to convey this message? Nobody knows me. Who will listen?"*

Then the Lord in His goodness encouraged me, telling me, *"You, My daughter, will be like a trumpet proclaiming My works. Blessed and joyful will be the ones to heed My words. The ones who will receive you, will receive Me, and who will reject you, will reject Me."*

Friends, these are not my words, but God's words, who loves Romania.

The Lord spoke to me, *"There are offerings and tears before Me, the blood of your forerunners, their fasting and prayers that were brought to Me and now I want to touch this country."* God wants to refresh Romania and to bring about change, because there are people who prayed and fasted for revival in the past.

God's Message For Revival

During that time, the Lord gave me a message from His Word to share with the Christians in Romania. This was the first verse that the Lord gave me:

> *"If My people, who are called by My name, will humble themselves and pray and seek My face and turn from their wicked ways, then I will hear from heaven, and I will forgive their sin and will heal their land." (2 Chronicles 7:14, NIV)*

This verse moved me deeply and I started weeping and sobbing under His guidance. Later, I found that the entire nations consider this verse as the golden verse for revival. I attended many conferences and I saw people of all communities, from many countries, who received this verse directly from God, just like I did. There is great mystery, blessings and conditions in this verse.

1. The main condition is humility.

Humility is becoming a rarity nowadays, but essential for our character as children of God. Those who learned the secret of humility received grace because He told us,

> *"For those who exalt themselves will be humbled, and those who humble themselves will be exalted." (Matthew 23:12, NIV)*

> *"Humble yourselves before the Lord, and he will lift you up." (James 4:10, NIV)*

> *"For this is what the high and exalted One says— He who lives forever, whose name is Holy: "I live in a high and holy*

place, but also with the one who is contrite and lowly in spirit, to revive the spirit of the lowly and to revive the heart of the contrite." (Isaiah 57:15, NIV)

"In the same way, you who are younger, submit yourselves to your elders. All of you, clothe yourselves with humility toward one another, because, God opposes the proud but shows favor to the humble." (1 Peter 5:5, NIV)

Humility is intertwined with fasting. We can humble our soul by fasting like David, Paul and many others from the Word. When we humble ourselves and we fast, we show that we do not want anything else but to repent, so that the Lord draws closer to us. When we fast, we separate ourselves from the world and we set ourselves apart for the Lord and His ministry. In humility, we renounce our traditions and opinions, learning from Him. Again, humility is becoming a rarity, but the Lord expects it from all the Christians. Nobody can attain it until they go to the Cross, until they are broken and crushed.

2. We are urged to intercede for others, especially for our countries.

Many of us pray, but we pray with a wrong attitude and this is what stands in the way of the response. When our heart is filled with pride or doubt, our prayers will lack faith. Some are discouraged because they have been praying for years and they see no answer. The enemy cannot wait to make doubting Christians blame God for His lack of response. He is waiting to sow seeds of doubt. He wants us to doubt God's goodness and love. In those moments, with disappointment, pain, anger and sorrow we say, *"Where is God? Why did He allow this trial? Why won't He answer? I have fasted, prayed and cried out. Where is His love? If He loved me, He wouldn't have allowed such hardships, injustices and accidents."*

Do you know what is happening in those moments? We *open the door to the enemy*, for him to dwell among us and torture us. If we do not take a stand immediately with God's Word, our state will only worsen. We lose our faith, hope, joy, and peace. The enemy rejoices because he knows that without those divine virtues, he has complete access and power over our lives. He then begins to fill our hearts and minds with sorrow, bitterness, disbelief, depression, anger and malice.

What should be done in such cases?

Look up all of God's promises for you. By reading His Word, you refresh yourself by reading about God's character and qualities. Then, repent and pray, ask God for forgiveness for opening the door to the enemy and for not standing firm in faith. Moreover, seek help from other Christians to encourage and pray for you. Do not forget, the Lord is good, and His mercy endures forever. He wants us the be able to shout it out:

> *"God, we are thirsty and hungry after You. No matter how much it costs, Lord, we ask You, come to us, show us Your glory and power, speak to us, Lord! Heal us, Lord! Answer us!"*

Pride closes heaven's door before we even start praying. Furthermore, the Lord expects humility, first and foremost. In other words, complete surrender with no hidden intention but only to seek His will.

3. The Lord urges us to seek His face.

As people, we acknowledge that many times, we tried to turn from our dirty ways, but we did not succeed. I tried to help other people, but they were not any better. Maybe they succeeded one day, two days or one month, and then they fell again. Why is that? We have to understand better what is happening in the spiritual realm. There is a law called the *"Law of the Forbidden Fruit."* The more we tell our children they are not allowed to go somewhere or touch something dangerous, the more they are attracted to doing so.

Saying, "do not take, do not taste, do not touch," is really of no help in dealing with the flesh (*Colossians 2:21-23*). We attract temptation through the things we forbid.

However, it is so wonderful to understand heaven's strategy - that of seeking God's face first. Why? Because here is a greater miracle:

you do not have to fight with your own strength, but you receive from God another light, strength, joy and love which will overflow in you. The old things will be cast out, because we are filling our minds and hearts with His presence, light, protection and faith. The more we concentrate on a problem or sin, the stronger it will get and it will hold us captives.

By seeking God's face, we find peace and freedom because we surrender to Him. We ask for His help, acknowledging that we cannot live without Him. When I found God, I found Christ and His love. Moreover, because I love Him and He loves me, I keep myself far from sin. I find rest and comfort in Christ, who holds me in His light, love and truth.

What a different and victorious lifestyle we would have if we only sought God first! Seeking His face means a life of worship. Whenever we seek Him, we offer Him a pleasing offering and it counts as an act of worship. We do not go to Him, begging. We go because we want to know and love Him.

> *"My heart says of you, "Seek His face!" Your face, Lord, I will seek." (Psalm 27:8, NIV)*

This verse attracts me like a magnet because there is so much love in it!

Worship leads us to singing songs of praise. There is a particular song which I enjoy the most, it says, *"Lord, show me Your face, I want to see just a ray of Your loving glance, I want the flames of Your love to become mine. Show me, Lord, Your beauty, to be amazed by You, so that I may never sin!"*

> *"Look to the Lord and His strength; seek His face always." (Psalm 105:4, NIV)*

> *"The Lord make His face shine on you and be gracious to you." (Numbers 6:25, NIV)*

The Lord knows there is great power in fasting, prayer and humility. If we encounter Him, He touches us and fills us up. Certainly, we will be able to steer clear from wicked ways!

I address this issue to all of you who are dealing with lust, desires, or sins that you cannot escape from anymore. A prison of sin. You might have a guilty conscience or not. Seek His face! Go in your room, close the door, kneel before God and pray. Spend time with Him in complete transparency. You will see how the Lord will set you free. Seek His face, knowing that you cannot live without Him. Trust in Him!

Many times, we try by our own strengths to be righteous and free, but we cannot succeed. Separated from Him we cannot do anything. True, there is a certain power in us that makes us handle things for a while, but this is far from surrendering everything to God. What does complete surrender mean? It's an abandonment filled with peace and faith, self-denial of everything we are or own. By surrendering ourselves to the Lord, He will have the freedom to work through us. We allow Him to work through us because we trust in His complete power and infinite love.

> SEEKING HIS FACE MEANS A LIFE OF WORSHIP.

When I was on a mission's trip in Uganda, together with the team, we climbed a mountain to pray. It was a "prayer mountain for all nations". As soon as we set foot on the mountain, a divine, supernatural peace overflowed through us and we started praying fervently and with power. We started interceding for Uganda and for the children who were being sacrificed to the demons. After two hours of intercession, with tears and anguish, suddenly I saw the verse from 2 Chronicles 7:14 written in the blue sky. The verse was written on the entire expanse with bright, shiny, capital letters. When the words *"Seek My Face"* appeared in the sky, they drew closer to me, towards earth. The words were alive, bright and inviting. In that moment, the Lord spoke to me to tell His people to seek His face. This is the most beautiful part of the verse, it is His urge to abide in His presence.

4. Turn from our wicked ways.

Why doesn't the verse say, *"Turn away from your sins?"* Because this verse is addressed to the people of God who must not *live* in sin anymore. By divine revelation, we become sensitive to God's desires and will concerning our lives. The Lord asks us to turn from our *ways*. What does that mean? It is about the religious system, which we inherited from our culture, ancestors or from personal experience. In church today, we see a lot of formal services that lack the life and power of the Holy Spirit. We sometimes wonder why God does not respond to us. He does not respond because we live and pray according to our own ways. We have our judgments, services, opinions and systems, and these are not pleasing to the Lord if we exclude Him from them. How is that so? If we sing to Him, honor Him and talk about Him why wouldn't that be all right? Well, the presence of God dwells in the heart, which is completely surrendered to Him when everything is done in humility, love and faith. It is sad when the Lord says the following about churches:

> *"These people come near to Me with their mouth and honor Me with their lips, but their hearts are far from Me. Their worship of Me is based on merely human rules they have been taught." (Isaiah 29:13, NIV)*

Religious formalism seeks to put God in a box and make us believe that our system is the best in existence. However, the Lord is calling us to humility, to seek His face, to rid ourselves of our traditions, to allow Him to hear our pleas, to forgive us and to heal our country.

We need the Spirit of revelation in our churches today. If for years nothing happens, if people do not change, if they do not repent and if they do not see the power and love of our Saviour, we must seriously ask ourselves these questions:

- *What is missing?*
- *Why are we stagnant?*
- *Are we fooling ourselves thinking that everything is all right?*
- *Why isn't God's presence pouring upon our church?*
- *Why aren't we seeing more souls saved?*
- *Why aren't we seeing more lives transformed?*

- *Why don't we see victory, healing and deliverance?*
- *Did God change?*
- *Or are we the problem?*

The answer is simple: the power of the Holy Spirit is missing. If we read Acts, we see how the Holy Spirit guided the ministry of the disciples. He was called upon, loved, and honored.

Why don't we allow something new in our churches? Are we afraid of change? Do we not trust in the power of the Holy Spirit?

It is imperative for the leaders of the church to seek God's face by fasting and prayer. They must listen, receive and see what the Holy Spirit wants to do in today's church, in our nations and in our personal lives.

The Lord wants us to change our "wineskins," which refer to traditions, customs and old services. Only then will He send the Holy Spirit, which is the new wine. What does this mean? I saw in many churches something new in terms of praise and worship, and in their practice of the Word. Those who are rooted in tradition cannot accept anything new because they were taught to reject everything. They cannot understand the Scriptures. They need a new mind and a new heart to receive the new wine from the Lord. (Matthew 9:14-17).

> *"Forget the former things; do not dwell on the past. See, I am doing a new thing! Now it springs up; do you not perceive it? I am making a way in the wilderness and streams in the wasteland." (Isaiah 43:18-19 NIV)*

Many times, the Holy Spirit has tried to bring something new, something powerful and profound! We are just not used to fresh revelation, and that is the reason why we reject it. It is such a shame, because we lose such grace, spiritual wealth, victory and healing from the Lord! At the same time, the ones who are thirsty after God step out in faith to new territories and make changes to their services, songs and sermons – while being grounded and committed to the Word of God.

This is a great secret: allow the Spirit to lead you in everything you do. If not, you risk having a form of godliness but you deny its power, and you grieve the Holy Spirit. The Holy Spirit never fails. He knows the Father's plans and the Father's will, and He wants to reveal them to us.

In the 1960s and 1970s, a sad event took place in Vancouver, Canada. Many Christians prayed for revival, and when it came, they did not recognize it and extinguished it. Why? God reached out to the lost youth, the drug addicts, hippies and rockers. They sought the truth. The Holy Spirit guided them to the church, but the Christians, when they saw how they looked, smelled and dressed, rejected them without feeling any love or mercy for them. Consequently, the Holy Spirit pulled back, and we haven't seen great revival in that city since that time. Despite this, there are Christians still praying and fasting, persevering in faith and expectation. There is a loud calling: *allow the Holy Spirit to work!* We have to be ready, not to be surprised, because:

> *"The wind blows wherever it pleases. You hear its sound, but you cannot tell where it comes from or where it is going. So it is with everyone born of the Spirit." (John 3:8, NIV)*

THE BENEFITS OF OBEDIENCE

Until now, we talked about the conditions the Lord has set for us. Often times we expect Him to fulfill His promises, but we do not take into consideration His conditions. If only we obey God, we would see His promises.

> *"…Then I will hear from heaven, and I will forgive their sin and will heal their land." (2 Chronicles 7:14, NIV)*

1. I will hear from heaven

Who does not want God to listen to their prayers? When we have the assurance that God receives our prayer, we are flooded with joy because this is a sign that God responds to us. If our sins make God say, *"I hide My eyes from you, even when you offer many prayers, I am not listening because your hands are full of blood" (Isaiah 1:15, NIV)*, then the beauty of the redeemed is that if we repent, He is faithful and He listens to our prayer. We surely have a God who hears because we have an Advocate with the Father, Jesus Christ, interceding for us.

2. I will forgive their sin.

Jesus is eagerly waiting for us to humble ourselves before Him with repentance so that we are forgiven. Forgiveness is a gift and it is God's grace. Jesus died to forgive us and to give us a new life. Why don't many people understand that? Why do only a few people experience forgiveness when it is enough for everybody? The answer is that people do not want to meet God's requirements; they choose to not repent and they refuse to believe.

3. I will heal their land.

Does your nation need healing? God's condition is that His people humble themselves, pray, seek God's face, and turn from their wicked ways. Through this God can heal your nation.

When the Lord spoke to me through this verse, He told me, *"Announce to all Romania to start fasting, praying and seeking My face!"* When I obeyed the Lord, a part of me was hurt to see those who did not take God's calling seriously, especially because the message did not come from *"Brother X"* or *"Pastor Y"* - from well-known people in the country. However, here is the mystery: God has His *ways* of working. He wanted to prepare our nation for great, mysterious and powerful works through all kinds of people.

At the same time, I was overjoyed to see that many churches, pastors and other insignificant people in the eyes of men received God's revelation of prayer and fasting. Many took action. Jesus deserves all the glory!

By writing this book, I want to refresh the desire and plan God has for your country. Let us align ourselves with heaven, and with many Christians who pray in secret.

STANDING IN THE GAP

This is the second verse that I received from the Lord.

"I looked for someone among them who would build up the wall and stand before Me in the gap on behalf of the land so I would not have to destroy it…" (Ezekiel 22:30, NIV)

When I read this verse, God's suffering overwhelmed me because He was looking for people who would hear His voice and I started weeping. In those moments, I felt the Holy Spirit's touch with power that entered every cell in my body. Then, under His divine presence, I fell facedown and I cried, *"Lord, I do not understand why You gave me this verse! What am I supposed to do about Romania? You moved me from Romania to Canada! Now I have a different citizenship, and many Christian friends and family. I belong in Canada! Don't You have enough Christians there to stand in the gap? Why are you calling me to pray for Romania?"*

The Lord replied profoundly, *"I desire an undivided heart, totally surrendered to Me, full of passion for Me and for My Kingdom. This kind of person will gladly stand in the gap for others because they love Me and care for them. I chose you, My daughter, to be one of those people, because I put in you love and passion for Me and for the lost."*

In this time, God revealed to me that He has a great plan for Romania, to bring revival in Romania that will spread to Europe and the world.

At that moment, I once again felt God's touch full of love and power. Again, the flame of His love started consuming me for Him and for my people. At the same time, I began to feel a great privilege to sacrifice everything for the Lord, for my country and for nations of the world. It is wonderful to serve from behind the scenes, from 10,000 km away, to listen to the Holy Spirit's exhortations, to pray, to weep, to intercede for the guilty and the sinful. I do not have anything to brag about. It is only His grace and His grace alone: you cannot suffer, weep, fast or torture your body and soul if God's love and grace are not with you.

When God's power touched me, I could not oppose it, but I had an immediate desire, passion and suffering because I wanted to intercede for the all people.

When you truly love the Lord, you are willing to sacrificing everything He tells you to. Here is the beauty of the intimacy with God: you cannot back down when He calls you, His yoke is easy and His burden is light, even when times are tough. True love and joy sees beyond the sacrifice. This truth ought to motivate us all!

The Lord is looking for others who are willing to stand in the gap. Are you one of those? The gap is large and many people are needed to fill it. Maybe you are thinking about your problems. However, the Lord is calling you to something new: come and align yourself and join the other watchmen standing on the walls, soldiers in the army of Christ. There is place for you too. Kneel and ask the Holy Spirit for a spirit of prayer and intercession for the lost and the broken-hearted.

We are all called to be intercessors. An intercessor is a person who understands the Father's heart and His desire, abandoning his problems for a while and focusing - body, soul and spirit - to intercede for others, a country and even the entire world. He knows that intercession makes a difference and can stop or delay God's judgment over a person, city or country guilty from sin.

Today, God needs powerful people whom He can use. God wants you to be like Esther. Maybe you come from a poor background, or you are an orphan, but you have been brought to the royal court and you had favour before the king who told you, *"Ask me anything and I will give it to you."* Esther asked for her nation. God saved a nation through her because she urged the Jews to fast, pray and humble themselves. God wants the same thing from us. He wants to work in us, to stand in the gap for our countries. When we go before the King, you will hear, *"What should I do for you?"* Then we can ask our nations to be radically transformed, lifted to a higher level from all perspectives: spiritually, financially and personally. God can heal our countries, but only if we fight. God changed nations because people stood in the gap, in fasting and prayer. Many revivals occurred on the face of earth only when the people took heed at God's words. He showed His glory through signs and wonders.

We were so glad to have the opportunity to visit different churches, conferences and see watchmen standing in the gap, in fasting and

STAND IN THE GAP FOR YOUR NATION!

prayer for revival in Romania. Many judge them, but they understand their destiny that of standing in the gap for their country, which is an offering of a pleasing fragrance to the heavenly Father. It is easy to stand on the sidelines, judging and criticizing other people's mistakes. But when you are on the battleground, you no longer have the time to criticize and judge, but to bear arms and fight.

We praise the Lord continuously because in all these years of mission, many souls were saved and set free, strengthened, encouraged and healed of diseases. As a result, many have started walking in their destinies God had in store for them.

Moreover, we were glad to see how God searches the hearts of many churches, fellowship groups, and women's conferences attendees. I saw the beauty of God when many sincere souls drew towards him, transforming their lives after God's holy face.

God started working. Before we went on mission, pastors from different countries came to pray for us. God showed them that a great fire will ignite in Romania. A revival will start with the youth; they will understand and receive God's ministry. Therefore, we must not pray only for ourselves, but for the young generation as well.

REVIVAL THROUGH THE HOLY SPIRIT

The third verse the Lord spoke to me was:

> "So He said to me, "This is the word of the Lord to Zerubbabel: 'Not by might nor by power, but by My Spirit,' says the Lord Almighty." (Zechariah 4:6, NIV)

I want to remind you that before Jesus' Ascension, He said that He would send us power, aid and a Comforter. In the book of Acts, we are told that through the Holy Spirit's power, the Christians multiplied because He was the One convicting them of their sin and the One performing the miracles. It is painful to see that we do not allow the Holy Spirit to work in our church services. I am so regretful that we have services without allowing the Holy Spirit to work with power and authority in our lives. Thus the Lord told me, *"It is time for My Spirit to work with signs and wonders, so that the Good News of the Gospel will be fully manifested."*

After I received all of this specific word from the Lord, I wrote everything down, shared everything with my husband, and then the Holy Spirit guided us to release this word to many Romanian churches.

THE TRUE RICHES

I want to encourage you: whoever you are, if you are going through trial, suffering, loneliness or depression, stop looking at yourself or your problem, and look towards Jesus, who promises, *"Never will I leave you; never will I forsake you" (Hebrews 13:5)*. You can do all things through Christ who strengthens you!

When you love Christ, He lifts your burden and is the only One who brings joy and happiness. You do not have to feel lonely anymore. Maybe you are poor and you say, *"Lord, what should I do?"* Maybe you are despised or chased away from home and worry about tomorrow. I have good news: Jesus Christ is for you as well. He wants to enrich you, not necessarily financially, but he will certainly provide for you if you trust Him. God wants to give you joy, peace and confidence. You are not alone; He wants to be a true Father to you. God's Word says, *" God will meet all your needs according to the riches of his glory in Christ Jesus" (Philippians 4:19, NIV)*. We are not alone with such a generous God.

> TRUE RICHES MEANS TO TRUST IN THE LORD EVEN IF HE DOESN'T ANSWER YOUR PRAYER.

My family and I still do not own a house, we pay rent but we are glad and thankful for what God has given us. We consider ourselves the richest and happiest people! Why? Because we have Jesus in our lives and He guides our every step and our every thought. We are His and our assurance in Him is worth more than this world's riches.

- True riches means to have peace in the midst of the storm.
- True riches means to have joy even through trial and tribulation.
- True riches means to love those who judge you and gossip about you.
- True riches means to forgive those who wrong you, and to bless those who persecute you.
- True riches means to trust in the Lord even if he doesn't answer your prayer.
- True riches means to lead others to Christ and make a difference in their lives.
- True riches means to serve the Lord and to serve others.

When you are touched by the power of the Holy Fire, you start to see what's truly valuable, that which remains forever. The world and its pleasures fade away, but whomever does God's will is blessed forever!

I desire God and only God, and I wish to do His will. He takes me by the right arm and guides me with His counsel.

The Miracles Of God

Like I mentioned before, I started a 40-day fast. Believe me, it is not impossible and it is not easy either. In those days, I experienced many wonders from God.

Throughout the fast, I felt heaven so close to me; I felt as if I could touch it. I would communicate with God at all times; I was praying and interceding incessantly. Truly, there is great power in fasting.

There were days when heaven seemed so far away, and I could only pray on a formal level and tone. You must recognize that during those times, the devil wants to destroy you with his weapons: exhaustion, grief, sadness and ungratefulness. He does not want you to pray because he knows that fasting empowers prayer. However, during this fast, the Lord did not abandon me and He dispelled the clouds that were burdening me. Then, I would intercede for hours for many lost and broken souls.

During those days of fasting and prayer, the Lord told me that it was time to begin our mission in Romania. When I heard those words, I was distressed and I made up excuses for why we should not go. I reminded the Lord about personal hardships and other needs, as if He did not know about this already. I told the Lord we did not have any money for plane tickets. I reminded him that we also did not have money to bring to the poor, to the orphans, and to the Christian Radio and TV shows in need. Moreover, we had to pay the rent and bills at home. I was beating my head with all these thoughts. Then the Spirit of the Lord reminded me that when God calls you to a ministry, you do not have to worry, sweat or fight.

The mind is the battlefield where the enemy wants to fight. He wants to disconnect you from God's plan, bringing about worry, doubt, fear and disbelief. However, the Lord provides. This was a big test for me.

The Lord, in His faithfulness, told me, *"People will come in turns and give you money because this is My ministry, not yours. I want you to go to Romania and declare My call to fasting, prayer and intimacy with Jesus. I will open up great doors for you, despite the fact that you are a woman."* I believed this word, although doubt tried to enter my heart.

I asked God when I was supposed to go, because I knew that the Lord provides every detail. His voice told me, *"On the 13th of June."* I called the agency and I found cheap flight only for the 13th of June. How faithful God is, blessed be His Name! I was so excited about this confirmation that I praised the Lord with all my heart. The plane tickets for my entire family only cost $7,400. I paid with my credit card and I said before the Lord, *"This is all Yours, Father. I have obeyed your voice. This is Your ministry. I trust You to provide."* He responded, *"Two days and two nights will pass and someone will come and give you some money. Nothing is up to chance; everything is scheduled and prepared by Me."*

The miracle of how we received the money

Two days and two nights after the Lord spoke, I was excited and joyful, highly anticipating God's promises. I went to a prayer meeting at our church. After the service ended, a sister who was new in our church came to me while I was going to my car, and she handed me an envelope with a card saying, *"You are a great blessing for me!"* I took the envelope and I thanked her on my way to the car.

I was fighting with myself and some questions were beating my mind. What is in the envelope? Does it contain what God promised? I was afraid to open the card. I was excited and curious at the same time. I got in my car and opened the card. What do you think I found in it? It was a $1,000 cheque! I looked again to see if it was not $10 or $100, but it clearly said $1,000! I started shouting for joy, singing a new song like the Lord in His Word exhorts us to do. I was weeping, overwhelmed by God's faithfulness and I could not stop praising Him and giving Him thanks.

However, I thought: *"Lord, thank You for this gift but I paid $7400 for the tickets and I need so much more!"* Two weeks had passed with no change. I was fighting with myself, should I trust the Lord or worry? It was not easy, but I chose to praise God and thank Him before I received the money I needed. I relied on the fact that He will provide completely.

After these two weeks, there was a women's conference at our church. During the fellowship, a sister approached me and handed me something, saying, *"Today I received a bonus at work and God told me, 'Give it to Rodica.'"* It was a $300 cheque! I was in awe to see God at work in this way! I was overwhelmed that I had an amazing God who made everything He promised become a reality.

After another week, a Christian family came to our house to pray together. When we got on our knees, they put a $2,000 cheque on the carpet, saying, *"The Lord put this on our hearts to give you this money."* I had no words to thank and express the wonderful way God was working! I thanked them for their obedience because through it the Lord is exalted.

Another day, when I went to the prayer meeting, the same sister who gave me the money, handed me another card. There was a $3,000 cheque inside! Then, another person gave me $10 - it was everything that person could give me.

Another day, I was overwhelmed by God's surprises and the generosity of a family with 10 children. They gave me $5,000, telling me they loved Romania (the wife is Italian and the husband is Romanian). They told us that the Lord put the desire in their hearts to give the money for the ministry that God called us to.

I was weeping because of their love and generosity, despite their difficult situation of raising 10 children. May the Lord bless them, because every time we were away, this extra-ordinary mother and her family helped us with our children, with food and with everything else we needed. How can you not praise God and trust Him? Who would have given you this amount of money if God had not sent it? We were overwhelmed by God's beauty and we praised Him with fear and reverence. This is how we received the money, step by step, because the Lord promised so. We did not ask for money, we did not advertise our need, but the Lord is so faithful to provide when we put our trust in Him.

The Lord provided miracles for us, but he also required us to lay everything down and give it all away for His purposes. We owned an apartment in Romania, but sensed from the Lord to sell it and to use that money for His mission. We knew that he required everything from us. Even though it was not easy for us to leave the children at home with trusted friends, the Lord told us that we had to leave everything to follow him (Luke 14:26).

We bless the Lord for His faithfulness!

The miracle with our passports

One week before we were to leave for Romania, our passports had still not arrived in the mail even though we sent the documents three months earlier. We were told they were lost and that we had to re-apply for new passports, which was a process that could take up to another three months. As a family, we fell on our knees and began to cry out to God for nothing short of a miracle! We went to the Passport Office, re-applied for new passports, and miraculously received them the next morning! We remembered that this was God's ministry and that God would work even in this situation.

How great and faithful is our God! He intervened and gave us favour, showing His divine hand at work.

Prophetic confirmation

When we arrived in Romania, a brother from Nigeria prayed for us and received a word from God for us. He did not know us or anything about us. The Lord spoke through him:

> *"I have sent you in this country; therefore, I will give you favour and influence. However, you need wisdom and tact. Woman, you will be a pioneer before other women. From now on, women will be seen differently, because I want to use women for the revival that is coming over Romania. I do not look at the exterior, but I search the heart. I am the one who chooses workers for My harvest!"*

In God's ministry and for the expansion of His Kingdom, it does not matter who you are. God wants us to be workers in His vineyard. He is Spirit and communicates through our spirit, not through our gender. The spirit God put in us has no gender or age. God seeks undivided hearts throughout the world (*2 Chronicles 16:9*). This prophecy strengthened me and I felt I "put my best foot forward" in the ministry, knowing that God Himself sent us there. He greeted us through His servant who confirmed God's plan, thus encouraging us. At the same time, those words had power and authority in the spiritual realm.

THE MIRACLE OF OPEN DOORS

Then, the Lord opened doors for us to bring His message and spread the Word to many people. The Lord allowed us to meet Pastor Petrică Dugulescu, who presented us to many churches. This pastor had a big heart, full of love, humility and compassion. We stayed at his place for a couple of days and we saw how busy he was helping everyone in need. His heart was burning for a revival in Romania as well. This brother was a special man, totally dedicated. He was in a continuous pursuit to help and bring joy to as many people as possible. He was working in Parliament, and was the first man to open a prayer meeting in Parliament. When he passed away, we were all sorry that Romania lost such a valuable man of God with great influence.

At that time, the Lord allowed us to meet Pastor Viorel and Vali Pentea. God Himself ordained this meeting. My relatives were supposed to go to Sucevița together with Vali and Viorel, but they could not go anymore and they connected us with them. We did not know each other, but I loved Vali because of her songs, which strengthened me many times when I listened to her CD. Going together to Sucevița, we became friends. The Lord opened doors for us everywhere she went to sing. In this way we spread the word of revival everywhere we went.

With the help of the Lord, we went to 30 churches and spread God's Word. Moreover, we spoke on the radio and on television. In all these cases, we wanted God's Name to be exalted and glorified. The Lord led us to spread the Gospel in prisons as well. Blessed be the Lord! We ministered in 9 prisons for women and men. The Lord touched many souls. Many were encouraged, others were saved while others received the seed from the living Word, which one day will grow for God's glory. Many convicted people declared, *"Thank you Jesus even that I'm in prison! It is here that I received Your grace and salvation! Outside this prison I was so busy and indifferent to You, but here in this harsh place You revealed Yourself to me."*

With the Lord's help, we helped many orphanages and we spread the Gospel even on the streets. I tell all this only for God's glory because He prepared everything.

Then, I understood why I had to fast and fight in prayer every day, in agony, in spiritual *"labor"* for the church of Christ and for all the people lost in sin and hopelessness.

The secrets of a life of victory are:

- Time spent with Christ
- Fighting through fasting and prayer.

RETURNING HOME AFTER THE MISSION

After these 3 months of mission in Romania, a time when we traveled throughout most of Romania, we returned home happy. We covered 10,000 km of ground in Romania. I praised God because He was with us and led us in triumph, even though our trip was not easy. A month after we returned to Canada, the Lord told me, *"Start fasting and praying 40 days."* I asked, *"Why, Lord?"* I thought everything was over and I can finally rest. The Lord told me, *"The seeds you and others planted needs water, health and protection to grow and bear fruit for My glory."*

I know for a fact that God ignited sparks and flames of revival in Romania, but I want to emphasize the truth: He sends His flames of trials to purify us and draw us closer to Him.

I went to several prisons and I saw desperate people, but after they were touched by God and received Christ in their lives, God's beauty started shining through them. When you go among them, you cannot judge them. Actually, if you have Christ's heart, you cannot judge anyone, not even the worst murderer, not even the worst prostitute. A true Christian has only compassion, mercy and the desire to lead such people to Christ's light and truth.

Together with our church in Canada, which is an international church with members from around 40 nations, we asked the Lord to touch Romania. In our church, there are people of Canadian, Native Indian, Filipino, African, Romanian, South American, Russian, Italian and Spanish descent, and many others. They prayed with passion for Romania since we left for mission. As proof that God loves Romania, He put in the hearts of people from other nations to pray for my country. The Romanians should pray even more, especially those who see the nation's pain, trouble, hardship, problems and sin.

A New Level: Calling Women

I started fasting and praying again for my country. You can imagine that it was not easy to stand in the gap once again for 40 days. For whom am I standing in the gap? For a sinful, hardened, religious country. For the people who hurt me, despised me and judged me because I am a woman and, in their eyes, was not allowed to speak up. If only you knew how painful it is for me to write these lines! It is God that made me to be woman and God that sent me to speak about Him (Acts 4:18-20).

People have made universal rules and laws about women not being allowed to speak in church. But in the Bible, when Paul told woman not to speak, it was a certain rule for a certain church at a certain time. It wasn't to be applied to every church, for the rest of history! The devil, who always sought to destroy the woman, has fought in all nations to choke the woman's voice (Genesis 3:15).

By setting these prejudices towards women, people judge God and do not believe His word, which says that he created all people in His image and likeness. We are all members of the Body of Christ. If the woman's role is to only do house chores (as some people say), how can the Body of Christ function? If only men are allowed to speak in church, then that body is sick and crippled, because a part of the body is not working according to the purpose God intended. Christ is the Head, and His Church (men, women and children) is His body. In every body, every member must work together (Eph. 4:16).

Why and for what purpose did God put such wisdom, love and gifts in a woman? Is it only to cater to her family and to do house chores?

Why did Jesus accept women to serve? Who was the first missionary? A woman and a sinful one: the Samaritan woman. Who was the first to witness Jesus' resurrection? A woman who was delivered from 7 demons. Jesus sent her to proclaim the greatest News, *"Go instead to my brothers and tell them" (John 20:17, NIV),*

"Go [women] and tell my brothers to go to Galilee; there they will see me" (Matthew 28:10, NIV).

The Bible tells us of another woman, Anna, who was serving at the Temple, telling everyone about Jesus. She did not stay quiet... *"She never left the temple but worshiped night and day, fasting and praying. Coming up to them at that very moment, she gave thanks to God and spoke about the child [Jesus] to all who were looking forward to the redemption of Jerusalem"* (Luke 2:37-38).

If Christians had not been guided by tradition and customs, God would have blessed us more through the women He chose, anointed and sent. Tradition kills us, but the Holy Spirit gives life! A misunderstanding of the Bible has destroyed many women and their gifts. This is how the church and the family were attacked. Do you think this was God's will? I am certain it was not! I met many women who have helped expand the Kingdom of God more than thousands of men (Men, please do not be offended). These women were dedicated to God and have saved many lives from death, hell, divorce and desperation. If they had not allowed the Holy Spirit to use them and they had followed tradition, would their souls have been saved? I repeat: Jesus commanded everyone who believes (men and women) to spread the Gospel of His Kingdom.

It is true that women must be in full submission of their husbands and the church. A woman must work under anointing and protection. There are many questions to be answered regarding the woman's role, but I ask you one thing: be open in finding the truth. Study the history and compare past events with today's world. In the light of the truth, God's Spirit of revelation will enlighten you.

Why did He call me, give me so many confirmations, and perform such great miracles in the process? If God would not have called me in this ministry, do you think anything would have happened? Do you think that without Him I would have been able to fast and pray or go to different countries to spread the Word? If you are looking from the exterior, you may or you may not be impressed by my life, but only my husband and I can confirm the reassurance of God's call, despite being a woman. He chooses whomever He wants. He chose to speak through a donkey. Why do we limit God so much by not understanding certain passages from the Bible? What is so wrong about allowing a woman to speak about our Lord Jesus? Can you not see that the passages in the Bible saying that a woman should not speak are referring to certain meetings and administrations because they were written at the beginning of building the church on earth?

God used women since the beginning. We can see this through the Old Testament. If women were so dangerous, Jesus would have mentioned it, don't you think? However, He restored a woman's position in society. I do not want to elaborate too much on the subject, but I felt it appropriate to share some thoughts about the woman's role in God's ministry.

WHICH IS MORE IMPORTANT: DOCTRINE OR LOVE?

To the ones who are judging women in ministry, I beg these people to fast with only water for 40 days and 40 nights, several times, for a sinful country full of criminals, murderers, prostitutes and abortion. They should sacrifice themselves for the Lord's sake: family, comfort, money, friends and stand in the gap for the lost at least 100 days a year for 7 years straight. Then, they should ask the Lord of Truth, what is the truth about a woman's role? I pray Jesus would open the eyes to those following in these teachings, who are hindering the outpouring of blessings upon many people who would come to Jesus through women.

You may say, *"God has His workers, therefore, women are not needed."* If only you knew how desperately the workers are in need!

What does the woman do when she is faced with the critical situation of having to *"preach"* to someone who is on the verge of suicide, desperation and death? If she has never been encouraged or allowed to speak, teach, or evangelize, how will she know what to say? It is because tradition urges a woman to keep quiet. If you do not have experience and freedom from the authorities, you will not have the ability, inspiration or courage to tell someone about Jesus. Which is more important: doctrine or love? What does a woman (or a man) do when she talks to someone and the demons start manifesting? To whom should she turn to? Don't we all need to be prepared, since we all have been given power and authority upon the enemy's power? There is a great need of workers! The harvest is ripe, we fight because of misunderstanding of doctrine and the enemy is rejoicing!

The enemy knows that when the Lord fills a woman with the Holy Spirit, she is danger against the enemy! That is the reason why he fights to stop her. Whose side are you on?

Remember what God said in the beginning:

> *"And I will put enmity between you and the woman, and between your offspring and hers; he will crush your head, and you will strike his heel." (Genesis 3:15, NIV)*

I fulfill God's plan with love for Him and His people. I say this with boldness and assurance: heaven approves and claps for a women's submission, love and ministry for the Lord and her sacrifice for others. This is obedience to God's heart and intent.

INTIMACY WITH CHRIST

Maybe you ask yourself what intimacy with Christ means. Here's the answer: to be madly in love with the Lord, to always walk in His presence. More exactly: to live a radical life for Jesus and to walk His paths for His sake only. The first step is to shift from religiosity to a personal relationship with the Lord and then to an intimacy with God. This word describes the communion between our Savior and us, just like the communion between a husband and a wife. Until they get married, they have a relationship of love, but after they get married, they have intimacy and have children.

> *"I am the vine; you are the branches. If you remain in Me and I in you, you will bear much fruit; apart from Me you can do nothing. (John 15:5, NIV)*

Throughout this book I will be discussing this matter continuously. He is the Spring and the Source, as soon as you turn from Him, you wither; you won't have power, love for the Word, for prayer and for worship. Through intimacy we can enter another level of intercession and travailing prayer.

UNDERSTANDING DEEP TRAVAILING PRAYER

In these days of prayer and fasting, God's Spirit came with great power upon me for intercession. I was full of sweat and tears. The state I can use to best describe what I experienced is a spiritual childbirth state - you can understand it only if you experience it, as Apostle Paul in Galatians 4:13 experienced, *"My dear children, for whom I am again in the pains of childbirth until Christ is formed in you."*

This type of prayer is the most powerful spiritual battle: it always brings forth results. When you take part in this kind of prayer, you are the Holy Spirit's vessel and He prays through you. You receive grace by feeling other people's pain, disappointment and depression. Your prayer becomes agony. You fight in prayer. In this fight, feeling so much pain, you start groaning while feeling spiritual and physical pain in your body, especially in your stomach. Women who have delivered a baby know what I am talking about. Praying with power, you feel the *"spiritual labor"* manifesting through the same kind of pain and cries, as if delivering a newborn. This agony of spiritual labor, or travailing prayer, can last from 5 minutes to 1 hour or even longer.

> ...THE HOLY SPIRIT. AT THE SAME TIME, IN THOSE MOMENTS OF INTIMATE FELLOWSHIP, THE HOLY SPIRIT SOWS A DIVINE SEED.

I will give more details for those who have never heard about this spiritual labor before. You cannot give birth to something if you have not had an encounter first, an intimacy of love, when you receive the seed. Spiritually, it is the same. Firstly, there has to be a real encounter between you and God. During this encounter a communion is established, a love between heaven and earth, between God and man, by the Holy Spirit. At the same time, in those moments of intimate fellowship, the Holy Spirit sows a divine seed. This can be a divine wish, a vision or a burden from the Lord that you are entrusted with until spiritual labor. You are like a pregnant woman carrying a cause, a burden, and a pain. Let us take evangelism for example: it pains you to see all those who go to hell, you suffer for them, you cry and you always pray that they receive God into their hearts and that they repent.

Maybe you are entrusted with God's glory:

- Maybe you desire to see the prodigal sons returning home,
- Maybe your heart burns for revival,
- Maybe you seek to bring love and peace to families,
- Maybe you want to help orphans and abandoned or abused children,
- Maybe you want to go on missions to third world countries,
- Maybe you want to help the poor with money and everything they need,
- Maybe you have the vision of seeing renewed churches,
- Maybe you want to see signs and wonders,
- Maybe you want to do anything for God's glory.

In those moments of profound revelation, God's Spirit puts the burden (seed) in your heart. You will feel the desire to pray and intercede for more and more. You will weep and fight for the cause. The "*pregnancy*" could last from little to a long time, depending on His plan and how fervently we pray. When the due date is approaching, meaning the fulfillment of "*on earth as it is in heaven,*" the agony, labor and pain start. In those moments, it is good to be alone or with people who are spiritually mature, who understand what is happening to you. Women do not give birth in public! People need to see only the fruit.

In those moments, you will start crying you will feel unbearable pain. You groan and try to breathe. Although it is difficult, you cannot help but deliver "*the baby.*" You experience great pain and you want to get rid of the internal torment. If you are not aware of what is happening, you will get scared and misinterpret the experience. If you know that you have been interceding for the cause by praying and fasting, do not be afraid. God's Spirit is in control, but the enemy wants you to abort the Spirit that was sowed in you a long time ago. Allow yourself to be used by the Holy Spirit! In the right time, You will cry and feel relieved and light. Your burden will be lifted. What the

Lord entrusted you with will be brought into the world through you. Everything that is from heaven can come on earth only through labor.

We are reminded of Mary who was in the same situation. She had a real encounter with God. The Holy Spirit shadowed her, filled her with His glory and sowed the divine seed. She accepted it and took care of it. Then, she bore the seed and the seed started growing and bearing fruit of its own. For Jesus to come on earth from the spiritual world, He had to be sowed in a special body prepared by God, allowing Mary to carry the seed. Even today, God is searching for hearts that can receive the seed of His plan and will.

DO NOT BE CONTENT IN YOUR COMFORT ZONE! DON'T BE SATISFIED JUST BECAUSE YOU GO TO CHURCH!

For example, the Lord wants to reveal His will concerning our country. He puts the seed of revival in many hearts. Then, we must carry it in fasting and prayer with tears and repentance until the due date. Since it is not easy to be assigned such pains, as they are by far the most terrible, many "abort" God's plan and will. We often give up in prayer because of unbelief or disappointment, or because we do not see anything happening. Satan sows the seed of disbelief and it is like poison, killing the "child" of destiny.

Maybe you ask yourself why it's necessary for you to suffer so much. Didn't Jesus suffer for our salvation? It is true, but do not forget that even though God is sovereign, He chooses to use human beings in order to fulfill His plans. In order to see spiritual revival in our personal life, church or nation, someone on earth must fight in prayer, for God's will to be *on earth as it is in heaven.* Many things are not fulfilled because God's children stop praying.

Do not be content in your comfort zone! Don't be satisfied just because you go to church! May the Lord stir up in your hearts a life of a victorious warrior to reach the highest peak, to win the gold medal!

A New Beginning

In 2008 the Lord told me to fast and pray for 8 days. The number "8" means a new beginning. The Lord spoke to me, *"I want a new beginning for Romania."* Then in April, God asked me to pray and fast for 40 days for Romania. This fast was a time of preparation for missions. I listened to His exhortation because I love Him.

Psalm 115:1 says, *"Not to us, Lord, not to us but to Your name be the glory, because of Your love and faithfulness"*

Had it not been for His grace, I would not have been able to do anything. Therefore, I do not need any praise, attention or anything else. I am but an unworthy servant who did her duty (Luke 17:10). At the same time, I am His beloved daughter because I felt God's calling - I had to submit and obey.

BEING TESTED

When I asked the Lord about the money we were supposed to use in the mission, He told me, *"This time you will receive all the money at once because this is My ministry and I want to show you My glory, yet at the same time you will be tested."* As it was so, the tests kept coming.

God cannot use you without testing you first. Maybe you will be persecuted or misunderstood, or you will go through troubles of all kinds - all these because He wants you to go higher and draw closer to Him. God does not want to take away your trouble and trial, He wants you to go triumphantly through trials because only then will your go to another level. In Psalm 110:2 it says, *"The Lord will extend your mighty scepter from Zion, saying, "Rule in the midst of your enemies!"*

This way we grow and we move gradually, until we reach where He wants us to be. I saw this in my life. He did not spare me from trials and sufferings because He wanted to make me a warrior for

Himself, for His Kingdom and for the people around me, so that they may be saved.

Now we were about to leave to Romania, but we did not yet have the necessary money, even though we believed He said that we would receive it in full. I heard the Lord saying, *"Trust Me that I am at work."* In this period of waiting, I attended conferences and prayer groups. I went to every place I was called. We saved up some money thinking it would be enough to cover the plane tickets. When I wanted to use them, God told me, *"Give the money to Me!"* Confused, I told God, *"Lord, You know how much we need the money for the mission trip and You want me to give it to other people? Why? Whom? This doesn't make any sense!"*

In my perplexity, I had to trust and obey Him. God guided us to give the sum to some missionaries who needed the money. In my mind, I was thinking about all these questions about the plane tickets and our needs, but God told me again, *"I told You the money will come all at once!"* God in His goodness said, *"Do not rely on anything that's on you, but rely on Me and My Word."*

GOD GAVE US TWICE THE MONEY WE GAVE TO THOSE MISSIONARIES. WE COVERED ALL THE EXPENSES FOR THE MISSION! HOW FAITHFUL IS OUR GOD!

I gave the money joyfully, but it was a great test. After I gave the money, I was overcome with joy. I knew that God was faithful, but soon faced another test. Our washing machine and fridge broke down. I was saddened and cried, *"I was expecting blessings and this is what I get."* At the same time, the Holy Spirit strengthened me, protecting me from all those negative thoughts and praising God. I said, *"I believe these are signs to show me that God is certainly at work, even if the enemy tries to trouble me."* I started praising God louder because God in his faithfulness prepared everything for us.

If you go through similar situations, remember that they are merely tests you must pass by trusting the Lord. Because God is faithful, He was not late in fulfilling His Word: on the last Sunday before leaving for Romania, our pastor called us in front of the congregation to pray for us. It was important to leave under their authority and anointing. The pastor encouraged the church to make a special offering for us, so that we could plant seeds in Romania. He put a flag before our feet and the brethren, one by one, came to the front and gave money. I wept because I saw myself as a wretch, asking myself, *"Who are we?"*

The Lord replied, *"You are My ambassadors."*

God gave us twice the money we gave to those missionaries. We covered all the expenses for the mission! How faithful is our God!

WALKING WITH GOD

One day I asked myself, *"What does it mean to walk with God like Enoch?"* The Lord answered me, *"Walk before Me! Walking with Me is not easy, but it is not difficult as well, it depends on your determination and desire."* Enoch walked closely with God, with determination and desire, he pleased God through everything He did, so that the very presence of God was somehow transmitted into his life, and he was taken straight up to heaven! This mystery should challenge us to walk before God like Enoch did.

God can do something wonderful through us if we surrender ourselves and desire to be used by Him. Our God is a God of wonders; He is faithful and full of goodness. It is worth trusting Him wholeheartedly! He expects a surrendered heart, which He could fill with His love - a heart full of faith.

The Lord told me once, *"Call upon My glory."* When Satan hears that we ask for God's glory to manifest on earth, he trembles and shakes because he knows he cannot have his way among us. God brings transformation, healing and liberty when His glory falls upon us. It is time we surpassed our limits and accepted the Most Infinite, Divine and Almighty God who is the same yesterday, today and forever, because He said, *"I, God, never change."* We want Him to be exalted and His glory to descend!

God wants us to move forward, to have mercy and compassion for the people around us who do not know God. We ought to be living testimonies. Let us think about God's plan for us: before creation, God desired all people to bear His likeness, He wanted to share with them His life, His nature, His purpose and vision.

You and I are called to represent Christ and Him alone. God desires to manifest His beauty in us.

Colossians 1:19 tells us, *"For God was pleased to have all His fullness dwell in Him."*

We have everything in Him, since Christ dwells and abides in us. We are filled with the wholeness of God the Father, Son and Holy Spirit. Amazing grace! This is the glory God prepared for our lives. If we are one with Christ, His glory will shine through us.

> *"If you remain in Me and My words remain in you, ask whatever you wish, and it will be done for you." (John 15:7, NIV)*

"Christ in you, the hope of glory." (Colossians 1:27, NIV) I absolutely love this verse! When we understand that Christ is in us, we obtain the hope of His glory in our lives. This glory is manifested from the beginning: in Moses, Joshua, and David and in the rest of us who seek Him. Today, Christ desires this glory to be reflected through us. Maybe you ask yourself how this is possible. The more you stay in intimacy with Christ, in communion and fellowship, His glory will be revealed in you. He will start shining through us, and we will bear the fruit of His character. Wherever we go, people will notice something special inside of us. Even if they cannot define that something, they feel drawn and they will know Christ abides in you. When this godly power is manifested through us, the world around us will see God's glory.

We must understand that we are living in a new season: God's glory ought to manifest through us. Are you ready for this? Do you see by faith all His wonderful revelations and plans for your life? Don't you think God chose you before the beginning of the world so that you may carry His glory and that He may manifests His glory through you?

> EVERY MORNING GOD RENEWS HIS MERCY, GOODNESS AND FAITHFULNESS TOWARDS US.

Wake up, brother and sister! Do not dwell in sin, disbelief or ignorance any longer. Look through the eyes of faith towards the wonderful destiny God has for you. Our God is the only Almighty God who does the impossible. You may feel weak, little, incapable or sick, but rejoice for God needs people like this! He wants to show His glory through the foolish things of the world to shame the wise. He chose the weak things of the world to shame the strong. Christ is our wisdom, righteousness, holiness and redemption.

The Lord told me to study Isaiah 60:1-2:

> *"Arise, shine, for your light has come, and the glory of the Lord rises upon you. See, darkness covers the earth and thick darkness is over the peoples, but the Lord rises upon you and his glory appears over you." (Isaiah 60:1-2, NIV)*

We will encounter darkness, wars, suffering, sin and difficult challenges, but at the same time God's glory will manifest like never before, at a higher level than anything experienced by Christians throughout time.

God wants to bring new things into your life, according to His promises in Isaiah 43:19:

> *"See, I am doing a new thing! Now it springs up; do you not perceive it? I am making a way in the wilderness and streams in the wasteland." (Isaiah 43:19, NIV)*

Stop thinking about what you went through in your life. Believe and act by faith, walking in His promises. Despite all your troubles, needs, or suffering, God is in control. He did not forget you and He promises that He has a new beginning in store for you, in your spiritual and material lives. He knows your ups and downs, strengths and weaknesses. He is ready to open new doors in your life. He is the God who spoke and the universe was created. Through Christ, you are a new creation; all things are made new. Look only to Him, embrace Him and accept by faith all these wonderful works that He wants to do in your life. Do not doubt and do not be afraid of new things.

I am telling you all these because I noticed that it is difficult for us to accept the things God brings into our lives. We need a renewal of the mind through the Word and prayer to leave the old things behind.

Every morning God renews His mercy, goodness and faithfulness towards us.

Maybe you face certain fights in your family. I hope that by reading this message, God has invigorated you, strengthened you and made you determined to seek a different relationship with Him, one of faith, power and authority. When God created us, He put all His power and authority in us. In Psalm 8:5-6, God speaks about man:

> *"You have made them a little lower than the angels and crowned them with glory and honor. You made them rulers over the works of Your hands; You put everything under their feet." (Psalm 8:5-6, NIV)*

God put His traits in us and we can do great things for Him and His glory.

How To Use Spiritual Authority

My husband and I have four children. As a mother, most of my attention is directed towards my children. For a long period I have studied the cause of rebellion and its manifestations. My eldest child always wanted to be independent, to do things his own way. He has a strong personality and character that needs to be shaped.

For example, one day my boy would not eat the vegetables with his soup. I was quite upset, because it had happened before. From a natural perspective, it is normal to be angry or irritated, but from the perspective of God's holiness, it is not all right. As I was talking to the Lord about it, I was weeping and suffering for my mistake, feeling guilty. I saw how the enemy attacked me through my own child. Then I realized that something wrong is happening to me.

Jesus said that the prince of this world is coming and that he has no hold over Christ. No matter how hard Satan tried to tempt Jesus, he did not succeed - therefore, nothing from the flesh ever entered Jesus' heart.

I understood that something was wrong because I got angry easily. It was clearly my fault and not my child's. At the same time I realized that there was some sort of power and opposition that wanted desperately to steal my peace and bring trouble in my family.

That day, I got up and I said with a firm tone that I would no longer allow the enemy to do all this. I looked straight into my boy's eyes and I told him, *"My boy, I am not talking to you. Now I am talking to the enemy, 'In the Name of Jesus Christ I command you, spirit of trouble, get out and leave!'"* My boy started laughing, but it was not his laugh, saying, *"Your prayers are in vain! Your prayer are not working!"* How was I supposed to react in that moment? The enemy tried to make me doubt, to believe that my authority was powerless. Then, full of holy boldness, I told him, *"No, I do not receive what you have just told me! My command has power! In the Name of Jesus Christ, I command you to leave! Do you know who I am? I am the daughter of the Most High God, I am empowered by the sacrifice at Calvary and I have power and authority over me! In the Name of Jesus Christ, I command you to leave and never return!"*

Suddenly, my boy was completely different. He sat down and ate all the soup and vegetables. Everything was quiet, peaceful and joyful. After he finished, he kissed my cheek and joyfully went to play.

We are not fighting against people, flesh or blood, but against evil spirits. We must go to a higher level and believe that God is with us in those situations. He tells us, *"I gave you power to trample on the enemy's powers. Why don't you use it? In my Name you will perform miracles, cast out demons, heal the sick; people will be delivered and healed."*

The authority is from Jesus Christ, but it is manifested only if we have faith, an obedient life and humility. Many times, we do not receive our answers because instead of using our authority against the enemy's powers, we beg for things in prayer. The enemy will not leave until someone stands up with authority to cast him out. We all want power, but we must learn obedience and humility just like Christ did (*Philippians 2:5-11*) to have His authority over the enemy. Many times we pray to be healed from a certain disease, but behind it lies a demon. You must cast out the demon and then the person will be healed.

A similar situation happened to me when I was in Uganda. A mother brought her 2-year-old toddler who was deaf and dumb so that we could pray for healing. In the meantime, she asked for prayer from the pastor because she had pain in her body. Suddenly, the spirits that were the cause of her aches started manifesting. She became extremely violent. Two pastors were holding her down and we came to their aid, leaving the child in the care of the grandmother.

We fought for 20 minutes until she was delivered. The battle was long and heavy. We commanded the demons to leave in the name of Jesus, but still she was not being delivered. Suddenly I asked the Holy Spirit for His strategy in this situation. I heard myself saying, *"Lord, send Your fire and burn them!"* At that moment, the spirits from that woman cried out, *"We are the spirits from the water!"* After a few minutes, the spirits began to shout out through that lady, *"We are burning! We are burning!"* The spirits left the woman and she was set free.

Later, the pastor told us that the moment the mother was delivered, the child was delivered as well because he started hearing and talking. Jesus' Name is higher than any other name!

THE AUTHORITY OF CHILDREN

In 2013, the Lord taught me new lessons by taking me through different tests and trials. My youngest daughter (10 years old) has a special gift of faith and is a prayer warrior, with a gift in leadership. Can these qualities be formed in a child? God allowed her to learn from us as her parents and through our tests and trials. We spent a lot of time with her and advised her not to neglect the Word and prayer.

One night as we were praying, God baptized her with the Holy Spirit. You could clearly see a spirit of intercession with tears. One day when the other children were agitated and would not listen to me, she managed to catch their attention and urge them to obey. She then went into her room. After an hour, she came to me with her eye red and swollen from crying. She told me she suffered a lot seeing the disobedience of her siblings and she shut herself in the room, praying and weeping. I was so moved!

One night she watched a movie based on a real event about a plane crash. It scared her so much that she could not watch it anymore and started crying. She felt the pain of the casualties. We prayed for her, but she barely fell asleep. From that moment, for about one month a spirit of fear tormented her. As soon as the night set in, she came to me saying, *"Mommy, let's pray, because I'm afraid."* I taught her how to use the Sword of the Spirit, which is the Word of God, to command the spirit of fear to leave. She would then calm down. After a while, she learned how to fight on her own. I will recount some of her prayers that are still vivid in my mind, which brought her deliverance and maturity.

"Spirit of fear, I command you in the Name of Jesus Christ to leave my mind. You have no right over me. I have the thinking mind of Christ. Jesus' Blood destroyed you at

Calvary and you have no right over me. No weapon formed against me shall prosper because I am a daughter of God.

Spirit of doubt, I command you to leave my mind. I believe and trust my God who fights for me.

Spirit of deceit, I command you to leave my mind. You have no hold over me. I stand in truth and declare Christ's truth upon me. I do not accept any lie. Nothing wrong will happen to me or my family. Jesus is my Helper and Shepherd and I fear nothing.

Lord, if I have sinned and opened the door to the enemy, please forgive me. I am closing it right now so that the enemy won't be able to come in."

I would marvel when I heard how she fought in prayer. She was desperate because of fear and she knew that only prayer with authority in Jesus' Name and Word can set her free.

In the meantime, we were also praying for her. From time to time, when I saw her in a state of fear, I prayed to God to understand why this was happening.

Then, I received God's peace and assurance that He is in control and He prepared her to fight. How can you learn to fight if you do not have a cause?

I thank God that after a long and serious battle, she was delivered. Now she is powerful in prayer and she understands what authority in spiritual warfare means. Every morning and night she reads the Bible aloud and prays without me reminding her. When I am away, she is the leader with devotional time. She is firm and serious. I see God's heart in her and the Holy Spirit guiding her. I thank the Lord for her because God will one day use her with power for His glory together with our other children because every one of them is special in their own way.

THE MIRACLE OF HEALING

One of our children was born with a lump on the back of his knee. We went to the doctor many times because the more my child grew, the more the lump grew. The doctors said they must operate on it, but they did not know how serious the lump was. At that time I had just finished reading a book about the power of faith.

This book that I read stirred up my faith greatly and it challenged me to go to my child and pray for him, *"God, you are the same God like you were 2,000 years ago! You can heal today with the same Hand you used before! You can heal my child!"*

I asked my child, *"Do you believe that God can heal you? There is great power in your words. Declare: In Jesus' Name I am healed!"* And he declared those words.

I declared upon my boy from God's Word from the book of Isaiah 53:5, *"By His stripes we are healed."*

I said, *"Jesus, by your stripes my boy is healed!"* And I declared, "Bless the Lord, my soul… who heals all your diseases" (Psalm 103).

I had faith and I was sure the lump would disappear, but nothing happened. I had so much hope, faith and holy stubbornness, that I did not give up and I kept telling the Lord, *"I chose to praise You and I thank You for healing him!"*

What is faith? It is the assurance of the things unseen! We must declare as if we received them already! Remember, it is *"God who gives life to the dead and calls into being things that were not" (Romans 4:17).* I did the same thing - I saw my child as healed.

What does God do in this situation? He tests us. He wants to increase our faith. This is beyond healing or any wonder. The next day, I told myself, *"Maybe the Lord is testing me, but surely my child will be healed tomorrow."* I anticipated and I thanked Him. On the third day, I had an even stronger hope. I remembered that Jesus rose from the dead on the third day. I rejoiced as I made some references to written events in the Bible.

I went to my child and… nothing. I felt doubt approaching me, but at the same time a wall and a shield protected my mind and heart. God says that His Word is a sun and a shield. Indeed, in those moments

God was my shield. I said, *"Lord, I praise You and thank You, even though I do not see anything. I will continue declaring healing over my child."*

After two weeks, we were all in the living room and my children were playing. Suddenly, the Lord told me, *"Look at your son's leg."* I got up and I was shocked to observe that the lump, which was as big as an egg, had completely disappeared! Blessed be the Lord, our Healer!

The doctors said that it was impossible for the lump to go away without surgery, but we witnessed God's hand! What is more important is that we passed the test. I encourage you to declare God's Word! Even if you do not receive your answer, continue to believe and declare that a miracle will happen. God promises in Jeremiah, *"For I am watching to see that My Word is fulfilled"* (*Jeremiah. 1:12*).

I will share with you the secret I learned from this experience, pray using God's Word and declare His promises!

> ...PRAY USING GOD'S WORD AND DECLARE HIS PROMISES!

We do not have to describe what we see or feel; we must declare His Word. Sometimes we complain that we cannot do certain things, but God wants us to do what Paul said, *"I can do all things through Christ who strengthens me!"* (*Phil. 4:13*). We do not have reasons to complain, because the Lord said, *"You are more than victorious! By My stripes you are healed!"* If you are cornered by trials, remember what God said in

Deuteronomy 28: *"If you fully obey the Lord your God… You will be blessed…They will come at you from one direction but flee from you in seven… The Lord will send a blessing on your barns and on everything you put your hand to… The Lord will make you the head, not the tail!"*

The Lord said to me, *"My angels are waiting to hear My Word through your mouths. When they hear it, they fulfill it. Therefore, do not complain. Cut out the disbelief and doubt. It is time you declared My power and glory. Meditate day and night on My Word until it becomes reality!"*

THE FIRE OF THE HOLY SPIRIT

Make time for God and He will make time for you. He wants you to experience great, extraordinary things. *"You will seek Me and find Me when you seek Me with all your heart."* (*Jeremiah 29:13, NIV*)

The Lord is calling us today to a real relationship with Him. Through the fire of trial, He cleanses us from our impurities to make us pure gold. Then, He is ready to send His fire, the fire of the Holy Spirit with a passion for Him. This supernatural fire will change you, transform you and you will no longer be common. Many people will judge you, but people will desire the same passion you have because of God's power manifested in you. This fire is the passion one has for God. If you are totally dedicated to God, sold to Him, you will ignite a fire in the hearts of the ones who are thirsty after God because God's power will accompany you.

God once told me, *"My fire is ready to fall down, but will it find something to burn?"* If we try to ignite a stone, we will not succeed, but if there is wood or gas, the fire will burn. What do the wood and gas represent? They are the offerings (fuel) set on altars, which we bring as worship: prayer, giving, praise and thanksgiving. God is the One who sends fire to scorch the offering. God wants us to be one with Him, to be a piece of wood thrown into the fire. This communion is intimacy with God, oneness with Him. You will start loving like Him, feeling as He feels and doing what He tells you to do.

What a great thing it is for a mortal sinner to enter into communion with He who is Holy, Eternal and Limitless! This can only happen because of the love He showed on the Cross.

Other than in your church, do you have a prayer altar in your house? Do you have an altar in your car, or at your workplace where you can isolate yourself and commune with God, a place where you bring Him offerings, praise and intercession?

Are you ready to receive the fire of the Holy Spirit to be at His disposal when He calls you? Maybe He will wake you up in the middle of the night and tell you to go on a certain street because somebody needs your prayer, or maybe you must give somebody money, or maybe He urges you to tell somebody about Jesus. This flame of His love will lead you into many situations where you will be a witness for God. We have a mission field in our homes, workplace, and neighborhoods. We do not necessarily need to be preachers in the pulpit to talk about God.

What do we do when nobody sees us? This is the greatest test. We are people always dealing with identity crises and seeking acceptance from the people around us. We like to do something for the Lord, only if people see us, or if we receive something, or if we sit in the front row at church. However, to get to those seats we must pass the test before the Lord, not before men. God was and is faithful. He rewards you even for a glass of water. We must be obedient and faithful in everything, knowing that God in heaven sees us, watches over us and rejoices. Then, the reward will follow.

Let us do all things as if we do them for the Lord! Let us not do something to impress people, but out of unconditional love that does not seek anything in return. Let us glorify the Lord through our love and do everything He asks of us even when people do not see us serving. Thus, we no longer seek the praises of men. If they come, we lay them down at Jesus' feet. We do everything with love and joy, for our Lord and Lover of our soul. When we are not seeking the praises of people, we are full of peace and freedom, and we are in a very safe place.

How would society look if we were all set free from our flesh and ego, which is proud and vain in appearance, but weak and without identity in essence? How would our churches be if we all loved each other, accepted each other, helped each other and did everything for His glory?

> I AM TELLING YOU THAT YOU WILL NOT DEFEAT GOLIATH UNTIL YOU FIRST CRUCIFY YOUR OWN FLESH.

Why are we not like that? It's because we don't have the fire of the Spirit in our lives! Yes, we call ourselves Christians, we go to church regularly, we give tithes and offerings, we do good, we sing in the choir, we play in the orchestra or in the worship team. Yet, why don't we have fire, passion and radical love for the Lord and for those around us? What is happening to our churches today? Why do people rarely give their lives to Jesus? Why? Because traditions, fear of men and fear of the unknown have replaced the fire of the Holy Spirit in many churches.

What is the Christian's role on earth? Firstly, to love God and secondly, to love our neighbors like we love ourselves. If we love, we are light and we abide in truth. We will certainly bear fruit and we will be a light in this darkness.

Let us take David's example. He had a close relationship with God and did great wonders even when other people did not see. He defeated the lion and bear before destroying Goliath in front of an audience. What is your lion or bear that you need to destroy? It can be pride, jealousy, fear, doubt, indifference, or lust. These need to be defeated in private.

I am telling you that you will *not* defeat Goliath until you first crucify your own flesh. You first need to conquer the enemy within you, before you conquer the enemy outside you. If you do not die to yourself, your flesh will destroy you.

Before entering the ministry that the Lord called me to, I had a vision. I was in a big room and there was a giant lion as big as an elephant lying dormant. A person told me, *"Before you go out in public, you must fight this lion."* When I saw how huge this lion was, I was terrified. I was thinking, *"How is anyone supposed to fight this gigantic lion?"* Immediately I said, *"I know what I have to do!"* I went near a wall in front of the lion. The lion got up and came towards me. Then, with peace and divine faith, I stretched my arms towards him and I said, *"In Jesus' Name I command you to get out because you have no power over me."* Exactly that second, the lion went out, as if it did not see me. Then I went out from the room and I saw a big, green field. I realized that it was the mission field the Lord had prepared for me.

There are steps of maturity in our lives. We cannot get directly into 10th grade from the 5th grade. It is the same with being a Christian. We grow, we learn, we pass tests and go into a different classes, where the expectations are higher. The tests will become more and more difficult, but if we learn our previous lessons well, we will be victorious.

The Principle Of Sowing And Reaping

The Lord says in His Word, *"Give, and it will be given to you. A good measure, pressed down, shaken together and running over, will be poured into your lap. For with the measure you use, it will be measured to you"* (Luke 6:38, NIV).

I witnessed God's miracles when I was generous and gave people money. I understood that it is better to give than to receive. After a while, you start reaping what you've sown. Do not forget, if you sow a seed of corn, you will reap a hundredfold. Sow in God's fields by helping the poor, orphans, churches, missionaries, and Christian radio and TV stations.

THE MULTIPLICATION OF 20 DOLLARS

It was April 2012 and I was fasting for 30 days for an upcoming mission trip. I was making plans to set for Romania, but I was penniless. The Lord allowed different trials in my path to teach me lessons, to test me and to reveal His glory through me.

In the beginning of April, God told me that the money would come when the month ends. On April 25th, as I was washing dishes, I clearly heard the Lord saying, *"Go buy the plane tickets online."* I was confused. *"But Lord, we don't have the money yet!"* I sensed his affirming words, *"Walk by faith, My daughter, because I will provide! Remember where all the money for missions came from. Who gave it to you? Remember what I told you in 2007, when I called you to mission, and provided every penny? People will come one by one and give you the money for everything you need."*

I searched for flights and I found the cheapest flights for June 19th. They only cost $1,060 each. Usually ticket prices around that time were around $1,500. I bought them through faith. I was highly anticipating God's work and provision. Each year, the Lord sent money in a different manner, through different people or our church. It was now April 30th. After my children went to school and my husband went to work, I started my devotional time with the Lord. I was so curious, wanting to see how God will fulfill His words. I was not interested in the money, but in working together with God to further His Kingdom here on earth. In my mind, the enemy tried to bring confusion and fear, *"What if nothing happens, what if you heard everything wrong?"* The voices were faint and could not scare me because God's voice was loud and clear in my heart and the Holy Spirit was in command, having control over my mind and emotions.

> MANY TIMES WE ASK GOD FOR A TREE AND HE GIVES US A SEED.

At 10 am, someone knocked on my door. Joyfully I exclaimed, *"Lord, I knew You would never forsake me and that You are faithful!"* There was a widow at my door who was part of a prayer group from the school my children attended. She gave me a $20 bill saying, *"This is from the Lord"* and then she left. I could not believe it. I said, *"Lord, just $20? I was expecting from you something more…"* Nevertheless, everything happened according to His words, but I only received $20.

In those moments, the enemy started crawling and attacking me, *"Where is your God? Can't you see that He betrayed you?"* I felt that these thoughts were trying to choke me, steal my faith and make me doubt God's goodness. At the same time, the Lord intervened through the Holy Spirit and gave me a fresh revelation. A ray of light penetrated the darkness that was over me. The Lord reminded me what He told me a month earlier about the principle of sowing and reaping. I was overcome with divine joy and I said, *"I praise You Jesus for I understand the mystery of this $20 bill! You gave me a seed and if I sow it, it will multiply - especially because it was the seed of a poor widow. I know what I am going to do with it, I will plant it in good soil."*

Many times we ask God for a tree and He gives us a seed. If we do not understand His principles and laws, we could throw away or neglect the seed. Then we complain. Genesis 1 says:

"Then God said, 'Let the land produce vegetation: seed-bearing plants and trees on the land that bear fruit with seed in it, according to their various kinds.' And it was so. God blessed them and said, "Be fruitful and increase in number and fill the water in the seas, and let the birds increase on the earth." God blessed them and said to them, "Be fruitful and increase in number; fill the earth and subdue it. Rule over the fish in the sea and the birds in the sky and over every living creature that moves on the ground." Then God said, "I give you every seed-bearing plant on the face of the whole earth and every tree that has fruit with seed in it. They will be yours for food.

We learn from these verses that God established a principle: seeds that are sown multiply after its kind. God reminds us about this principle because He wants us to sow even the little we have:

- Money
- Encouraging words
- Food
- Time
- Energy
- Talents
- Prayer
- Wisdom
- Appreciation
- Joy

Whatever you sow, whether it is good or bad, you will reap.

Coming back to my experience, I took the $20 and I put them in my Bible. I then said, *"Lord God, I know You are a God of multiplication, I thank You for this seed and I thank You that I did not doubt Your goodness and faithfulness. I put this seed in Your hands, Lord, and I ask You to multiply it a thousand fold – to $20,000 - for Your glory. You know our needs for the mission. Father, I thank You for the faith You have given me and I praise You as if I already received the fruit of this money. Father, I ask that You multiply this $20 bill."*

I was overcome with Holy Spirit's divine joy and I could not stop praising God and giving Him thanks. By faith, I saw how all of the expenses for the mission could be paid with this money. I knew we would have money to give to radio stations, TV stations, and churches, and to help the poor and the orphans. I could not leave God's presence for another two hours. I praised and thanked Him continuously.

Later, when I took my Bible to study it, I realized I had put the bill in the chapter about faith from the appendix. I was thrilled and I started declaring each verse, which only strengthened my faith. Here lies another principle we must know: if we persevere in God's Word, by memorizing and repeating His verses, the power of the words will affect our subconscious mind and our faith will align with God's will.

On Sunday morning, I took the seed and I sowed it at church. Life went on and I saw no multiplication yet. We humans are so impatient. Does a seed grow instantly? No, it needs time. After two weeks, I found an envelope on my doormat, which said, *"Seed for Romania."* There was $2,000 in that envelope! How great is our God! I praised Him for His goodness and faithfulness. I felt from the Lord that I needed to continue to sow from that money.

God's Word says:

> *"Now He who supplies seed to the sower and bread for food will also supply and increase your store of seed and will enlarge the harvest of your righteousness."* (2 Corinthians 9:10, NIV)

I sowed another $200 to different ministries and in places I knew God's glory was praised. It is very important where you sow!

A widow came to me and told me that God put in her heart the urge to pray for us and for Romania. She told me lovingly, *"You know I do not have money to give, but I want to give you all that I have."* She put some coins in my hand - $5.90. There was one week left and we did not have the money yet. I was a bit sad when I saw the $5. I expected God to do wonders that day and I only received $5.

Immediately, the Lord reminded me of the principle of sowing and reaping. This was another seed from a widow. With divine joy, I told myself, *"I know what to do with the money - I will sow!"* What do you think happened? At 10 pm, someone called me and said, *"Today, God told me what sum I must give you for your mission. I am going out of the province, so give me your account number to wire you the money."*

I started weeping because of God's beauty and might. He always fulfills His Word. The next day I went to the bank and I can't tell you how nervous I was. When I saw $5,000 in our bank account, I started weeping and praising God joyfully, shouting unto Him, as His Word urges us. I could not stop praising Him and thanking our Almighty God. Then, other brothers and sisters in Christ came to church and pledged us money, even though there was not a special offering for us. Even the pastor from our church called me, joyful, because many brethren from the church gave generously towards the mission like never before.

God multiplied the money and it was more than enough to cover all our expenses for our missions – more than $20,000! I want to thank the church I attend and all the brothers and sisters who obeyed God and joyfully gave money for His glory and for the fulfillment of His plan through us!

How did everything start? It started with a step of faith and obedience. Then, I declared steadfastly that the Lord will provide and He will fulfill His promises. I stood in faith, praising God.

> *"Blessed be God, who in His goodness amazes us with His wonders! (Psalm 65:5)*

FIRST FRUITS

There are different kinds of offerings.

This kind of offering means giving the Lord your first paycheck that you earn. You will be abundantly blessed in this manner. Or if you have a business, the money earned from the first sale or quarter must be given to the Lord. You will certainly receive more in return.

I remember my parents. They earned money from agriculture. From November to March or April they had nothing to sell, so they had no money until the first vegetables came in spring. Still, after the sold the first harvest, they set money aside for the Lord and they were blessed for the whole year. God always demands the first hours of the morning, the first income, the first newborn, the first love, the first priority for His Kingdom. He is God and He deserves primacy.

You may ask, *"Where should I offer my money?"* You must ask God and expect His guidance.

TITHES (10%) OF YOUR EARNINGS

Usually you give the tithes to the local church where you are a member. If you do not feel that you have to give the tithes there, give them where the Lord guides you, but you MUST give tithes because they are God's.

OFFERINGS FOR THE POOR

It means that you must give where the money is desperately needed (there is a need everywhere, but you must have the heart to do it). God's Words says, *"Whoever is kind to the poor lends to the Lord, and he will reward them for what they have done." (Proverbs 19:17, NIV)*

THE PRINCIPLE OF SOWING

The parable of the Sower teaches us that the seed that falls on good soil brings fruit, 30 times, 60 times and 100 times. The seed sprouts when you plant it in good soil: ministries, churches, conferences, and mission trips where souls turn to God, where people are delivered, healed, encouraged and who bring glory to God. By investing in such ministries you will surely be rewarded. God rewards us every time we give, but I noticed that the seed sown on good soil bears more fruit faster.

You may not see the results immediately, or receive money in return, but God will surely open a door through which He can bless you. He will decide how to solve your health problems. Dare to sow in the field of evangelism because many souls will hear about the Lord and will be saved partly due to your obedience and generosity.

You may not have the time or are not gifted to preach or evangelize, but by supporting those who do, your reward will be great in heaven. Did you know that almost all successful Christian businessmen understand the principle of tithes and offerings? They keep on giving, and therefore they have abundance. You might say that they give because they have the financial power. This is partly true, but did you ever think that they have money because they offered it in the first place?

With those $200 I sowed a part in Africa. The next day I received $500. Who is behind this miracle and why do things work like this? Firstly, we know God is the provider. Secondly, this is His plan for the mission He called us into. Moreover, faith and obedience worked their part as well.

The Power Of Words

The principle of sowing and reaping does not necessarily refer only to the financial aspect, but it is connected to everything we do and speak. Pay attention to your words, because what you speak you will one day reap in a greater measure, be it good or bad.

> *"The tongue has the power of life and death, and those who love it will eat its fruit." (Proverbs 18:21, NIV)*

> *"But I tell you that everyone will have to give account on the Day of Judgment for every empty word they have spoken. For by your words you will be acquitted, and by your words you will be condemned." (Matthew 12:36-36, NIV)*

Words have creative power, because they have life. Why do you feel pain when someone says something bad to you, insults you or humiliates you? Don't you feel it's like a knife stabbing your heart tormenting your entire being is?

> *"The words of the reckless pierce like swords, but the tongue of the wise brings healing." (Proverbs 12:18, NIV)*

If you doubt that words have power and life, why do they hurt you? Let us take heed, because we cannot play with words. They have the ability to destroy when used in the wrong way.

At the same time, if you are sad and burdened and someone comforts you and encourages you, you immediately come to life. Why? The same reason: words have a creative power and they can heal you.

> *"Like apples of gold in settings of silver is a ruling rightly given." (Proverbs 25:11, NIV)*

"A gentle answer turns away wrath, but a harsh word stirs up anger." (Proverbs 15:1, NIV)

"The soothing tongue is a tree of life, but a perverse tongue crushes the spirit." (Proverbs 15:4, NIV)

"A wife of noble character is her husband's crown, but a disgraceful wife is like decay in his bones." (Proverbs 12:14, NIV)

The tongue can be either our friend or enemy. Many Bible verses show us the consequences of our words. If this is the case, we should surrender our tongue to the Lord and speak only kind, gentle and positive words. The Word urges us, *"If anyone speaks, they should do so as one who speaks the very words of God" (1 Peter 4:11, NIV)*. His words are always positive and work for our best. When the Scriptures say that God's Work is alive and active, it means it is moving, it has creative power and always takes action.

Words are like *seeds*. Whenever we badmouth someone, the immediate effect is that we hurt that person. At the same time, we grieve God, because our words will come around against us and eventually hurt us and our family. Therefore, we are urged to speak in such a way that we edify, strengthen and never destroy others or allow the enemy to come after us. In our daily endeavors, we must be careful about what we think, and what we talk about with our spouses or children. If we keep complaining that they are bad, disobedient, what results are we expecting? We are nurturing those states and they come to life because we keep repeating, believing and uttering them.

If we do not have the money and we keep complaining, we remain in the same state. The same principle applies when we are sick and talk to other people about our disease.

Let us be careful! Our words have an attractive power. You either believe it or you do not, but the truth is, words have power and God gave this law. Therefore, God's Word urges us to walk by faith and speak words of faith. Instead of talking about our problems, troubles, sickness, or lack, let us declare the His truth and His realities for blessing. Jesus clearly said, *"Ask and it will be given to you; seek and you will find; knock and the door will be opened to you." (Matthew 7:7, NIV)*

EXPAND YOUR VISION

How is our spiritual vision? What is the Holy Spirit showing us before our spiritual eyes?

- Do we see stadiums filled with people who turn to God, shouting for joy because they have Jesus?
- Do we see God's power manifesting like He did in the apostles' times with our spiritual eyes?
- Do we see simple men like Peter who are used mightily by God?
- Do we see the enemy's power bound?
- Do we see the crippled being healed and the dead being resurrected?
- Do we see God's promises becoming a reality in our lives?
- Do we see God's angels working for us and conveying messages from God to us?

Do not think this is foolish: godly men and women do not mind being called crazy for Christ. These sentences and phrases are revelations received from God and He desires to perform miracles. I encourage you to stand up in faith and declare these truths in Jesus' Name. If we think in this way, the wonders will become a reality for us. If we doubt, we ought to pray, repent and ask the Lord to open our eyes, to increase our faith and see His glory and power.

I am addressing this to the Church: the revival is happening around the world, including our country. Let us continue believing and praying, anticipating and thanking God for His work around the world. Let us pray for the workers He will use. Let them be baptized with Holy Spirit - fire, passion and zeal. Let them listen to His voice and take action according to His Word, standing day and night in the gap at His altar. Moreover, I pray that the Lord increases our faith and love for Him, to stand in the gap in fasting and prayer with faith.

It is time we put aside our theological disputes! Let us approach the sole Truth - Jesus Christ! In Christ there is no fighting, debate, contention or disunity, only love discernment. Satan is fighting against us, and his purpose is to make us lose our target, and the plan God has in store for us. Only when we are balanced in the *central truth* of Christ can we be used to change humanity.

The most important thing happening during a spiritual revival is the manifestation of a thirst and hunger after God. We must be desperate after His presence, after fellowship and communion every second of the day. When this desperation fills our hearts, it is a sign that the Holy Spirit is free to work in us.

I was glad to see people seeking God. Christians are fed up with formalism and religion, they want something more and they want to see God in His perfection. This is what God wants from every church.

- Are you one of those souls who desire to know Him more than anything else?
- Are you thirsty, hungry and desperate after Jesus Christ and intimacy with Him?
- Does a desire burn in your heart to love Him wholeheartedly with all your being and strength?
- Do you desire to stand in the gap for your country, protecting it from destruction?
- Are you praying for a revival in your country?

If yes, then be certain that God's love, goodness and faithfulness will fill your life and you will be able to testify to all men that you have found true fulfillment.

- Let us desire to know God.
- Let us walk guided by the Holy Spirit.
- Let us die to ourselves.

"If you remain in Me and My words remain in you, ask whatever you wish, and it will be done for you. This is to My Father's glory, that you bear much fruit, showing yourselves to be My disciples. As the Father has loved Me, so have I loved you. Now remain in My love." (John 15:7-9, NIV)

I pray that God's spirit rests upon each and every reader and that He stirs up a thirst and hunger after Him for complete surrender!

PART II

THE POWER OF FASTING

"Even now," declares the Lord,
"Return to Me with all your heart,
With fasting and weeping and mourning."
Joel 2:12

"When I heard these things, I sat down and wept.
For some days I mourned and fasted and prayed
before the God of heaven."
Nehemiah 1:4

"Anna was a widow, and until she was eighty-four,
she never left the temple but worshiped night and day
with fasting and prayer."
Luke 2:37

Fasting In The Bible

In the second part of this book, I will discuss the importance of fasting and the way in which we can discover God's beauty through fasting. I am aware that while some Christians have a disciplined fasting lifestyle, other Christians hardly ever fast, or only fast out of obligation.

Through my personal experiences and those of others, I will attempt to explain this topic in detail and I will try to give answers to some questions that have come along the way regarding this subject. By writing this, I do not want to put myself in the spotlight. I write this book with the earnest desire of encouraging, touching, strengthening and blessing other people. I pray that after reading this, you will be motivated to add fasting to your prayers, which will change your spiritual lifestyle for the better, and will improve your physical state as well.

Moreover, I want the name of Jesus Christ, which is higher than every other name, to be glorified and exalted. In His Word, God commands us to tell people about His works and wonders so that He receives glory and so that the Church is strengthened.

Fasting has solid foundation in the Bible and we need to focus on the Word to understand its true value. The Bible is the fundamental book for each and every believer who desires to learn how to fast according to God's will.

FASTING IN THE OLD TESTAMENT

Moses' fast. This was a 40-day and 40-night fast to receive the 10 commandments.

> *"Moses was there with the Lord forty days and forty nights without eating bread or drinking water. And he wrote on the tablets the words of the covenant—the Ten Commandments."*
> *(Exodus 34:28, NIV)*

Samuel's fast. The Day of Atonement, which was a day of humility.

> *"This is to be a lasting ordinance for you: On the tenth day of the seventh month you must deny yourselves and not do any work—whether native-born or a foreigner residing among you—" (Leviticus 16:29, NIV)*

David's fast. When he interceded for his sick child, and when he humbled his soul.

> *"David pleaded with God for the child. He fasted and spent the nights lying in sackcloth on the ground." (2 Samuel 12:16, NIV)*

> *"Then David and all the men with him took hold of their clothes and tore them. They mourned and wept and fasted till evening for Saul and his son Jonathan, and for the army of the Lord and for the nation of Israel, because they had fallen by the sword." (2 Samuel 1:11-12, NIV)*

> *"When I weep and fast, I must endure scorn;" (Psalm 69:10, NIV)*

> *"When they were ill, I put on sackcloth and humbled myself with fasting" (Psalm 35:13, NIV)*

Elijah's fast. Elijah ate and drank and started a journey of 40 days and nights with no food to eat in preparation to meet with God.

> *"So he got up and ate and drank. Strengthened by that food, he traveled forty days and forty nights until he reached Horeb, the mountain of God." (1 Kings 19:8, NIV)*

Ahab's fast. He humbled himself and as a response, God postponed judgment.

> *"When Ahab heard these words, he tore his clothes, put on sackcloth and fasted. He lay in sackcloth and went around meekly." (1 Kings 21:27, NIV)*

Jehoshaphat's fast. He proclaimed a fast for Israel and the Lord fought for them.

> *"Alarmed, Jehoshaphat resolved to inquire of the Lord, and he proclaimed a fast for all Judah."* (2 Chronicles 20:3, NIV)

Nehemiah's fast. Strengthened him to rebuild the walls of Jerusalem

> *"They said to me, "Those who survived the exile and are back in the province are in great trouble and disgrace. The wall of Jerusalem is broken down, and its gates have been burned with fire." When I heard these things, I sat down and wept. For some days I mourned and fasted and prayed before the God of heaven." (Nehemiah 1:3-4, NIV)*

Ezra's fast. God answered their petition for protection.

> *"There, by the Ahava Canal, I proclaimed a fast, so that we might humble ourselves before our God and ask him for a safe journey for us and our children, with all our possessions. So we fasted and petitioned our God about this, and he answered our prayer." (Ezra 8:21, 23, NIV)*

Ezra's second fast. He did not eat or drink because of the sins of the people.

> *"Then Ezra withdrew from before the house of God and went to the room of Jehohanan son of Eliashib. While he was there, he ate no food and drank no water, because he continued to mourn over the unfaithfulness of the exiles." (Ezra 10:6, NIV)*

Joel's fast. This was a national fast for repentance, restoration and obedience.

> *Even now," declares the Lord, "return to me with all your heart, with fasting and weeping and mourning." Rend your heart and not your garments. Return to the Lord your God, for he is gracious and compassionate, slow to anger and abounding in love, and he relents from sending calamity. Who knows? He may turn and relent and leave behind a*

blessing— grain offerings and drink offerings for the Lord your God. Blow the trumpet in Zion, declare a holy fast, and call a sacred assembly." (Joel 1:14, Joel 2:12-15, NIV)

Esther's fast. Through this fast God spared the entire nation.
"Go, gather together all the Jews who are in Susa, and fast for me. Do not eat or drink for three days, night or day. My attendants and I will fast as you do. When this is done, I will go to the king, even though it is against the law. And if I perish, I perish." (Esther 4:16, NIV)

Daniel's fast. A fast of mourning, followed by redemption and divine revelations.
"So I turned to the Lord God and pleaded with him in prayer and petition, in fasting, and in sackcloth and ashes." (Daniel 9:3, NIV)

"At that time I, Daniel, mourned for three weeks. I ate no choice food; no meat or wine touched my lips; and I used no lotions at all until the three weeks were over." (Daniel 10:2-3, NIV)

Isaiah 58 fast. True fasting chosen by God that brings reward.
"Is not this the kind of fasting I have chosen: to loose the chains of injustice and untie the cords of the yoke, to set the oppressed free and break every yoke? Is it not to share your food with the hungry and to provide the poor wanderer with shelter— when you see the naked, to clothe them, and not to turn away from your own flesh and blood?" (Isaiah 58:6-7, NIV)

FASTING IN THE NEW TESTAMENT

- Fasting is described in contrast to the religiosity of the hypocrites.
  "When you fast, do not look somber as the hypocrites do, for they disfigure their faces to show others they are fasting. Truly I tell you, they have received their reward in full." (Matthew 6:16, NIV)

- Fasting is a necessary ingredient in servanthood.
  "…In beatings, imprisonments and riots; in hard work, sleepless nights and hunger;" (2 Corinthians 6:5, NIV)

- Fasting in marriage is a normal activity for a family.
  "Do not deprive each other except perhaps by mutual consent and for a time, so that you may devote yourselves to prayer. Then come together again so that Satan will not tempt you because of your lack of self-control." (1 Corinthians 7:5, NIV)

- Fasting is necessary for increasing our faith and for deliverance.
  "However, this kind does not go out except by prayer and fasting." (Matthew 17:21, NKJV)

- Jesus' 40-day fast was followed by His consecration in the ministry and His filling with the Holy Spirit.
  "After fasting forty days and forty nights, he was hungry." (Matthew 4:2, NIV)

- Hannah served the Lord by prayer and fasting, waiting for the Messianic promise.
  "…And then was a widow until she was eighty-four. She never left the temple but worshiped night and day, fasting and praying." (Luke 2:37, NIV)

- Paul's fasted, for three days, in which he humbled his heart and evaluated his life leading to his renewal.
  "For three days he was blind, and did not eat or drink anything." (Acts 9:9, NIV)

- The fasting of the prophets of Antioch opened new opportunities to minister.
  "While they were worshiping the Lord and fasting, the Holy Spirit said, "Set apart for me Barnabas and Saul for the work to which I have called them." So after they had fasted and prayed, they placed their hands on them and sent them off." (Acts 13:2-3, NIV)

- The elders' fast for the consecration of servants.
  "Paul and Barnabas appointed elders for them in each church and, with prayer and fasting, committed them to the Lord, in whom they had put their trust." (Acts 14:23, NIV)

- Fasting was seen as part of a committed, dedicated Christian life.
  "I have labored and toiled and have often gone without sleep; I have known hunger and thirst and have often gone without food; I have been cold and naked." (2 Corinthians 11:27, NIV)

FASTING FOR THE WRONG PURPOSES

- Queen Jezebel fasted with an impure, negative intention.
  "In those letters she wrote: 'proclaim a day of fasting and seat Naboth in a prominent place among the people. They proclaimed a fast and seated Naboth in a prominent place among the people.'" (1 Kings 21:9, 12, NIV)

- Fasting with a hard heart and stubborn mind.
  "Although they fast, I will not listen to their cry; though they offer burnt offerings and grain offerings, I will not accept them. Instead, I will destroy them with the sword, famine and plague." (Jeremiah 14:12, NIV)

- Fasting to impress people.
  "When you fast, do not look somber as the hypocrites do, for they disfigure their faces to show others they are fasting. Truly I tell you, they have received their reward in full." (Matthew 6:16, NIV)

FASTING SPECIFICALLY FOR REVIVAL AND BLESSING

- The Lord is expecting us to fast and repent, so that He will forgive and heal our country.
  "If My people, who are called by My name, will humble themselves and pray and seek My face and turn from their wicked ways, then I will hear from heaven, and I will forgive their sin and will heal their land." (2 Chronicles 7:14, NIV)

- The people of Nineveh believed God's message and fasted, so the Lord relented and forgave them.
  "The Ninevites believed God. A fast was proclaimed, and all of them, from the greatest to the least, put on sackcloth. When Jonah's warning reached the king of Nineveh, he rose from his throne, took off his royal robes, covered himself with sackcloth and sat down in the dust. This is the proclamation he issued in Nineveh: "By the decree of the king and his nobles: Do not let people or animals, herds or flocks, taste anything; do not let them eat or drink. But let people and animals be covered with sackcloth. Let everyone call urgently on God. Let them give up their evil ways and their violence. Who knows? God may yet relent and with compassion turn from his fierce anger so that we will not perish. When God saw what they did and how they turned from their evil ways,

he relented and did not bring on them the destruction he had threatened" (Jonah 3:5-10, NIV).

- God poured out his blessing on those who humbled themselves and fasted.
  "I am sending you grain, new wine and olive oil, enough to satisfy you fully; never again will I make you an object of scorn to the nations…And afterward, I will pour out My Spirit on all people. Your sons and daughters will prophesy, your old men will dream dreams; your young men will see visions. Even on My servants, both men and women, I will pour out My Spirit in those days" (Joel 2:19, 28-29, NIV).

All these verses above describe the importance of fasting for God's people. Of course, there is power in prayer, but when prayer is paired with fasting, its power is multiplied and mountains can be moved.

What Is Fasting

Fasting means abstaining from food and drinks for a period of time. Webster's Dictionary defines it as "an abstaining from food." Water and food are two different things. I want to emphasize this fact because there is a lot of confusion about it. Some people believe that God only accepts a full fast, which is abstaining from both food and water, therefore they don't fast at all because they think it is too difficult.

IT IS IMPORTANT TO DRINK AS MUCH WATER AS POSSIBLE THROUGHOUT THE FAST.

Many people ask us if they can drink water when they fast? Yes! Why not? The enemy comes and condemns us because of our lack of knowledge. If you fast 1-3 days and you are healthy, it is all right to abstain from drinking water. But if you work a lot, if it's hot outside or if you feel unwell during a fast, you can drink water whenever you want during the fast. The fast will be received by God.

Our body is the temple of the Holy Spirit, thus we need to detoxify our bodies from the flesh; we must not abuse our body, it needs water. Otherwise it will get sick. It is important to drink as much water as possible throughout the fast.

You can fast for several days while drinking only water. Why?

• Our body is 70-80% water.

If we want to be healthy and able to pray during the fast, we must drink 2-4 liters of water a day. You must drink it gradually, not just in the evening.

• Water helps the metabolism.
• Water is necessary for detoxification.

- Drinking water on an empty stomach helps clean the colon and leads to an acceleration of the process of creating new cells in our body.
- Water balances the body. The absorbent glands help maintain the balance of the liquids in our body and fight off infections.

Many people claim that they fast by simply not watching TV, using the Internet, drinking coffee, etc. But this must not be confused with the Scriptural act of fasting; it is merely temporary and voluntary abstinence.

> …FASTING *DOES NOT* REPLACE JESUS' SACRIFICE ON THE CROSS.

Fasting means abstinence from food in order to dedicate oneself to a spiritual cause. It is a form of *sacrifice* and this is the reason why many Christians don't want to pay the price. As a result, many Christians don't get any benefit from it.

WHAT FASTING IS NOT

I need to specify from the beginning that fasting *does not* replace Jesus' sacrifice on the cross. Redemption is received only by the sacrifice of the Lord Jesus Christ, through his blood.

When people fast out of personal reasons and misconceptions, the result will not be like the ones mentioned in the Scriptures.

- We cannot manipulate God with our fasting;
- We do not fast to be forgiven of our sins;
- We do not fast to boast or to stand out as holy people;
- We do not fast to lose weight;
- We do not rely on fasting more than the sacrifice of Jesus.

WHY FASTING IS IMPORTANT

Firstly, we fast because we love the Lord and we desire to get to know Him more. We fast to be transformed for His glory, so that Jesus

Christ is exalted and glorified. When we fast we are given the perfect opportunity to praise God and worship in Spirit and in truth.

Maybe you only fast when you have a problem or a specific prayer need. Today the Lord wants to teach you something new: the most important thing about fasting is to get closer to God, to love and praise Him. This mindset will make a difference in your life. The Lord calls us His "*first* love" (*Revelations 2:4*). He urges us to first seek His Kingdom (*Matthew 6:33*). By fasting and praying we fall in love with Jesus once again.

I was once in a great trial and I added fasting to my relentless prayers. From the first day, I sensed from the Lord that this fast would be one of praise and thanksgiving, despite my need. Therefore I cried out to the Lord only once so that He would answer my plea. Immediately I praised and adored Him, the One who is worthy of it all for the duration of the fast. I understood that when we praise Him and give Him thanks, even before seeing a solution to our problems, we show faith, which will always bring fruit and results. The next day the Lord started to work on my situation. It was a miracle. This was a 7-day water fast.

> WE FAST TO RECEIVE NEW AND FRESH REVELATIONS FROM HIS WORD, AND FROM HIS THRONE OF GRACE FOR OUR GENERATION.

Fasting is setting ourselves apart for the Lord, for a period of time. Moreover, fasting is a *radical consecration*. Consecration doesn't mean only abstaining from food or merely fasting, but it has a deeper meaning: we isolate ourselves from the world's system, the mundane, our desires, casual talks and normal activities to stand before the Lord in solitude. Meanwhile, we are a living sacrifice. We are on His altar and we ask for His purging fire to clean us of any impurities that stand in the way of our fellowship with Him.

- We fast to be hungry and thirsty after God, after His love, holiness and truth.
- We fast to receive new and fresh revelations from His Word, and from His throne of grace for our generation.
- We fast to humble ourselves and to crucify our flesh.

- We fast to have faith, for Him to be pleased with us and to do His works.
- We fast so that we could be set free from addictions, lust and evil spirits.
- We fast for our personal causes, for the Church's causes, and our nation's causes.

The Effects Of Fasting With Prayer

If we do our part, if we persevere in His Word, if we fast and pray, these blessings will be manifested "on earth as it is in heaven."

- Fasting and prayer moves the hand of God, the hand that controls the universe.
- Fasting opens God's heart and the spiritual realm, bringing His power to our aid.
- Fasting and prayer solve impossible situations, tearing down strongholds and hurdles that come our way.
- Fasting and prayer heal our body and soul.
- Fasting and prayer purify us, cleanse our soul from worldly flesh and help us forgive and rid ourselves of addictions (sex, alcohol, drugs, smoking, spending money recklessly, etc.).
- Fasting and prayer keep us humble.
- Fasting and prayer help us discern God's voice and will for our generation.
- Fasting and prayer bring answers to our petitions; those pleas that are after His will and glorify Him.
- Through fasting and prayer, prodigal sons return home.
- Fasting and prayer create a deeper hunger and thirst after God, after the spiritual realm.
- Fasting and prayer open an account in heaven's bank.
- By fasting and prayer we have more passion and determination for God's ministry.

> FASTING AND PRAYER MUST BE AN INHERENT PART OF OUR SPIRITUAL LIFE.

- Fasting and praying produce faith that leads to spiritual power.
- Fasting and prayer bring divine revelations.
- Fasting and praying bring spiritual revival.
- Fasting and prayer help us walk in the Spirit.
- Fasting and prayer open the doors to His promises.
- Fasting and prayer lead us to through spiritual battles, which always lead to victory.
- Fasting and prayer bring loss to the enemy; he always loses the battle.
- Fasting and prayer help form the discipline and fruit of the Holy Spirit.
- Fasting and prayer touch God's heart; they are a pleasant sacrifice before Him.
- Fasting and prayer lead us to a deeper level of His presence; they help us forgive, endure, love, give and worship in Spirit and in truth.
- Fasting and prayer are the Christian's secret weapons, which he uses to defeat the enemy.
- Fasting and prayer must be an inherent part of our spiritual life.
- Fasting and prayer are like a light switch bringing life; they fulfill God's plans.
- Fasting and prayer rejuvenate us, awakening the passion and determination for Christ for the weak and weary
- Fasting and prayer are vital aspects in spiritual warfare for deliverance.
- Fasting is powerful and necessary for recapturing lost territories; corporate fasting is required for this kind of victory.

The one who fasts and prays becomes:

- A channel through which the Holy Spirit works;
- An instrument in God's hands;
- A vessel which is cleansed of impurity and is completely surrendered to God;
- An anointed servant;

- An ambassador of Heaven, with the call to go throughout the world and proclaim the Gospel and to do even greater works than Jesus!

Fasting without prayer is doesn't carry the same power as fasting with prayer.

Prayer without fasting is well received, but prayer with fasting becomes all the more powerful. Prayer must be a total surrender and trust in the Lord. It strengthens our spirit to fight off the flesh.

OBSTACLES THAT STOP US FROM FASTING

These are some obstacles that could stand in the way of our fasting:

- Disbelief;
- Doubt;
- Fear;
- Worry;
- Lack of knowledge;
- Lack of self-control;
- Lack of passion
- Unforgiveness;
- Physical fatigue;
- Sleep;
- Weariness.

All these are strongholds of the old man, the flesh. If our flesh is crucified and our life is hidden in God, we shouldn't be fooled into avoiding fasting. We have to meditate on Galatians 2:20 daily, declaring this verse until it becomes a reality. Only then will we see our life transformed.

> *"I have been crucified with Christ and I no longer live, but Christ lives in me. The life I now live in the body, I live by faith in the Son of God, who loved me and gave himself for me. (Galatians 2:20, NIV)*

155

"Those who belong to Christ Jesus have crucified the flesh with its passions and desires. Since we live by the Spirit, let us keep in step with the Spirit. Let us not become conceited, provoking and envying each other."
(Galatians 5:24-26, NIV)

Fasting is the most powerful method of subduing our flesh, which battles with the Spirit and stands in the way of God's blessing. Fasting humbles our worldly flesh. David would humble his soul by fasting.

"Yet when they were ill, I put on sackcloth and humbled myself with fasting." *(Psalm 35:13, NIV)*

After fasting, our prayers become more passionate and bring results. Prayer changes the spiritual reality. Fasting and prayer moves the hand of God.

> I HAVE BEEN CRUCIFIED WITH CHRIST AND I NO LONGER LIVE, BUT CHRIST LIVES IN ME.

Believers of other religions also fast zealously and faithfully with reverence, and they see the effects of their fast. For Muslims, fasting is one of their "pillars of faith". During the Ramadan, every Muslim fasts for 30 days. This is one of the reasons they are so faithful to their religion. Throughout their fast, they read the Quran and declare its words. During the day, from dusk till dawn, they don't eat or drink. It is true that during the night they feast until dawn!

It is sad that many Christians today do not put an emphasis on fasting anymore. Many do not know the effects of fasting. If you are a missionary, preacher or pastor, and if you fast at least once a year for 21-40 days, you would see a greater difference in you life and in the lives of others. May God enlighten us so that we may understand the importance of fasting for longer periods of time! May we practice fasting and see a difference in every area of our lives.

Descriptions Of Fasting From The Bible

The Bible explains stories of many different people of God fasting. Fasting is an extensive theme throughout Scripture.

MOSES' FAST

The Bible tells us that Moses was the meekest and most gentle man on Earth. The Lord gave Him a great task: that of getting the Israelites out of Egypt. At the same time, he was given the grace to be God's mouthpiece for the people. Moses loved the rebellious Israelites even when God wanted to destroy them. He stood in the gap so that God would take back His anger:

> *"Then once again I fell prostrate before the Lord for forty days and forty nights; I ate no bread and drank no water, because of all the sin you had committed, doing what was evil in the Lord's sight and so arousing his anger. I feared the anger and wrath of the Lord, for he was angry enough with you to destroy you. But again the Lord listened to me."* (Deuteronomy 9:18-19, NIV)

The lack of faith and rebellion of the Israelites saddened God so much that he decided to destroy them. However, Moses' 40-day fast coupled with prayer saved the entire nation. Moses had a burden from the Lord for the people because of their evil deeds.

When we feel a burden from the Lord for a certain cause, we must come before Him with prayer and fasting.

"Moses was there with the Lord forty days and forty nights without eating bread or drinking water. And He wrote on the tablets the words of the covenant—the Ten Commandments." (Exodus 34:28, NIV)

This fast was special, because Moses stood before God in His presence on the mount. The Bible doesn't use the word "fast" in this passage, but it is mentioned that he didn't eat or drink. In this unique experience, Moses abstained from all food and drink for 40 days, and encountered the powerful presence of God in an extra-ordinary way.

> WHEN WE FEEL A BURDEN FROM THE LORD FOR A CERTAIN CAUSE, WE MUST COME BEFORE HIM WITH PRAYER AND FASTING.

I am certain that if the Lord chooses us to stand before Him on the Mount, like Moses did, we won't need anything because His nature will manifest in us, as if we are living in the spirit alone. God becomes like the air that we breathe, like our food and life source.

"For in Him we live and move and have our being." (Acts 17:28, NIV)

God's presence was so real to Moses after his encounter with God that his face shone. He didn't need anything else, because *"You make known to me the path of life; You will fill me with joy in your presence, with eternal pleasures at your right hand." (Psalm 16:11, NIV)*

I love the history of Enoch, who walked with God for 300 years. How beautiful and desirable is this lifestyle! He was taken away without ever experiencing death. I wholeheartedly believe that because Enoch walked with God, His nature was in him and Enoch emanated God's divine presence wherever he went. Moreover, at one point he became one with his Creator. Oh, how I desire that kind of relationship with God!

THE NUMBER 40

Why did Moses fast for 40 days?

The number "40" is very important because it is deeply connected to life and the human race; it is equivalent to a generation of people.

The Lord cleansed the earth by the flood for 40 days. Likewise, it is natural to fast for 40 days because we need 40 days to detoxify our bodies of all its toxins.

The following are some Biblical examples regarding the number "40". We will understand the importance of this number through God's perspective:

OH, HOW I DESIRE THAT KIND OF RELATIONSHIP WITH GOD!

- The Great Flood lasted for 40 days and 40 nights. (*Genesis 7:17*)
- Noah opened the ark's window to see if the water level decreased after another 40 days. (*Genesis 8:6*)
- Moses lived for 120 years. It is divided into 3 time periods of 40 years (time spent at the Pharaoh's, time spent in the desert and time spent with the Israelites in the desert).
- Moses fasted for 40 days and 40 nights.
- The Israelites wandered the desert for 40 years until the entire generation – except for Joshua and Caleb - died. (*Numbers 13:33-34*)
- The spies of Israel kept the Promise Land under watch for 40 days. (*Numbers 13:25*)
- The maximum limit for a punishment was 40 lashes. (*Deuteronomy 25:3*)
- When the people cried out to God, He gave them rest for 40 years. (*Judges 3:11, 5:31, 8:28*)
- Goliath circled the camp and threatened the Israelites for 40 days. (*1 Samuel 17:16*)
- Saul was a judge for 40 years. (*1 Samuel 14:18, Acts 13:21*)
- David (*1 Kings 2:11*), Solomon (*1 Kings 11:42*) and Joash (*2 Kings 12:1*) ruled for 40 years.
- Elijah ate the food the angels prepared and walked for 40 days and 40 nights. (*1 Kings 19:8*)

- Ezekiel bore the sin of Judah's people for 40 days. (*Ezekiel 4:6*)
- God gave to the people of Nineveh a deadline of 40 days to repent. (*Jonah 3:4*)
- Jesus fasted for 40 days and 40 nights. (*Matthew 4:2*)
- Jesus was tempted for 40 days and 40 nights. (*Luke 4:2*)
- Jesus remained on earth, from resurrection until ascension, for 40 days.

From the Scriptures, we understand that "40" is used by God to determine a set period of time in which He judges His people through flood, desert, drought, battles, etc. At the same time, it is a time of testing and communication with Him. The number "40" means a period of waiting, cleansing, preparation, punishment, death and renewal.

A person reaches a different level of wisdom after the age of 40. Many people realize that after a man turns 40, he enters a new season in his life; he "*enters in his destiny*" provided that he is ready.

I can tell you with joy that my life was transformed and touched by God when I was around 40 years old. Until then I had periods of waiting, testing, discipline, cleansing and equipping.

Additionally, it is recommended to use insecticide for a period of 40 days to fully destroy bacteria and bugs infecting crop fields. Why? Only after 40 days does the next generation of insects stop from reproducing.

I think we now understand why this 40-day fast is so important.

ELIJAH'S FAST

Elijah fasted for 40 days, having a divine encounter afterwards. The Lord's angel brought him food:

> "*So he got up and ate and drank. Strengthened by that food, he traveled forty days and forty nights until he reached Horeb, the mountain of God.*" (1 Kings 19:8, NIV)

This fast was his preparation for his encounter with God. How wonderful to have God before him as a sweet and gentle whisper! Surely many of us desire to have such encounters with God, to hear Him, to feel Him... but how many of us really want to pay the price?

Why did Elijah have to fast for 40 days and 40 nights? He had considerable faith, but Elijah still allowed fear, disappointment and dissatisfaction to come into his life.

This is a lesson for each and every one of: No matter how much God uses us, we are still vulnerable. God didn't disqualify Elijah because of his weakness or vulnerability; He took care of Elijah and used him. How did God take care of Elijah? He offered Elijah a chance of getting close to Him during the fast.

Fasting is a powerful weapon used for liberating us from bondage. In Elijah's case, God wanted to purify him so that He may speak to him. Elijah had to be prepared to discern God's voice, that gentle whisper. Had he remained in his state of fear, frustration and sadness, most certainly he wouldn't have heard and discerned God's voice.

> NO MATTER HOW MUCH GOD USES US, WE ARE STILL VULNERABLE.

We want to hear God and we desire to do many things for Him, but we can clearly see in Elijah's example that we first need a strong and deep relationship with God. Fasting and prayer deepens this relationship and it prepares us for our walk on the mount with the Lord (*Psalm 15*). If we want to walk with the Spirit like Elijah did, we need to sacrifice and surrender ourselves as well.

Lastly, we must acknowledge Elijah's beautiful ending. Who wouldn't want to be taken away in a fiery chariot? Who wouldn't want to be taken up to heaven and never experience death? The Lord's servant Elijah had that honor! God is the same even today. He rewards His people by the intensity of their passion and pursuit of Him. May the Lord help us live our lives like Elijah's and may we be used by Him!

AHAB'S FAST

Although he was an utterly evil king, he had the chance to witness God's goodness due to his fasting and humility.

> *"There was never anyone like Ahab, who sold himself to do evil in the eyes of the Lord, urged on by Jezebel his wife. He behaved in the vilest manner by going after idols, like the Amorites the Lord drove out before Israel."* (1 Kings 21:25-26, NIV)

God sent Elijah to Ahab to threaten him with a harsh punishment.

> *"He says, 'I am going to bring disaster on you. I will wipe out your descendants and cut off from Ahab every last male in Israel—slave or free."* (v. 21, NIV)

After he heard Elijah's words, Ahab tore his clothes, put on sackcloth and he fasted. He would sleep in his sackcloth and would walk around meekly.

> *"When Ahab heard these words, he tore his clothes, put on sackcloth and fasted. He lay in sackcloth and went around meekly. Then the word of the Lord came to Elijah the Tishbite: "Did you see how Ahab has humbled himself before me? Because he has humbled himself, I will not bring this disaster in his day, but I will bring it on his house in the days of his son."* (v. 27-29, NIV)

When I read those verses I understood the power in fasting and humility. God's heart was moved. He was glad to see a radical change in Ahab's life and He wanted to discuss it with the only one who could hear Him - Elijah. The Lord spoke so beautifully: *"Did you see how Ahab has humbled himself...?"* As if He was surprised by Ahab's action! In this situation, we see that God's mercy triumphs over His justice (*James 2:13*). God promised Ahab that judgment would be delayed because of Ahab's humility and fasting.

What amazing grace! Who is like our God? If He relented before this unmerciful, godless and evil king, imagine His mercy for us! When we sin, what God is looking for is a broken and contrite heart (*Isaiah 57:15*). After we repent, we can be boldly approach the Throne of God because we have an Advocate with the Father - Jesus Christ, the Righteous One and the Worthy Lamb. He will forgive, cleanse and change our lives, regardless of our sinful lives. *(1 John 2:1-2, Heb. 4:15-16).*

JEHOSHAPHAT'S FAST

We can learn many things from King Jehoshaphat. The Lord was pleased with Him, because he followed in his father's footsteps, King Asa. But God wanted to show His glory in the life of the new king. The Lord displays His power and might through our trials, and with His victory, we no longer need to trust in man for help. He is our help.

The Bible tells us that the Moabites and Ammonites started a war against Jehoshaphat (*2 Chronicles 20:1*).

> *"After this, the Moabites and Ammonites with some of the Meunites came to wage war against Jehoshaphat."* (v. 3, NIV)

King Jehoshaphat reached out for the powerful weapon and *he proclaimed a fast*! This was the signal for the nation to humble themselves before God. The Lord loves those who are broken in spirit. Then, Jehoshaphat declared God's Word, reminding God of His promises to them. He knew what great power was in God's Word.

The Lord gave us this wonderful example so that we learn that in spiritual warfare, we always fight based on what He has promised us. Again, the question is: where did Jehoshaphat learn all these details? Most certainly his parents taught him these secrets because God's command was that parents teach their children God's ways.

Sometimes I ask myself:

• How many parents know about God's promises in His Word?

- How many parents know God's battle strategies in times of need?
- How many fathers teach their children God's ways and commands?
- How many families have prayer, praise and worship altars in their homes?

Jehoshaphat's prayer proves a clear understanding of God's ways:

> *"Our God, will you not judge them? For we have no power to face this vast army that is attacking us. We do not know what to do, but our eyes are on You." (v. 12, NIV)*

How beautiful it is for us to come before the Lord with sincerity and child-like faith, knowing that God has everything we need! That's what Jehoshaphat did. The fast gave him faith, and when he declared God's Word, he received the assurance that God would fight for him and for the nation.

HOW MANY FAMILIES HAVE PRAYER, PRAISE AND WORSHIP ALTARS IN THEIR HOMES?

Jehoshaphat knew the great power in fasting, God's Word, prayer and praise. He used all 4 of these weapons. Praise is a very powerful weapon; it strengthens faith. Faith motivates us to praise God, and to experience God's goodness and mercy. The moment people start praising Him, God Himself sends His angels to fight for them.

Knowing God's battle strategy is vital. It is helpful when we are tested, attacked or found in unexpected situations without help or resources. The Lord teaches us to run to Him and to seek His support, to continuously seek His Face (*Psalm 105:4*).

> *"God is our refuge and strength, an ever-present help in trouble." (Psalm 46:1, NIV)*

In Jehoshaphat's battle we clearly see how these divine strategies are used:

- Fasting;

- Knowing and declaring God's Word;
- Humble prayer;
- Praise and worship.

All these led to victory.

ESTHER'S FAST

In the fast proclaimed by Esther, nobody ate or drank water for 3 days and 3 nights. As a result of this fast, the entire nation was redeemed (*Esther 4:16*). Esther was adamant in her fight and she understood that she had to risk her life for an important cause, to save her people.

What would have happened if the Jewish people had not fasted? Would they have been wiped out? We don't know for sure. By the simple fact that their fasting was written in the Scriptures, we understand that God responds powerfully when people fast. That is the reason why we are challenged to fast with determination for our personal causes, the causes of the Church and for our nation.

We don't always understand what great battles are fought in the spiritual realm. Through some examples from the Bible, we understand that the dark forces cease and relent when we fast and pray.

When the Lord called my husband and I into the ministry, this was God's exhortation: *"Call the people to fasting and prayer!"*

It's never too late to humble ourselves in fasting and prayer. If Christians today would fast and pray, just like the Jews did in Esther's time, imagine what kind of victories could take place in our nation!

NINEVEH'S FAST

An example of a radical fast takes place in the city of Nineveh. Jonah shouted to the nation: *"…forty more days and Nineveh will be overthrown." (Jonah 3:4)*

In this case we are talking about an absolute fast. Nobody ate or drank anything during the fast.

"The Ninevites believed God. A fast was proclaimed, and all of them, from the greatest to the least, put on sackcloth… The king of Nineveh, he rose from his throne, took off his royal robes, covered himself with sackcloth and sat down in the dust. This is the proclamation he issued in Nineveh, 'By the decree of the king and his nobles: Do not let people or animals, herds or flocks, taste anything; do not let them eat or drink.'" (Jonah 3:5-8, NIV)

The Bible doesn't mention how long they fasted, maybe one day, 3 days or even several days. The important thing to know is that they knew what to do when they heard the Lord's judgment. The entire city humbled themselves through fasting, including all of the animals!

Nineveh was an isolated pagan city. Knowing this, we may ask ourselves a question: how did they know the secret of fasting and that they ought to fast? Maybe they knew they had to repent because of their guilty consciences. But how did they know about the power of fasting?

What was the result of their fasting and humility?

"When God saw what they did and how they turned from their evil ways, he relented and did not bring on them the destruction he had threatened." (Jonah 3:10, NIV)

Do we fully understand God's goodness?

Do we realize how limitless His grace is for some pagans who cried out to Him?

What exactly determined God to relent and not bring the destruction He intended to bring?

When we fast, we humble ourselves and seek His face. We become aware of His sovereignty, we repent and we turn from our wicked ways.

Oh, if only more cities would humble themselves before the Lord like the Ninevites did!

Many people have received prophetic words for their countries, but how many have humbled themselves before the Lord through fasting and prayer regarding the prophecies? In humility and desperation, how many have begged the Lord for mercy and grace like the city of Nineveh? How many have turned from their wicked ways?

> *God, help us not be so careless and indifferent. Call the nations of the world to humility through fasting and prayer, so that Your judgment towards our sin will be relented.*

EZRA'S FAST

> *"There, by the Ahava Canal, I proclaimed a fast, so that we might humble ourselves before our God and ask Him for a safe journey for us and our children, with all our possessions."* (Ezra 8:21, NIV)

Some observations from Ezra's proclaimed fast:

- These people prayed and fasted for the Lord to guide them in the right way. This applies to us as well: when we want to bring the Gospel to other countries, we have to be guided by the Holy Spirit because the enemy wants to deceive us.
- They fasted and prayed for the protection of their children, for the next generation. It's important to ask for our children's protection and safety every day. God will make them mighty warriors and giants for His Kingdom.

> CHRISTIANS ARE BECOMING MORE AND MORE MATERIALISTIC AND SELFISH, LIMITING THE EXPANSION OF THE KINGDOM.

- They fasted and prayed for the resources they needed for their return to Jerusalem. We also need resources to spread the Gospel and we need wisdom to manage the money we receive.

Unfortunately, Christians are becoming more and more materialistic and selfish, limiting the expansion of the Kingdom. We must be generous and selfless. We must give freely, and bless those on the mission field.

Ezra fasted, suffered and interceded. He stood in the gap for the sins of the people, just like Moses and Daniel did. There is a great need for us to intercede before God to forgive the sins of the people in our churches and in our countries!

> *"Then Ezra withdrew from the house of God and went to the room of Jehohanan son of Eliashib. While he was there, he ate no food and drank no water, because he continued to mourn over the unfaithfulness of the exiles."* *(Ezra 10:6, NIV)*

NEHEMIAH'S FAST

> *"They said to me, 'Those who survived the exile and are back in the province are in great trouble and disgrace. The wall of Jerusalem is broken down, and its gates have been burned with fire.' When I heard these things, I sat down and wept. For some days I mourned and fasted and prayed before the God of heaven." (Nehemiah 1:3-4, NIV)*

Nehemiah wept when he heard about the sins of his people, the destroyed walls of the city, and the burned down gates of Jerusalem. He fasted and prayed desperately before God, seeking aid and forgiveness. The Lord gave him favour before the king, and Nehemiah succeeded in rebuilding the walls of Jerusalem. God's reaction to Nehemiah's humility and pain was truly wonderful!

In the same way, when trouble, hardship or destruction enter into the lives of our family, church or city, we must learn from Nehemiah's example. When Nehemiah heard of the terrible news, he not only fasted and prayed, but he also decided to take action. We need the same passion and determination as Nehemiah to take a stand and make a change in our nation.

DANIEL'S FAST

In the book of Daniel we find many references to a lifestyle of fasting and prayer. God showed him wonderful and important revelations for the times to come. Daniel had many divine visions and encounters.

Daniel's fast is called the "partial fast." Usually it is held for 21 days.

Daniel put God first in his life.

- He knew how to stand in God's presence.
- He knew what to eat and what not to eat.
- He took good care of his body, because he understood that whatever defiles the body, affects the soul and spirit also.
- He chose a simple menu: vegetables. Even this helped him draw closer to God, and it also enabled him to receive divine revelations.
- He fasted and prayed and received strength to stand his ground.
- He was disciplined and determined.
- He understood dreams, visions and revelations because God gave him this gift.
- He had a deep relationship with God.

Even when the enemy wanted to destroy Daniel's life, he was not afraid. He was faithful, disciplined and obedient, and he continued to draw near to God.

How about us? When persecution comes, how do we respond? Are we afraid? Or do we draw near to God and receive His strength and courage? When we fast and pray we can stand strong in times of trial or persecution. We honor God through our obedience and faithfulness.

> *"So I turned to the Lord God and pleaded with Him in prayer and petition, in fasting, and in sackcloth and ashes."* *(Daniel 9:3, NIV)*

In the Old Testament, sackcloth and ashes are symbols for humility.

Now test yourself: eat little food and mostly vegetables for 2 weeks. Drink lots of water, pray throughout the day, and see what happens.

Or you can try this: eat a lot of greasy food for 2 weeks. Eat everything you want, and mix all kinds of ingredients together. Your body will feel lazy, sick, heavy and tired, and you will see that your spiritual life is affected.

The food we eat affects not only our physical bodies but also our spiritual lives. That is why a lifestyle of fasting is so important. In times of fasting, we become more aware of the spiritual realm. People often have visions, revelations from God, and even encounters with angels during extended fasts. Fasting enables us to separate ourselves from our flesh and to walk in the Spirit.

DAVID'S FAST

After David was anointed as king, he had to go through many trials. Through the trials, I believe he developed a profound lifestyle of prayer, fasting and praise. In Psalm 109 he says:

> *"I fade away like an evening shadow; I am shaken off like a locust. My knees give way from fasting; my body is thin and gaunt." (Psalm 109:23-24, NIV)*

We reason that David fasted for many days, maybe even 40, because only extended fasting weakens your knees and brings this kind of fatigue. During this time David received profound revelations concerning God and His Word, especially regarding praise, worship and thanksgiving.

When opposition came, David's heart was weary, yet he still chose to fast.

> *"When I weep and fast, they mock me. When I put on sackcloth, people make sport of me. Those that sit on the gate mock me, and I am the song of the drunkards." (Psalm 69:10)*

"Yet when they were ill, I put on sackcloth and humbled myself with fasting. When my prayers returned to me unanswered, I went about mourning." (Psalm 35:13, NIV)

Another episode in David's life recounts his sin with Bathsheba. When his newborn child got sick, David prayed and fasted (*2 Samuel 12:16-20*). He fasted for 7 days, hoping God would intervene. Still, his child died. Why didn't God react to David's plea? Why didn't the fast do the trick?

Many people can say they have fasted for a certain cause, but didn't receive the answer they wanted. After such an experience, many are disappointed, unhappy, and no longer wish to fast and pray.

Discouragement is like a snakebite that poisons us. It's like a thief who steals our joy and peace. It's like a giant who holds us captive in his prison. The enemy cannot wait to discourage us, especially after we don't get an answer after a fast. We must realize that we hold the key to the prison of discouragement – the key of God's promises.

We must surrender completely to our Master, even if we don't receive our answer. We must trust in Him because He is sovereign and He never fails us! Moreover, we must trust that all things work together for our good, provided that we truly love our Saviour!

If we study the Word, we understand why David's infant died. God already told him that the child would die because he was born out of adultery. David received a heavy punishment for his sins of murder and adultery, and also for giving opportunity for his enemies to blaspheme God (*2 Samuel 12:14, KJV*).

After his child died,

"David got up from the ground. After he had washed himself, anointing himself with lotions and changed his clothes, he went into the house of the Lord and worshiped. Then he went to his own house, and at his request they served him food, and he ate" (2 Samuel 12:20).

We can note some important conclusions for us.

- First, *David got up from the ground*. We must approach God with facedown humility and surrender, and then accept and trust the will of God even if He says no.
- Second, *David washed himself.* We must wash ourselves of all negative thoughts, words and actions, and from all the hidden sin in our hearts. This cleansing is done at the Cross by repenting, renouncing our sins and radically turning towards holiness. The Word is like clean water that washes and rejuvenates us.
- Third, *David anointed himself with lotions.* We must understand the importance of the Holy Spirit's anointing in our lives. This anointing comes from broken-heartedness, humility and it does wonders:

"The Spirit of the Sovereign Lord is on Me, because the Lord has anointed Me to proclaim good news to the poor. He has sent Me to bind up the broken-hearted, to proclaim freedom for the captives and release from darkness for the prisoners." (Isaiah 61:1, NIV)

When I was in Israel I saw how they make olive oil: the olives are put in a press, they're crushed and then the oil is collected into vessels. The press is heavy and repeated actions are needed to obtain the olive oil. Where does the anointing come from in our life? You get it from intimacy with Christ and from crushing. Only when you go to the Cross can you truly love and sacrifice yourself for others. Then, when you preach the Word or praise God, your words will be filled with anointing, fire, passion, zeal and power. The lives of others will be changed. But first, we need to be crushed and purified in order to bear fruit.

> WHERE DOES THE ANOINTING COME FROM IN OUR LIFE? YOU GET IT FROM INTIMACY WITH CHRIST AND FROM CRUSHING.

- Fourth, *David changed his clothes.* We need to change our garments of bitterness, sadness and disbelief with garments of faith, peace and joy. Instead of bitterness, we must put on the garment of praise to worship our God.

- Fifth, *David went into the house of the Lord.* After we finish a fast, it's good to go into the house of the Lord, or in your secret place, to spend more time with God in worship and thanksgiving, accepting His will.
- Sixth, *David worshiped.* Worship is one of the most powerful keys in the Christian life. David learned to worship God when he was alone, when he was at work, when he was in trial and when he was at war. David learned to worship God in every circumstance. This is how he became a man after God's own heart. Why? Because God is in the centre of worship and worship changes the atmosphere. God dwells in the praises of his people.

My life started to change when I started to listen to worship music. The more I listened, the more I understood the power of real worship that exalts God. During moments of deep worship, God revealed Himself to me in very real and tangible ways. Even today, God has been emphasizing to me the importance of worship.

THIS FAST STRENGTHENED HIM TO ACCEPT GOD'S WILL.

The Lord recently spoke to me:

When you worship Me, expect revelations from Me.

When you worship Me, you create an atmosphere for Me to reveal Myself to you.

When you learn to worship Me in the midst of your trial, you can expect miracles.

When you focus on Me and trust in Me, you cannot give up.

David fasted and repented for the healing of his child. This fast strengthened him to accept God's will. After the child died, David was calm because he knew that his child was in God's hands.

*"But now that he is dead, why should I go on fasting? Can
I bring him back again? I will go to him, but he will not
return to me." (2 Samuel 12:23, NIV)*

We certainly need more people like David today! If we meditate
day and night on His Word, we will have abundant life in God. Don't
you want to be like David, to stand before God in fasting and prayer?
He will surely make you a fighter and a worshiper like David, but you
could only be a fighter if you are a worshiper.

You will be in love with God.

You will say:

*"You, God, are my God, earnestly I seek You; I thirst for You,
my whole being longs for You, in a dry and parched land
where there is no water." (Psalm 63:1, NIV)*

We are thankful for David's writings and we appreciate this great
man of God, *"a man after God's heart."* But what made him so special
before God?

It was his relationship with God. Ever since he was a young boy, he
nurtured his relationship with God and prepared his heart for God's
works. Alone with the sheep, he must have talked to God a lot! I believe
it was during that time when he really meditated on God's works and
wonders. Even when he was young, his faith grew strong and he clung
to the one true God.

How did David know all the details about the Jewish people when
he wrote the Psalms? He fervently studied the Law of God!

How did David fight the bear and the lion when they came after
his sheep? Or how about Goliath? I believe that it was because he spent
time with God through:

- Studying the word of God;
- Prayer and fasting;
- Praise and worship.

Through all this he received faith, trust, strength and bravery.

Oh, how I wish the youth retreated from the chaos and noise and
spent a couple of days in fasting and prayer. In this way, God would
reveal Himself to them like He did to David. Not only the youth, but

also Christians of all ages! If leaders and pastors would fast, they would be strengthened and would receive fresh revelations from the throne of grace and mercy.

I have read about great men of God who retreated from the hustle and bustle of life for a period of time. They wanted to "charge themselves with the Lord," to be in His presence, and to hear His voice. They would go somewhere in the mountains, a lodge, a quiet and peaceful place in the middle of nature and fast, pray and hear God's voice. All of these men were blessed and have blessed other people in return.

PERSONAL EXPERIENCE - ALONE WITH GOD

I cannot express through words the experience I had with the Lord. After 7 days of fasting, only with water, I desired to spend extended time with the Lord and to write this book. From the Lord's urge and my husband's approval, I spent a week in a cabin built especially for Christians to spend time with the Lord alone. The moment I arrived in my room, the presence of God filled me and I spent 2 hours in deep and powerful prayer and worship. His presence was so real, alive, warm, sweet and fresh that I did not want to leave that place. It was so quiet: the mountains, the cabin, and my inner self. It was wonderful not to be disturbed by anyone, and not to talk to anyone for a week except God. There I started writing this book, and there the Lord showed me new heights and depths of His blazing Love. I would weep out of joy; His presence was so real and so profound! I could not ask Him for anything. I felt as if I was in the Holy of Holies, where peace, love and joy are absolute. His presence was more than enough. I wanted to enjoy His waves of grace, mercy and love, which He would overflow upon me. I would write, pray and praise the Lord. It was a divine atmosphere.

The nature, mountains, trees and sun seemed like they were singing together with me. I felt like I was in oneness with creation, completely aware of the Creator's beauty, who created everything for His glory. In that divine splendor, I asked the Lord for a real and tangible sign. He is so wonderful! He surprised me deeply! The sky was bright, but I could see one tiny, white cloud. Suddenly, coming from the treetops from the right, there was a breeze carrying with it a shower of hail (it was warm and sunny). I looked around and I noticed that it was raining only on me, an area of about 2 meters.

When I saw this miracle, this divine sign, I shouted out of joy and I praised my beloved God even more. I heard the Holy Spirit speak within me: *"In the same way I will answer your prayers. Suddenly, I will reveal Myself. Suddenly, My blessing will come. I am present and I know your needs. I am so real. I am so close to you. I listen to you and I'm happy to respond."*

The raindrops showered for about five more minutes and then they stopped. I cannot tell you how much I joyfully prayed after that! I prayed for at least two hours with power, passion and tears. The Lord told me many things and strengthened me in my ministry. I felt like I was in heaven.

Many people want God to reveal to them more about the future or the end times, and that becomes the reason why they fast and pray before the Lord. But I didn't ask Him for that. By fasting and praying, I wanted to fill myself with His love, in order to serve and love Him more. My fast was for His love alone, to proclaim Him and show love wherever He would call me to go.

FASTING PREPARES US FOR TRIAL AND TEMPTATION.

I recommend every Christian to pull away from the noise of the world, and to spend days alone with the Lord in fasting and praying. When you go in the solitary place, I encourage you to have your Bible and notebook in hand, and also to have praise and worship music with you. The Lord will surely reveal Himself to you, and you will come out from that place changed, refreshed, and ready for battle.

JESUS' FAST

Jesus' example in the New Testament is written in all four gospels. He fasted for 40 days and 40 nights:

"Jesus, full of the Holy Spirit, left the Jordan and was led by the Spirit into the wilderness, where for forty days He was tempted by the devil. He ate nothing during those days, and at the end of them He was hungry." (Luke 4:1-2, NIV)

We must ask ourselves this question: *"Why did Jesus, the Son of God, who had no sin, need to fast?"* After Jesus was baptized, and just before he entered into ministry, He was filled with the Holy Spirit, and was led into the wilderness to fast. Now, He was led by the Spirit into the desert to be tempted and tried. The Bible doesn't mention that Jesus didn't drink water. Many scholars believe that Jesus did drink water during this time or it would have been mentioned in the Bible.

Fasting prepares us for trial and temptation.

If Jesus who had no sin had to fast, how much more so do we, sinners redeemed by grace, need to fast?

By grace, I visited the desert where the Lord was tempted in Israel. The heat was unbearable, and it was hard to breathe. There was no grass, but only rocks and mountains all around. The desert lived up to its name.

Jesus was temped and tried with the most common temptations, which are lurking to get us even today. He, our forerunner, gave us the perfect example of how to fight using His Word. He had the courage to stand His ground against Satan, who fled from Him. Jesus knew the Word from the Old Testament, and He quoted Deuteronomy 6:13, 6:16. 8:3.

Do we know the Word to the extent of quoting it in times of temptation? Do we have the determination to endure hunger, cravings and fleshly desires for His sake?

> WHILE FASTING WE WILL ALWAYS BE TESTED AND TRIED, BUT AT THE SAME TIME WE WILL RECEIVE THE POWER AND STRENGTH TO WITHSTAND TEMPTATION.

While fasting we will always be tested and tried, but at the same time we will receive the power and strength to withstand temptation. Many of us rely on our knowledge, our faith, our goodness and our strength. However, the only thing that can help us gain victory is a life spent at the feet of Jesus, in His Word, in worship, in prayer, in fasting and in surrender.

In a particular situation, Jesus told the bewildered disciples that they couldn't cast out the demon because they lacked faith, prayer and fasting.

> *"And Jesus rebuked the demon, and it came out of him; and the child was cured from that very hour. Then the disciples came to Jesus privately and said, "Why could we not cast it out?" So Jesus said to them, "Because of your unbelief; for assuredly, I say to you, if you have faith as a mustard seed, you will say to this mountain, 'Move from here to there,' and it will move; and nothing will be impossible for you. However, this kind does not go out except by prayer and fasting." (Matthew 17:18-21, NKJV)*

We can clearly see how important fasting is to our faith. The demons here probably refer to the many powerful legions of demons, and to cast them out you need great faith. The key is to engage in praying and fasting.

Jesus did not perform any miracle or work until He was 30 years old. What did He do in the meantime? Let us not forget that He is the Son of man, He was fully human and at the same time He was fully God. Since childhood, in His house and hometown, He learned obedience and discipline.

He started His ministry after the Holy Spirit filled Him, and after He fasted and overcame temptation. Jesus' example reveals to us what true dependence on God looks like. He often prayed alone at night on the mountain. He talked to the Father and prepared for the miracles He would perform the following day.

> *"Then Jesus answered and said to them, "Most assuredly, I say to you, the Son can do nothing of Himself, but what He sees the Father do; for whatever He does, the Son also does in like manner. For the Father loves the Son, and shows Him all things that He Himself does; and He will show Him*

greater works than these, that you may marvel. For as the Father raises the dead and gives life to them, even so the Son gives life to whom He will. For the Father judges no one, but has committed all judgment to the Son, that all should honor the Son just as they honor the Father. He who does not honor the Son does not honor the Father who sent Him."
(John 5:19-23, NKJV)

Most certainly, God wants to reveal His plans for us. But how can we know His will? We must learn from Jesus, who spent time in solitude, prayer and learning about His Father's will. If you are called to any kind of ministry, be it large or small, this exhortation is for you: You must discipline yourself in fasting and prayer, even if you have never done it before. This is how you will see a difference in your life. Great revivals throughout history took place because people humbled themselves through prayer and fasting.

My Experience In Uganda

By the grace of God, in February 2011, I went on a mission trip with my pastor's wife from our church. A pastor from Uganda named Medad Berungi invited us to minister in remote places, in Anglican churches, conferences, and in many individual lives.

After we arrived in Uganda, we traveled 7 hours away from the capital because there was a huge mission field in that place. They rented a Jeep and we were four women with a driver. After half an hour of driving, the engine began emitting smoke. The driver got out, but did not know what was wrong, so we continued with our journey. We started praying because we were scared. The smoke grew thicker and thicker. The driver drove at high speeds because we had a lot of ground to cover; the road had potholes and there were no street lights.

GOD URGES US TO RELY ONLY ON HIS GOODNESS

After a while, the driver stopped again. He looked at the engine again, but he still did not know what was wrong with it. We traveled by faith. We prayed ardently for a long time. In the meantime, I had a vision in which the car seemed to be on fire. Then I told God, *"Lord, You didn't bring us here so we could die! You have a plan for us; I know You want to stir our faith. You fight for us!"*

A sister in Christ who was with us told us: *"The enemy is hindering us from reaching our destination because someone truly needs deliverance from demonic forces. The enemy sees that you have a Greater Power and he doesn't want you to succeed in ruining his game. He's fighting with you."*

I told myself: *"God is for us and He will fight for us!"*

Then the Lord reminded me what He revealed to me during my 21-day fast prior to entering Uganda. He guided me into learning more about His goodness. I was surprised to learn about the goodness of our Lord. In Psalms, David repeatedly mentions the importance of praising God for His goodness and faithfulness. In Psalm 107, it says that God longs for us to praise His goodness. It is as if God is gently sighing because we do not know His goodness and we do not praise Him for it. In Psalm 65:5, God urges us to rely only on His goodness, so that we experience wonders and miracles.

> *"Let them give thanks to the Lord for his unfailing love and his wonderful deeds for mankind"*
> *(Psalm 107:8, 15, 21, 31, NIV)*

> *"You answer us with awesome and righteous deeds, God our Savior, the hope of all the ends of the earth and of the farthest seas" (Psalm 65:5, NIV)*

In those moments of panic, I understood why God allowed me to meditate on this. Suddenly, I began to see God in a different light: full of power and kindness. When I remembered Psalm 145:7, I understood for the first time how much we lose because we do not truly understand God and His goodness. Moreover, I felt that He suffers due to our lack of knowledge. That is why He asks us to proclaim His infinite goodness, and to remember it.

Moreover, the Spirit of the Lord guided me to Jehoshaphat's example. What did the Israelites do when they faced danger? They ran to the Lord and to His goodness: *"Our God, will you not judge them? For we have no power to face this vast army that is attacking us. We do not know what to do, but our eyes are on you." (2 Chronicles 20:12, NIV)*.

Then, they praised God by saying, *"Give thanks to the Lord, for his love endures forever." (v 21)*

All these revelations went through my mind and suddenly I felt His presence and I started praising Him and declaring 2 Chronicles 20:21, which is often repeated in the Psalms,

> *"Lord, You are good and Your mercy endures forever! Lord, I praise You for Your goodness! I know you are good and that You will help us. Hallelujah!"*

I repeated these words with joy, together with the sisters.

As we were singing about His goodness, a small car came in front of our car. The driver made a sign with his hand for us to stop. The man came to us and told us to lift the car's hood. Dark smoke came out. Surprised, he told us, *"The car could've burst into flames had you traveled further for a little while. I am an engineer mechanic and I know what's wrong with your car."*

He immediately called two boys who were sitting in his car. They took their overalls and tools and got under our car to fix it. We were extremely glad that the Lord performed such a miracle!

I got out of the car and went to him to ask, *"Please, tell me who you are. Are you human or an angel?"* He started smiling, and full of peace, he told me, *"I saw the smoke coming out from your car and I knew you were in danger. That's why I came to your help."*

After he fixed our car, I asked him: *"How much does it cost?"* He replied gently: *"You don't have money to pay me and my time."* (He couldn't have known that we had no money on us. We only had a cheque in Canadian Dollars, which needed to be converted into their currency.) We were amazed, especially the driver and the sisters from Uganda, because they knew it was rare for something like this to happen in their country.

I asked that man whether he was a Christian, and he said he wasn't. Then I told him: *"You are an angel!"* After we got in the car, he told us: *"I will go follow you to make sure you reach your destination safely."* His words amazed us even more. I said to God, *"Lord, it's a miracle! We praise You and thank You. Your goodness has saved us! You clearly sent an angel to help us!* Your Word says *"The angel of the Lord encamps around those who fear him, and he delivers them." (Psalm 34:7, NIV)* We all saw that car behind and in front of us for the next two hours until night came and we didn't see him anymore.

Starting the next day, we met poor, sick and lonely women. Many were set free from demons, diseases and disbelief. Blessed be Jesus' Name! A 16-year old girl was tormented by many demons. She had many traumas and was tortured by the enemy even though she was a Christian and a pastor's daughter. Her past was extremely painful and it was difficult to imagine that a 16-year old girl could go through such things. Praise God that He set her free and restored her!

Before leaving for Uganda I fasted for 21 days, I prayed and I declared God's Word. I didn't have time to fast there, I only prayed. I began to understand that it wasn't enough. Then the Spirit of the Lord made me understand that we had to praise Him more for who He is, for His goodness and mercy.

We deal with different situations in our lives. That is the reason why we must be equipped, anchored and vigilant to become victorious. You may ask, *"The Lord knows what I need; why won't He help me?"* Here is the secret: God expects our collaboration. By fasting, praying and trusting His Word, we activate our faith and we proclaim things that are yet to come into existence. God inspires us and we ask, believe and take action.

You demonstrate faith if you act as if you already received what you asked for.

> *"May the God of hope fill you with all joy and peace as you trust in Him, so that you may overflow with hope by the power of the Holy Spirit." (Romans 15:13, NIV)*

Different Types Of Fasting In The New Testament

The Word shows us that at the beginning of the New Testament, Jesus fasted for 40 days and 40 nights. I mentioned His fast in the previous chapter. However, there are other people who understood the value of fasting in the New Testament:

John the Baptist was a man of prayer and fasting. His fasting was partial, but powerful, with long-term effects. His fasting was more of a lifestyle of eating wild honey and locusts in the desert (*Matthew 3:4*). He received favour for being the one who paved the way for Christ's coming. Jesus called him the greatest of the prophets. It's true that not many people have a calling like John's, but God desires to have more dedicated and consecrated men and women just like John the Baptist.

Jesus fasted 40 days and 40 nights in the wilderness. (Matt. 4:2)

Hannah served the Lord at the temple by fasting and praying. (*Luke 2:37*)

Saul of Tarsus (Apostle Paul) fasted for three days before his transformation: *"For three days he was blind, and did not eat or drink anything." (Acts 9:9, NIV)*

The Christians from Antioch fasted before ministry. *"While they were worshiping the Lord and fasting, the Holy Spirit said, 'Set apart for me Barnabas and Saul for the work to which I have called them.' So after they had fasted and prayed, they placed their hands on them and sent them off." (Acts 12:2-3, NIV)*

The Apostles fasted to set apart elders in the church. *"Paul and Barnabas appointed elders for them in each church and, with prayer and fasting, committed them to the Lord, in whom they had put their trust." (Acts 14:23, NIV)*

Paul talks about the fast which brings victory: *"I have labored and toiled and have often gone without sleep; I have known hunger and thirst and have often gone without food; I have been cold and naked."* *(2 Corinthians 11:27, NIV)*

How Fasting And Prayer Have Brought Spiritual Revival

There have been many spiritual revivals related to fasting and prayer. You may all have heard about the Azusa Street Revival in Los Angeles in 1906. Before the outpouring of the Holy Spirit, there were people who fasted and prayed for a long period of time. Moreover, they praised God by singing heavenly songs, which drew God's presence. The revival spread like wildfire, the Lord worked with signs and wonders and many were baptized with the Holy Spirit.

A woman named Emma "Mother" Cotton was involved in this revival. She was completely dedicated to the Lord and lived a lifestyle of prayer and fasting. In order to encourage Christians to fast, she put a poster up at her church, stating: "Fasting on Fridays!" (Franklin Halls' book, *The Fasting Prayer,*" recounts the whole event).

Another man who was used by God in the same revival was William Seymour. He fasted a couple of weeks before the revival. He occasionally ate, but was completely thirsty after God and the Holy Spirit. At that time, other Christians got together, resembling Pentecost, and fasted and prayed for 10 days. Then the Holy Spirit came upon them with power and they experienced a transformation.

These brothers and sisters were fasting and praying, and were united by the Holy Spirit who was the leader of their meetings. When the Lord anointed someone, that person got up and started speaking. There were no denominational barriers, they were not judging nor hurting each other. The Holy Spirit worked, bringing such unity, collaboration and joy that they did not even think about eating.

This is what happens to people who fast and pray: they experience the touch of the Holy Spirit. In those moments, you cannot get enough of His presence; it is like a magnet pulling you closer to Him.

Many churches today do understand this secret of fasting, praying and worship. They experience the power of the Holy Spirit, like at Pentecost. They are ready to pay the price, and they are determined to fight in prayer until they experience a move of God.

Another person who has motivated me in the ministry is John Hyde. As I was reading *"Praying Hyde, Apostle of Prayer[5]"*, I was profoundly moved by this kind of lifestyle, and by the fruit of his prayers and fasting. This man experienced the filling of the Holy Spirit, which led him to a greater love for God and for the lost. The author says that John Hyde was the man who ate and slept the least. He fought in prayer for days and nights. For example, before a conference in India, he, together with another 3 men, prayed fervently for 36 hours, with only short breaks. God told John to pray continuously even after the conference had ended for the seeds to grow. The seed is the word of God.

I was overjoyed when I read these testimonies because it is exactly what God told me to do. Every year, for the last 7 years, after we have returned home from our mission trip, the Lord has spoken to me to enter in a 40-day fast. When I ask the Lord why, He revealed to me the importance of continually fasting and praying for the seeds that have been sown to grow in the hearts of people. Every year we see

SOMETIMES HYDE WAS PRAYING AND FASTING ON HIS KNEES ALL DAY LONG.

people changed and transformed to deeper levels of love and faith. This has challenged me to never give up and to really believe the importance of fasting and praying even after a meeting, conference, or mission trip.

The Lord wants us to understand the necessity of fasting and prayer. We must step out of our comfort zone and put ourselves to His disposal, interceding for others. Many people won't understand us. We have to be ready and aware of the fact that we will be judged and misunderstood by others. The most important thing is not to

---

[5]   The book was edited by E. G. Carre, who collected the recollections of John Hyde's friends.

neglect prayer and our personal relationship with God. (Many times others have criticized me because of my radical relationship with God). One thing is certain: when you fall in love with God, you will not be understood by all people. However, don't give up. You must sacrifice much and take many risks for His sake.

Sometimes Hyde was praying and fasting on his knees all day long. When the spirit of intercession fell upon him with a heavy burden, he wouldn't sleep nor eat for 2-3 days. He would fight for a long time in prayer and then he would get up and start praising and worshiping God. Only by the power of the Holy Spirit was he able to pray to that extent.

From my experience, I can confirm that this kind of lifestyle is not easy. In order to be fully used by the Holy Spirit in prayer, you need solitude and time set apart so that nobody bothers you. Moreover, it is necessary to surrender yourself to the Holy Spirit: body, soul and spirit.

In such events, hours pass like minutes. I couldn't believe how fast five or six hours of prayer would pass as I was fighting and interceding, praising and thanking God. All these hours would seem like thirty minutes. When you are in the spirit, time doesn't exist because you are in another dimension. You feel like you could spend all the time with God in fellowship, talking to Him, praising Him, weeping and rejoicing in Him.

Praying Hyde continued with his long-term fasting and prayers. In 1908, he told God, *"Give me a soul a day or I will die!"* During the night he would fight in prayer, and the next day a soul would return to the Lord and would be baptized. In 1909, he asked for two souls a day. In 1910, he asked for 4 souls a day. The number of the believers grew each and every day!

WHY DO WE NEED ALL THIS FASTING, PRAYING AND SUFFERING, IF CHRIST DIED AND SUFFERED FOR THE LOST? ISN'T HIS SACRIFICE MORE THAN ENOUGH?"

I asked myself: what was Praying Hyde's secret? He was full of love and passion for Christ and for the lost! This fire consumed him in such a way that he wanted to fast and pray until all people were saved. He had the vision of Jesus' love and sacrifice on the cross for the lost. Moreover, he saw the destiny of the lost souls, how they would end up in hell because nobody fought for them, nobody talked to them about the Savior's love. He had a Father's heart for the lost sheep. Although he won many souls every day for Christ, he was not content and wanted more and more people to turn to Christ. However, he paid a great price to see those souls saved. John took no pleasure in worldly affairs. When there were conferences, he stood in prayer. He had a lot to talk about to the crowd and people wanted him to preach, but he never rushed to the spotlight. He kept on praying even while many were waiting for him to preach. John knew that the secret of fasting and prayer is the key to a free and transformed life.

Maybe you ask yourselves, "Why do we need all this fasting, praying and suffering, if Christ died and suffered for the lost? Isn't His sacrifice more than enough?" Yes! His sacrifice is perfect, but it is powerless if we do not believe and do not repent. In order to repent, we need someone to tell us the Gospel. Moreover, in order to receive this truth, someone has to pray and fight in the spiritual realm by fasting and praying by faith.

Where can we find such persons today? Why are they so rare? Who stole this all-sacrificing love from us? Why is it so difficult to partake in Christ's suffering? I always hear God asking: *"Whom shall I send?"*

When I heard God ask me this question for the first time, I felt His divine power together with suffering and love that overflowed my being. I fell facedown, prayed and sobbed for the desperate, lost and unsaved souls tortured by the enemy. In that moment, all my desires vanished. The desires to live a comfortable life started to seem unimportant. I felt God's deep burden, and I was sinking into a different world that I never knew existed, a world that needed desperate help. It was the desperate, lost world, with no Saviour, no hope and no prayer, in which suffering and pain reign. In that world, the enemy tortures God's creation.

I started praying with desperation. I was in agony. I felt like I was in labor in hours. I experienced the pain of childbirth for the lost world. I fell facedown and wept for the pain and suffering of the lost souls who are going to hell, and for the lukewarm Christians. Then, I told myself, *"Here I am, Lord! Send me!"* In an instant, I felt all of heaven enter into action. I felt heaven open so that I would receive more of God's love for those who are suffering. I knew that God was mobilizing me, preparing people, and opening doors for me to enter into His mission.

I realized that if we draw closer to God and have profound intimacy with Him, we start feeling His suffering. The Apostle Paul said, *"I want to know Christ—yes, to know the power of His resurrection and participation in His sufferings, becoming like Him in His death." (Philippians 3:10, NIV).*

We need His heart, pain and tears, His suffering, *not ours.* He is praying and weeping through the Holy Spirit in us. Only people who reach this point can understand what I am referring to. If you do not understand, do not be quick to judge. Read further. Also ask the Lord to give you a spirit of intercession for the lost souls to return to Him. The Word encourages us by saying: *"Ask and you shall receive."* Have you ever thought about asking God to give you His tears, pain, and heart for the weak, lost and broken world? (Even as I am writing this, I am reliving those painful moments. I am writing these sentences with righteous tears because I understand His sorrow. Jesus is standing on the Father's right and He is interceding for us).

Why did God ask Isaiah: *"Then I heard the voice of the Lord saying, "Whom shall I send? And who will go for us?" (Isaiah 6:8).*

From this passage, we understand that God chooses to use people to work together with Himself for the salvation of the world.

Jesus came to save the world, but gave us this command: *"Go!" (Matthew 28:19, Mark 16:15);*

> *"How, then, can they call on the one they have not believed in? And how can they believe in the one of whom they have not heard? And how can they hear without someone preaching to them?" (Romans 10:14, NIV)*

Ever since I told God that I am at His disposal and that He could send me wherever He wants, He opened the doors to many villages, cities and countries. Many times the enemy has come and brought opposition and trials to the ministry, trying to cause me to give up on God's mission. However, through the opposition and trials, even when I want to give up, I relive the sorrow and burden of the Lord that has been given to me for the lost.

I remember His deep calling, and when I responded: *"Here I am, Lord! Send me!"*

I want to remind you that the most important thing is our relationship with our Saviour. Only after you are in love with God, are you ready to go wherever He wants you to go. Only then are you ready to sacrifice your money, comfort, family and reputation for His sake. After God called me to ministry, my greatest desire became to spend more time with Him. Many times, I wanted nothing to stand between God and me, be it friends or family. Thus, fellowship with Him is the sweetest, most vital and most powerful thing in our lives.

> Any Christian who does not spend at least one hour in prayer per day is a weak Christian.

Any Christian who does not spend at least one hour in prayer per day is a weak Christian. His faith, love and power are weak as well. If you want to experience God's greatness, you must prioritize - God first and then family, friends, job or money. This is the only way for you to have a loving relationship with your Creator and Saviour. It is worth giving up everything for Him!

GREAT MEN OF GOD FASTING

Here are some names of the heroes of faith, who were men who prayed and fasted: Tertullian, Martin Luther, John Calvin, John Knox, Charles Finney, Jonathan Edwards, John Wesley, George Müller, Charles Haddon Spurgeon, Frank Bartleman, David Brainard, Rees Howells, Evan Roberts, John Hyde, Andrew Murray and Sadhu Sundar Singh. Together with other great men, they understood the importance of fasting and praying. God performed great works through them. I encourage you to read their biographies because their life stories will motivate you.

Just like in the times of Elijah, God has set aside people who do not bow to other gods, and who stand in the gap through fasting and prayer. A pastor once told me, *"If a sinful country is still in place, it's because they have people standing in the gap, praying for them and fasting from 10-40 days for the nation."* This is true. May God bless those people!

Don't you want to be one of those who could save a nation?

Through this book, the Lord is encouraging and motivating you to step out of your comfort zone and to learn to stand in the gap, to sacrifice yourself and to work together with Christ for the expansion of His Kingdom. There are many Christians who are not written in history books but have understood and practiced fasting and have prayed passionately. They have left spiritual legacies and testimonies worthy of being followed. They lived admirable lives before God and men. They understood that a fasting lifestyle will bring them closer to God, it will humble them and it give them power over the enemy. The ministry God called them to do had an impact and was visibly powerful in their times and for generations to come.

> DON'T YOU WANT TO BE ONE OF THOSE WHO COULD SAVE A NATION?

I have met a lot of people who have embraced fasting and prayer. Wherever they go, they spread Christ's perfume. I have noticed a big difference between the ones who fast and pray with power, and the ones who barely survive. The latter do not have any testimonies by which they can praise the God of wonders. They do not have many victories or peace in the storm. They get easily disappointed when they are tried. I want to encourage you through this book to shake off your indifference and to join the battle. This way we can live in God's promises, and the enemy will fear Christ who abides in us.

A MOMENT OF SELF-EXAMINATION

You are now put to the test:
- What's the number one priority in your life?
- Why don't you have enough time to spend with the Lord?
- What are the obstacles that stand in the way of your prayer and fasting?
- Do you believe that these obstacles can be removed?
- What is more important for you *than your relationship with God*?

- What got you stuck in this prayerless state, to live like a victim instead of a conqueror?
- Have you ever experienced a burden for the lost?
- How many souls have you led into the Kingdom of God?

The Lord is telling you: "*Abandon everything that is not from Me. Cast your worries onto Me. Run to Me because I cannot wait to bless you with My joy and love. I want us to be workers together for the expansion of My Kingdom. Are you ready to leave everything behind? Are you ready to risk everything for My sake and to go wherever I send you? I will open the eyes only of those who walk by faith, so that they may see My wonders and rejoice in them. The greater the sacrifice, the greater the joy and victory. Anything that's keeping you bound will eventually burn one day. Whatever you gather today will be wasted another day. Whatever you are keeping hidden in your heart will dry your prayers out of power and will steal your blessings and My joy. Therefore, says the Lord, come to Me all of you who are weary and burdened and I will give you rest.*"

What exactly made Praying Hyde leave America behind and go to India, to fight in prayer for the salvation of the lost souls with fasting, tears and weeping? Neither food nor sleep was important to him, although they are vital in order to live. The love of God brought him to that place a sacrifice. In times of sacrifice we also enjoy great times of divine joy and victory which many Christians never experience.

> WHAT IS MORE IMPORTANT FOR YOU *THAN YOUR RELATIONSHIP WITH GOD?*

When John Hyde got sick, the doctor discovered that his heart had moved from the left to the right. He was told he needed to give up the ministry of intercession, or he would soon die. Instead of being afraid, he smiled and was glad to be able to suffer like Christ and to continue praying with passion, tears and power. His friends wrote that after nights of prolonged prayers with tears and sorrow, he would get up so overjoyed and excited, that other people were amazed and attracted to him. He was full of kindness, humility and meekness just like Christ. He became one with Christ, in suffering and in love. The Lord took him home when he was only 47 years old. What great celebration took place in heaven when he entered through those golden gates bringing thousands of souls to Jesus.

The Lord wants us to be in that state. It would be perfect if no human desire were greater than that of loving God, of becoming one with Him and serving Him with joy. When we are one with Him and have deep intimacy with Jesus, our lives become the fragrance of Christ. Only when we are one with Him, when we partake in His death and suffering, can we intercede and love like Him.

As mentioned above, I advise you to read about the lives of great men who understood the power of fasting and prayer. The purpose of their biographies is not to exalt the human. They are examples, living witnesses that allowed God to work through them with freedom and liberty, for His glory and for the betterment of others. Few people today are truly sacrificing themselves for others.

> FEW PEOPLE TODAY ARE TRULY SACRIFICING THEMSELVES FOR OTHERS.

If you want to see a difference in your life and in the lives of others, start fasting 10, 21, 30 or 40 days with water or with natural juices. You will see that it is difficult, but you cannot receive the prize of glory without suffering and sacrifice. I encourage you through the written examples of the Bible, my personal experiences and those of others to fast for a longer period of time. You will see great change in your life, in your family and in your nation. Long-term fasting is one of the most powerful weapons and it will undoubtedly bring a difference in your prayer life and in your faith.

THE FOUNDATION OF THE CHRISTIAN LIFE

Since the beginning of His ministry, Jesus offered us many principles to follow. Matthew 6:3, 5 and 17 present three powerful and necessary practices that every Christian must follow. Jesus talks about giving (*v. 3*), prayer (*v. 5*) and fasting (*v. 17*). He does not say, "*if you do these things*", but He expresses His expectation of us doing what He commanded.

Jesus emphasized the matter because He knew the importance. Without neglecting prayer and giving, In this book I want to emphasize the importance of fasting, because it is discussed and understood too little. Why is fasting so neglected? It is neglected because you cannot discuss it if you do not practice it. Otherwise, it's just empty words.

Out of these three disciplines mentioned by Jesus, fasting is the most difficult and the most powerful. When we fast, we are compelled by God to both pray and give. Giving or prayer without fasting does not contain the same power.

When it comes to fasting, although necessary for the Christian life, we practice it too little because it involves too much sacrifice. Long-term fasting has a hidden truth, unknown by many people. This is why the Lord urged me to write this book. He told me in 2007 that I would be writing a book, but I was not ready for it because I had to experience fasting myself in order to write about it.

My prayer for you is to discover the beauty of God through a simple lifestyle, in which we feed ourselves with spiritual matters. We ought to seek God's face by fasting and prayer to see His works and to live a life of victory.

Since the beginning, we see how the enemy tempted Eve with food. Satan knew man's weakest point - the lust of the eyes. That is how Esau sold his birthright as a firstborn for food and lost everything. The enemy tried to tempt Jesus with food. Jesus did not fall into temptation, although He was hungry.

Usually when you are weak, the enemy brings before you what you desire. That is the reason why you must discipline your body to withstand and abstain. We have to control our flesh so that we do not become its slaves. If we are not careful, we can be dragged into all kinds of sins and diseases because we have no self-control. When we are guided by the Holy Spirit, we can control the lust of the flesh and our soul's desires:

> *"Dear friends, I urge you, as foreigners and exiles, to abstain from sinful desires, which wage war against your soul."*
> *(1 Peter 2:11, NIV)*

"What causes fights and quarrels among you? Don't they come from your desires that battle within you?" *(James 4:1, NIV)*

"So I say, walk by the Spirit, and you will not gratify the desires of the flesh." (Galatians 5:16, NIV)

Why Is Fasting Powerful?

For your encouragement, I will tell you three personal experiences by which the Lord allowed me to understand the power of fasting.

1) THE STORY OF MY SON'S DEMONIC ATTACK

Years ago, in 2005, when the Lord started equipping and shaping me profoundly, something extraordinary happened. Together with my husband and children, we went for a walk in a park in the mountains, from where you could see the ocean, the city and the mountains. The scenery was incredible. We were happy, relaxed and carefree, we were rejoicing in the beauty of God's creation and we played with the children.

Marian and I sat on the grass while the children were playing. Richard, my eldest boy, came to us and showed us a plate that said, *"This is the playground of the gods."* We got up and took the kids elsewhere. Afterwards we noticed something was odd with our boy who touched the plate. In the area, there were many columns and pillars, "idols" of the native Indians. In that very place people came every night to perform rituals. I did not know that the columns had any actual power.

Suddenly, Richard started running way ahead of us. I called to him, but he would not listen. He was running towards the forest, and the park's boundary. We were upset. We tried calling him, but he avoided us. We could not do much because there were other people there. Finally we decided to go back to the car and go home. He got into the car without saying a word. We told him that we would discuss about his strange behavior when we get home.

When we got home, we asked him why he behaved so oddly. He told me that he saw a witch on a broom drawing him into the woods! When you hear such things, you want to laugh or think it is just a figment of his imagination, as he was only 8 years old, and especially if you do not know what is happening in the spiritual realm.

Dear parents, *be careful*! When you see a strange behavior coming upon your child do not scold him, punish him, chase him away or treat him carelessly, because there might be *something else* taking place trying to destroy your child's life. I heard about many charms, curses and spells cast upon people, objects and houses. Many young people go to witches, palm-readers, and mediums or some even enter satanic circles and cults to gain power. They don't realize that the enemy never gives something without asking something else in return. He wants to ruin their lives because he comes to steal, kill and destroy.

When our boy told me what happened, I started praying. I do not know what kind of power touched him and why it was after him. At night, he went into his sisters' room to sleep early. I asked him what was up. He told me with desperation: *"Mommy, there are witches lined along my wall!"* When I heard that, I knew something bizarre and serious was happening. Then, the Spirit of the Lord came to my help. I raised my right hand and I commanded the witches to go away in Jesus' Name. I could not see them, but my child could and he told me that they disappeared. Thank God!

After a few minutes, Richard stood up in his bed and gazed at the door. He told me, *"Mommy, there is a big, ugly spirit that looks like a scary goat staring at me."* Then I called Jesus' name and I commanded it to leave. Richard told me it would not go away. I called my husband to anoint our boy. Back then, I was not aware of the power of the Word, but the Lord was with us. Then Richard told me, *"Mom, I know what I have to do! I have to fight! I am getting ready and putting God's armor on: the helmet, the belt, the breastplate, the shoes, the shield... what else, mommy?"* I told him, *"Get your sword and charge!"*

When I saw how the Holy Spirit worked through my 8-year old boy, I took heart and got courage and faith to command the spirit to leave. We asked Jesus' blood to be upon our boy. After a while, Richard exhaled and said, *"Mommy, it's gone! I can see a big angel standing by the door and he has a bright sword in his hand."*

We then calmed down and took our boy to sleep with us. He was happy because he could see the angel standing by the door, protecting us. I do not know what the enemy's plans were, but God allowed a greater good for everyone. I thought everything would be over the next day. Not a chance! Richard told me, *"Mommy, did you know it is interesting to see the spiritual realm?"* I replied, *"Yes, sweetie, but I need to know who opened these evil eyes because it can be either the Holy Spirit or the enemy."* He replied, *"I know! It was the enemy because I can see a huge eye, and 'THE EVIL ONE' was written on it."* When I heard that, I realized the battle was extremely serious, but I had peace because I knew the Lord was with us. I knew the Lord wanted to teach us something and prepare us for future ministry.

The following day I had to go shopping and I took Richard with me. When we went out, my boy shouted, *"Mommy, I can see a very big witch in the sky casting spells and curses upon the earth, houses, churches, schools, shops and people."* Everything was clear to me then, that the enemy is fighting so hard to destroy us. After this, I understood the source of suffering and evil in our world.

Who is fighting against these witches? Who is countering their curses with blessings? Friends, this is not a joke. Do not think these are mere fairy tales! Later, I heard testimonies of former Satanists who practiced these kinds of things. Most Christians have no idea about demonic strategies, and if they happen to know them, they don't know how to fight against them. The enemy is content that Christians do not know about his plans or that they are too afraid to fight. We wonder why there are so many sins, diseases, sufferings and suicides! Satan enjoys torturing God's creation! The enemy is not afraid of Sunday-only Christians. They are afraid of people who contain the fire of the Holy Spirit and the light of Christ.

The Spirit of the Lord is calling all lukewarm Christians to lay down their comfortable lives and spiritual weaknesses. We must understand our position in Christ. Then, by fasting, prayer, and with the Sword of the Spirit, we can help those caught in the enemy's snare.

In Richard's situation, he described whatever he saw in the spiritual realm, and I would pray. When we entered a shop, my boy told me he saw evil spirits of different kinds in adults and children as well. After four days of suffering, I told him, *"We must abide in prayer so that this eye will shut and you will be free!"* He told me, *"Mommy, prayer alone is not enough; it does not have enough power, we need to fast as well. I know what I need to do: I will fast for three days.*" Imagine an 8-year old boy saying this!

In that moment, Richard saw the leader of the demons kneeling before him, telling him, *"Richard, please, please, do not fast, because if you fast, I die and I lose my grip over you."*

According to Richard, this demonic leader had smaller spirits under his reign. When they heard about fasting, they all started shrieking, *"We want food, we want food! We can control people through food. We do not want you to fast! Do not fast, for we die!"*

Do not think these are merely stories! The Lord allowed these events in my life because He called me to a life of fasting and prayer. He called me and He gave me the grace of fasting many times from 3 to 40 days, for different situations, people and nations.

You may ask what credibility an 8-year old has. I know my boy and I know such reactions and words could not be made up. What I told you here is the truth. The Lord urged me to write this book for you to dare to fast, to believe in the power of fasting, and to live in His victory.

When I understood how important fasting is, and how it destroys the enemy's power, we fasted as a family. The following day, I asked Richard how he felt. He told me the witches were fewer and smaller and that the spirits were further away and powerless.

Blessed be the Lord! We saw that our fasting was effective! The following day, Richard told me, *"I am not fasting anymore."* Surprised, I asked him why. *"Because the powerful leader is lying on the floor, exhausted and faint; he no longer has power over me."* I encouraged him to persevere because the evil eye was not shut yet, since he could see the demon. He would contradict me, when suddenly, he shrieked, *"O, mommy! He is getting up!"* When I heard that, the power from the Spirit of God came upon me and like a lioness defending her cub, I commanded with all authority for the evil spirit to be destroyed in the Name of Jesus. Richard rejoiced, *"Hallelujah! Look! The same angel appeared and thrust his fiery sword into the spirit's chest. It's gone! He disappeared!"* Suddenly an ugly stench filled the room. The smell was horrible.

Blessed be the Lord, because right then Richard was free. The "evil eye" was shut and Richard could no longer see the spiritual realm. He still had headaches and earaches for a while, but he stopped seeing the spiritual world. The Lord healed him and set him completely free.

From that point on, I received new insight and I saw the power of fasting and prayer.

2) EVIL SPIRITS MANIFESTING THROUGH A CHRISTIAN LADY

I had a different experience in February 2013. God allowed me to minister to a family who was in great trouble with depression, suicidal thoughts and divorce. The experience was unique for me. After I prayed for the couple, the evil spirits started manifesting and speaking through her.

The deliverance was long and difficult. The first session took three hours and the second one another two hours. The battle was difficult. Many spirits would manifest and present themselves and their rights over the person. Only by God's grace, goodness and guidance, I cast those spirits out and lead that person to repentance, forgiveness and deliverance.

The spirits would talk back and mock, saying, *"We will not come out because she is sold to us. She has been sold to us 7 generations ago."* Her situation is difficult to narrate, due to generational curses and spells cast by her ancestors. Even though she followed God, the spirits kept chasing her.

When I asked for the power of Jesus' blood and I commanded them to leave, they shrieked and left. At one point, I told her she had to fast. Immediately, the spirits said, *"We will not let her fast!"* I asked why, and they said with a sad and faint voice, *"When you fast, it burns us and we have to come out!"* I asked, *"What happens if we fast longer, what happens with you?"* They replied in a desperate and weak voice, *"Then we won't have any power over you..."*

When I heard this confirmation from their mouths with a different voice, I was overjoyed and I remembered what the Lord said,

> *"This kind can come out only by prayer and fasting"* (Mark 9:29).

This was yet another confirmation that fasting has power over demons.

I thank Him for delivering that person. I taught her how to fight, to abide in God's Word, to fast, pray, praise and worship God, and to be careful not to leave the door open to Satan. This way the enemy has no stronghold over her life.

Demons know everything that we do and do not do. I told that same lady to take the Word and to start fighting the spirits with the Word of God. After I said that, the demons started mocking me through her saying, "*She does not have power to fight; she is too weak because she has not read the Word of God for a week.*" She recognized that what they said was true. It is hard to believe that evil could talk through someone's mouth. However, you cannot play with sin. When we open the door to the enemy, he attacks us and activates any curses that have been cast upon us.

3) DELIVERANCE AFTER 7 MONTHS OF TORTURE

As I was writing this book, a friend of mine called me to tell me of her experience with fasting. She was a faithful girl. She prayed a lot and preached the Gospel on the streets and bus stations to people and wherever else she had the opportunity. She was full of passion for the Lord. However, something happened to her. She still does not know the cause, but spirits of insomnia, agitation, doubt, disbelief and even death attacked her. She could not sleep for months! She saw and heard evil, ugly and deceiving things. I fought with her in prayer, with tears and sobbing and I fasted for many days, believing God would set her free. At the same time, she went to different churches for prayer. She was still agitated and burdened. She lost her faith, peace and joy. Suicidal thoughts bothered her. She gave away all her clothes believing that she would soon die. After 7 months of torment, God in His goodness completely set her free.

I remember that as I was praying, I received a message that the dawn is coming, and soon God will set her free, but she needed to persevere in fasting and prayer. She tried to fast, but she could not do it. However, the Lord gave her grace and fasted half a day. She then saw a spider (symbol of witchcraft) and she stomped it. She was encouraged and she declared: *"I will fast longer!"* At the same time, she heard spirits saying, *"Don't fast! Your fasting is burning us."* In that moment, she was determined to fast even more. After her second day of fasting, she felt relieved. She kept fasting, even if she ate at noon or in the evening. Day by day, she felt more powerful, happier and her passion, love and desire to pray doubled in measure. She did not see anything evil anymore; she did not have any more thoughts about dying. Instead, she started having visions and wonderful dreams about Jesus. Now she was rejoicing in the Lord, in fasting and prayer, and already God has started to use her mightily.

> THERE IS SUCH AMAZING GRACE AND SUCH GREAT POWER IN FASTING FOR WHOEVER PRACTICES IT!

There is such amazing grace and such great power in fasting for whoever practices it! I wrote these short, real experiences to encourage you to fast. Not eating is a pleasing sacrifice before the Lord. In the spiritual realm, the sacrifice of fasting is like a defense that does not allow the enemy to torment us. Of course, we need to fast and to take action in faith. The enemy does not fear the fast itself, but Christ in us.

Let us not forget for one second that we are forgiven, saved and cleansed of our sins only by Jesus' sacrifice at the Cross- by His holy blood. Fasting and prayer both represent our part of the fight here on earth. By fasting and praying we abide in His salvation and we maintain our freedom, leaving behind the old nature, which was used by the enemy to hold us captive.

A WONDERFUL LESSON ABOUT FASTING

Before leaving for a mission trip, every year the Lord would tell me to fast for 40 days and 40 nights with only water or juice. I fasted for Romania so that God brings revival, cleanses and heals the land. At the same time, I interceded for the salvation of the lost. Moreover, the Lord gave me plenty of opportunities to preach the Gospel and revival messages received from the Lord. I asked the Lord to use me with power.

Once, I fasted for 40 days, but on the 30th day I felt hunger pangs and took a bite. I told myself everything will be all right. I was tempted but I would not relent. I could not eat, but I occasionally took some bites. Then I was irritated about that and I started asking the Lord for help. The following day the same thing happened. I told Him, *"Lord, what is wrong with me? I fasted this 40-day fast so many times, and now I am not even able to abstain for a few more days?"* I tried my best to complete the fast and I commanded the hunger to go, but nothing happened.

Then the Lord told me tenderly,

> *"My daughter, you unknowingly began to rely more on your fast than on My sacrifice. I took the grace, which helped until now, so that you understand that you cannot do anything without Me. Slowly but steadily you fell into the trap of relying on your actions rather than on Me. You have everything you need in Me because of My sacrifice. You receive authority and power from the Cross. Only My sacrifice and your faith in Me will give you victory!"*

> *"What am I to understand, Lord? Should I not fast anymore?"*

> *"You ought to fast, but your mind and faith should be always focused on Me and My grace, not on your deeds. Always rely on what I did for you. Fasting is a part of the discipline in your life, to draw you closer to Me and grow in faith. Fasting attracts My presence and I fulfill your requests. Look vertically to Me, not horizontally. You must walk in the good deeds that I prepared for you beforehand."*

Only then, I realized how much the enemy deceives us. We think our conscience is clean just because we did something good. We think that if we give money to the poor and dress humbly we are appreciated and righteous before God. We must do good deeds, but the Lord explained to me that I should not rely on my own deeds, which are like dirty rags before Him. In other words, we should not replace His grace, love and sacrifice with our deeds.

This is how I was set free from the condemnation that began to torment me. I saw His faithfulness and He pulled me back to Him. He did not allow me to rely on anything else but Him and His love.

How great is our Saviour!

The Conditions Of The Fast (Isaiah 58)

This chapter describes the wonderful benefits of fasting. It also describes the conditions we must comply with to obtain our benefits. This is what needs to be done to get the benefits of fasting:

LOOSE THE CHAINS OF INJUSTICE

We are all wicked to some extent. Many times, we try to rid ourselves of this malice, but we cannot do it because our old nature is already rooted. However, His grace and goodness will help us break these chains when we completely surrender to Him and we fast.

Malice comes from the enemy. It destroys marriages and friendships; it divides people and the church. The word "wickedness" has the stem *wicked*, which leads us to the enemy: *the wicked one*. Therefore, it is understandable that you must flee from evil!

Where does wickedness dwell? Firstly, it dwells in our old nature and in our pride. It has an even deeper root - anger. Where does anger come from? It comes out of sorrow, long-term frustration, bitterness, dissatisfaction and many other places.

You can see how many chains bind us without even being aware of it. Many chains are wrapped in wickedness and inherited generationally, or because of abuse in one way or another in childhood. Other times, it builds up if someone experiences multiple injustices in their life. We all shout *"Justice!"* and when we do not find it, we get angry, and become bitter and unforgiving. We hate and we take revenge. Many people have fallen victim to the chains of wickedness and have eventually caused others to walk in evil deeds.

Jesus always has the solution. We must come to Him in humility and in repentance, admit our faults, ask for forgiveness and decide to forgive those who wronged us. Then, with the authority we have been given in Christ, we break the enemy's chains that tormented us. We are set free by faith in Jesus' blood and in His Name. Fasting helps seal this deliverance.

> *"See to it, brothers and sisters, that none of you has a sinful, unbelieving heart that turns away from the living God."* *(Hebrews 3:12, NIV)*

The wickedness that we bear in our hearts is dangerous: it separates us from God, therefore

> *"Get rid of all bitterness, rage and anger, brawling and slander, along with every form of malice. Be kind and compassionate to one another, forgiving each other, just as in Christ God forgave you." (Ephesians 4:31-32, NIV)*

Untie the cords of the yoke

Maybe there are persons who are indebted to us and cannot pay their debt back. What do we do? Put yourself in their shoes and do what the Word advises us to do: either give them more time or forgive their debt. It is not easy, but we ought to be careful, lest we become like the wicked, unmerciful servant (*Matthew 18:21-30*). God asks of us to show mercy. Nobody should be our slave. Let us love, help and forgive them.

> *"Give to the one who asks you, and do not turn away from the one who wants to borrow from you." (Matthew 5:42, NIV)*

SET THE OPPRESSED FREE

You may ask yourselves, *"Who are those we are oppressing? We live in modern times where there are no slaves!"* Usually someone who is higher ranked takes advantage of their status and oppresses others with a spirit of control and manipulation. Let us not take advantage of their weakness, status or poverty! It is sad because in some churches today the leader or the pastor oppress others.

By not forgiving, we indulge in oppressing them because we are holding them chained, tormenting them and ourselves.

> *"Give to everyone who asks you, and if anyone takes what belongs to you, do not demand it back." (Luke 6:30, NIV)*

BREAK EVERY YOKE

> *"But love your enemies, do good to them, and lend to them without expecting to get anything back. Then your reward will be great, and you will be children of the Most High, because he is kind to the ungrateful and wicked." (Luke 6:35, NIV)*

SHARE YOUR FOOD WITH THE HUNGRY

Jesus urges us to help the poor, widows and orphans. There are people in need all around us. The Lord tells each and every one of us, rich and poor: share your bread, food, and goods with those who do not have any. This means that if you have a slice of bread, you must give half to someone who does not have any at all. Help us do so, Lord!

If you are poor, you may excuse yourself saying you do not have anything to give. However, the Lord clearly states you ought to give, even if it is a little. If you are rich, remember that it was God who gave you power and wisdom to have everything in abundance (*Deuteronomy 8:17*). He gave to you on the condition that you give back abundantly.

What would you do if the Lord took your soul tonight? Who will inherit your wealth? What will you tell Him when He asks you why you took no notice of the poor? Jesus tells us that every time we did something for the least of His brothers and sisters, we did it for Him. (*Matthew 25:40*)

Do you know how many mothers cry out to God, asking for food to feed their children, or for money to pay the bills and other expenses, because they have no income? Whose ears are in tune to Holy Spirit's whisper to help those in need?

Do not judge the ones in need. God did not tell us to judge or criticize them. He asked us to share our food with them. Riches come and go. Therefore it is better to invest in Heaven and in God's Kingdom, and for His works, so that we could call ourselves spiritually wealthy.

PROVIDE THE POOR WANDERER WITH SHELTER

This is a great challenge for God's children: to help the homeless. How many of us bring homeless people into our homes for lunch or dinner? Blessed be the Lord, I met people who were not afraid or ashamed of bringing homeless drug addicts into their houses. Not only did they provide food, but a bed as well. May God bless those families! Fewer Christians have mercy for the homeless nowadays. They judge them, telling them it was their own choices that got them there.

> *"If you love those who love you, what credit is that to you? Even sinners love those who love them. And if you do good to those who are good to you, what credit is that to you? Even sinners do that." (Luke 6:32-33, NIV)*

In the ministry to which the Lord called us, we had plenty of opportunities to help the homeless, children and elders. They need so much love and acceptance! Who can provide them all with love? Their parents chased them away and rejected them. Since the church is not ready to sacrifice for them in a real, concrete way, the enemy bound them in the chains of sin, helplessness and loneliness. The Lord promised that He is the Father to the orphan. He empowered us to take action.

DO NOT TO TURN AWAY FROM YOUR OWN FLESH AND BLOOD

> *"Be kind and compassionate to one another, forgiving each other, just as in Christ God forgave you."* *(Ephesians 4:32, NIV)*

> *"Be completely humble and gentle; be patient, bearing with one another in love."(Ephesians 4:2, NIV)*

> *"Suppose a brother or a sister is without clothes and daily food. If one of you says to them, "Go in peace; keep warm and well fed," but does nothing about their physical needs, what good is it? In the same way, faith by itself, if it is not accompanied by action, is dead." (James 2:15-17, NIV)*

There are so many needy, poor, orphaned, lonely and abandoned people around us! Who can give them a lending hand? Who cares about their suffering and shortages? The Lord urges us not to turn our backs from the needy. How many times did we turn our backs thinking that others might have compassion for them? Lord, change us and give us the grace and power to do every good deed.

When we start a lifestyle of fasting and prayer, Jesus' heart, which is full of compassion and mercy, will beat in us and we will rejoice in helping others wherever the need arises.

The Rewards Of The Fast (Isaiah 58)

We read above what God requires of those who fast. If we take heed, we will also experience the benefits of fasting and obedience. This is what we have to do to obtain the benefits of fasting, as they are presented in Isaiah 58.

YOUR LIGHT WILL BREAK FORTH LIKE THE DAWN

"Then your light will break forth like the dawn, and your healing will quickly appear; then your righteousness will go before you, and the glory of the Lord will be your rear guard. Then you will call, and the Lord will answer; you will cry for help, and he will say: Here am I. "If you do away with the yoke of oppression, with the pointing finger and malicious talk, The Lord will guide you always; He will satisfy your needs in a sun-scorched land and will strengthen your frame. You will be like a well-watered garden, like a spring whose waters never fail." (Isaiah 58:8,9,11, NIV)

During and after a fast your spiritual eyes are open to see things that you weren't able to see before. The Lord will show you new revelations from His Word, He will tell you unknown mysteries:

"Call to Me and I will answer you and show you great and mighty things, fenced in and hidden, which you do not know (do not distinguish and recognize, have knowledge of and understand)." (Jeremiah 33:3, AMP)

211

At the same time, the Lord's light will reveal many of your heart's secrets - sins, moods, attitudes and wrong motivations that sadden the Lord and the Holy Spirit. He will make you more aware of things around you, especially the pain of others that you may have caused. His light will reveal everything. When the power of His love cleanses and enlightens your heart, you will be able to see the heart of others. When you talk to people, you will suddenly see what dwells in their hearts. With the eyes of your heart, you will recognize what hides behind their reactions, habits or glances.

You will see what others do not see: spiritual truth. You will see Satan's strategies, how he works and deceives people. At the same time, you will observe how the Holy Spirit works through you and through others. Moreover, you will see God's potential in other people. You will no longer notice only their weak points, but their gifts that God has placed in them. Your vision will broaden. When you contemplate on His creation, you will rejoice and say, *"Lord, You are so wonderful!"*

When God's light penetrates our hearts, it exposes our motivations and attitudes. Then, without anyone pointing at us, we will fall at the feet of Jesus. We then understand that many things, which we thought were from God, are only worldly. Maybe they are "good" things, but they are not from the Holy Spirit. Prolonged fasting enables us to see like God does.

The proud and arrogant man is still in darkness and cannot see Christ. Those who are in the light humble themselves. They obey, they do not argue and they try to live in unity with those around them.

When true light shines upon us, the truth about our flesh and ourselves is revealed. Many people find excuses for their state, proving they are still in the dark. Therefore, we must be disciplined and enlightened by the Holy Spirit, in order for Him to reveal more of Himself and what is hidden inside us.

One day, the Lord told me, *"I want you see that I'm in in everything, absolutely everything, because I am omnipresent. All things live and move because of Me. Whomever will see Me will be aware of My presence and sovereignty and will not fear anything. Every living creature must bless My Name because I am in the snowflake, the raindrop, the sweet whisper of the dawn, in the sunrays and rustling of the leaves. Stop and realize that I am everywhere; that is why My goodness fills the earth."*

"For in Him we live and move and have our being."
(Acts 17:28, NIV)

"The Son is the radiance of God's glory and the exact representation of His being, sustaining all things by His powerful word. After He had provided purification for sins, He sat down at the right hand of the Majesty in heaven."
(Hebrews 1:3, NIV)

"There is one God and Father of all, who is over all and through all and in all." (Ephesians 4:6, NIV)

Lord God, how great You are! Who can know and understand You, Lord? We ask that You help us understand Your omnipresence through the Holy Spirit! When we receive this divine light, we will shine for You and attract people wherever we go. The darkness shall disappear because there is no room for darkness in the light.

Darkness is the absence of light. Why is it so dark around us? It is because we are not in the light, because we do not follow Jesus' teachings. Let us imagine for a second how the world around us would be like if we were light and if His light shone through us.

"For the fruit of the light consists in all goodness, righteousness and truth" (Ephesians 5:9, NIV)

"The Lord is my light and my salvation— whom shall I fear? The Lord is the stronghold of my life— of whom shall I be afraid?" (Psalm 27:1, NIV)

"For with you is the fountain of life; in Your light we see light." (Psalm 36:9, NIV)

"Your word is a lamp for my feet, a light on my path." (Psalm 119:105, NIV)

"The unfolding of Your words gives light; it gives understanding to the simple." (Psalm 119:130, NIV)

"Arise, shine, for Your light has come, and the glory of the Lord rises upon you." (Isaiah 60:1, NIV)

"The Lord said, 'Let there be light!' And there was light." (Genesis 1:3)

Your healing will quickly appear

Another reward of the fasting done after His will is healing. Psalm 41:1-3 illustrates the sacrifice we make for the poor, and the blessing that comes as a reward:

"Blessed are those who have regard for the weak; the Lord delivers them in times of trouble. The Lord protects and preserves them— they are counted among the blessed in the land— he does not give them over to the desire of their foes. The Lord sustains them on their sickbed and restores them from their bed of illness." (Psalm 41:1-3, NIV)

What a wonderful promise! You are the first to benefit from the blessing of sacrificing yourself when you fast and pray. By fasting, you have the promise of being healed of many diseases. Why? It is because during those 21-40 days when you fast, your blood and body are cleansed and regenerated.

I can testify to that account. The Lord healed me from anemia, headaches, liver pain and stomachaches. I always feel well. I said in the first part of the book that the Lord healed my tonsils and I never got sick since then. I believe this is because I maintain my health by prolonged, frequent fasting. Blessed be the Lord!

You have to give your stomach "a break". The benefits of this break cannot be put into words, but you will only rejoice and be amazed of the results. You will appreciate the healing and restoration done in your body and you will declare that the suffering and labor were worth it all.

I read many testimonies of people who fasted for 40 days and were later cured from cancer and tumors. How is that so? Here is the mystery of fasting: we detoxify our body and soul. The blood is cleaner, thinner and it can "attack" the diseases in your body. Therefore, we must drink as much water as possible during the fast.

It is important to mention that the food eaten today is not as healthy as it was when our grandparents lived. With all these chemicals and additives, food has become more and more poisonous and toxic than we can even imagine. Yet, even if we know all this, we cannot abstain from eating. Then we complain about unexpected pain and we get sick.

During the fast, the body is fighting all the "intruders and invaders", the toxins and poisons that we accumulated along the years by eating unhealthily. The "unwanted guests" pile comfortably in a vulnerable place in our body and produce a disease. When the stomach "takes a break," it is set free from all the viruses and germs, and our "temple" is clean and the flesh is crucified.

The stomach is one of the most hard-working organs in our body. It is like a slave working day-in and day-out and it never gets to rest. When your stomach takes a break, you renounce the natural for the supernatural. This is the fastest way of obtaining spiritual food from God. During the fast you are completely surrendered to God. You give Him your pride, weaknesses, flesh and natural desires. During this "break," you will experience great and wonderful divine revelations, you will have power in your prayers and you will be willing to meditate on His Word. Please dare enter this "starvation" of the body – sometimes - for His glory! The enemy's powers will be cast out and you will be unhindered in communicating with God. He will show you His power in the most profound ways!

Two of the archenemies of the Holy Spirit are doubt and lack of faith. If these two are cast out, the obstacles we encountered by now and the distance between Jesus and us disappear. He has free passage to speak, heal and help.

YOUR RIGHTEOUSNESS WILL GO BEFORE YOU AND THE GLORY OF THE LORD WILL BE YOUR REAR GUARD.

We can once again observe the beauty of obeying God's Word and commandments. When we rely on Jesus' sacrifice and we do His will, by faith, we are considered clean and righteous before God. From this reassurance, we are happy and confident in our Lord and His glory is always with us.

> *"…Christ in you, the hope of glory." (Colossians 1:27, NIV)*

There is no greater or more desirable promise than this one: God's glory is accompanying us. This means that God's power is manifesting, bringing about signs, wonders and healings.

Lord, make us worthy so that Your glory accompanies us, to be carriers of Your glory here on earth!

THEN YOU WILL CALL AND THE LORD WILL ANSWER; YOU WILL CRY FOR HELP AND HE WILL SAY: HERE AM I.

Every time I read these verses from Isaiah 58, my heart is filled with joy and faith. I weep every time. Who does not desire something like this? Who does not want to hear God speak?

Do you understand what this promise entails? The Creator of the Universe Himself shows up when we cry out to Him! More than that, when our pain is unbearable, we can cry out to Him and God in His infinite mercy and goodness will say, *"Here I am. I'm here for you. What do you want Me to do?"*

Don't you think it's worth doing everything He asks, for His sake, in order to experience this promise?

> *"What, then, shall we say in response to these things? If God is for us, who can be against us?" (Romans 8:31, NIV)*

Imagine that every time you kneel in prayer and cry out to God, you hear, *"Here I am. I'm here for you. What do you want Me to do?"* We lose so much because we do not take God seriously and we do not believe His promises of *"Yes"* and *"Amen"*!

Lord, forgive our ignorance and indifference. Too many times we allow the flesh to lead us. We now decide to put it behind us and in fasting and prayer, fulfill Your Word God. We trust in You, Lord, that when we cry out to You, You are right beside us. We thank You that You will help us, clean our minds, heart and ears and enable us to hear You when You say: "Here I am!"

THE LORD WILL GUIDE YOU ALWAYS

Here is another great promise. All Christians need it on a daily basis. Many times, we have to make decisions and we do not know what to do. However, our good Father is an Almighty God who has solutions and unlimited resources. He promises that He will always guide us. Therefore, another benefit of fasting is the elimination of confusion, disbelief and doubt.

> *"Yet I am always with you; you hold me by my right hand. You guide me with your counsel, and afterward you will take me into glory." (Psalm 73:23-24, NIV)*

> *"I will instruct you and teach you in the way you should go; I will counsel you with My loving eye on you." (Psalm 32:8, NIV)*

> *"Teach me to do Your will, for you are my God; may your good Spirit lead me on level ground." (Psalm 143:10, NIV)*

HE WILL SATISFY YOUR NEEDS IN A SUN-SCORCHED LAND

Here we can see the beauty of God's goodness and grace for everybody who listens to Him. He takes care of His children when they are in certain trials. What does it mean to be in a "sun-scorched land"? It means the desert and barren ground of any kind. Have you ever been in the desert? There is no grass because where there is no water and no life. All you can see there is wasteland. To these people, God promises the rain of His blessings.

I found myself in a spiritual desert once. It seemed like my entire life was lifeless and hopeless without spiritual water. However, the Lord came to me and spoke to me from His Word. He gave me water from His Word and refreshed my soul. God's Word is like a spring overflowing incessantly, bringing life wherever it flows.

> "See, I am doing a new thing! Now it springs up; do you not perceive it? I am making a way in the wilderness and streams in the wasteland." (Isaiah 43:19, NIV)

The Lord is encouraging you through this verse. He is saying that if you are lacking, He will saturate you, refresh you, grow you, and mature you so that you will bear fruit for Him. If you are in a spiritual wasteland, God, in His infinite grace will saturate you with His Word and revelation. If you trust God and seek His face, the wasteland will turn into an oasis with springs and a well-watered garden.

WILL STRENGTHEN YOUR FRAME

Walking through this world, we get tired, weary, weak and sick. We feel burdened because of our struggles, worries or battles. However, the Lord promises that He will give us *strength*. Even when we fail or fall, God will continually revive us.

> "He gives strength to the weary and increases the power of the weak. Even youths grow tired and weary, and young men stumble and fall; but those who hope in the LORD will renew their strength. They will soar on wings like eagles; they will run and not grow weary, they will walk and not be faint. (Isaiah 40:29-31, NIV)

His promise is that He never tires. He is always ready to forgive, strengthen and help His children.

YOU WILL BE LIKE A WELL-WATERED GARDEN

Have you seen a well-watered garden before? The flowers, vegetables and fruit create amazing scenery. Anyone is happy to visit or work in such a garden, and to enjoy its fruit. We must be like this garden, in case anyone needs fruit they might find it in us. If someone needs prayer, comfort, financial or spiritual help, we can supply it to them. If the Lord dwells in us, our garden must produce plenty of fruit.

Cleanse us, Lord. Water us, God, so that we may water other people. Amen!

LIKE A SPRING WHOSE WATERS NEVER FAIL

We know that the spring of our lives is Jesus Christ. We take water from Him daily. His Word is eternally rich and true. God is a spring of peace, forgiveness, love and grace. He dwells in us through His Word. We can become a spring that never dries.

What does a spring do? It brings life to its surroundings. The surrounding nature is rejuvenated. The thirsty quench their thirst. Water is used for washing, cleansing and refreshing. Do we want to be a spring whose waters never dry? If we abide in obedience, we will benefit from many blessings owing to fasting and prayer. We must thank the Lord for these benefits, owing to the grace of His sacrifice, which is constantly and incessantly flowing in us and pouring through us.

> *"For with You is the fountain of life; in Your light we see light." (Psalm 36:9)*

> *"The fear of the Lord is a fountain of life, turning a person from the snares of death." (Proverbs 14:27, NIV)*

"Blessed is the man whose delight is in the law of the Lord, and who meditates on His law day and night. That person is like a tree planted by streams of water, which yields its fruit in season and whose leaf does not wither – whatever he does prospers." (Psalm 1:2-3, NIV)

Jesus' promise to the Samaritan woman was clear: the water given by Jesus will quench her thirst and she will never thirst again. This water will become a spring gushing from inside out and she will never dry (John 3:38). Jesus was referring to the Holy Spirit. In this manner, we will bring life to every place we go.

Oh, Spring of our lives, how we thirst after You! We want in turn to become a spring that gives life to our surroundings. There is so much wasteland around us, Lord! We ask You, Spring of Life, pour Yourself in us, so that we may water and pour in others! Make us aware of Your promises! We want to fulfill the necessary conditions so that Your promises manifest in our lives. We passionately and fervently ask You, our heavenly Father!

YOU WILL BE REPAIR THE BROKEN WALLS

People who fast will be called to action. What kind of action? To rebuild ancient ruins and to repair broken walls. We are called to rise up and put into practice what we know. We are to be bold and courageous, and we are to help others who have been broken and need help in restoration, and healing in their lives. We are also called to bring the truth of Jesus and a Biblical foundation into the broken walls of media, education and government that have been distorted by sin.

An Encouragement To Fast

Our bodies were not designed to eat 3-4 times a day, every day, without stop. From time to time, we need to give it a break. The more we stuff ourselves, the more our faith and His works weaken - we become lukewarm and waver in faith.

The absence of fasting and prayer in our life leads to spiritual coldness, contention and strife in the family and church, gossip, envy, ungodliness, fleshly lust, doubt, lack of faith, lack of joy, worries, spiritual pride, a shallow and powerless form of Godliness, hardened hearts and sin.

Christians who do not practice fasting and prayer severely lack in love, faith, divine revelation and cannot say that they sincerely worship God. Therefore, we are called to repent and return to the Lord, to seek His face in fasting and prayer. Let us begin obeying His Word; let us bring Him praise, worship and thanks, to be His faithful witnesses in this lost world!

Abstinence from food enables our prayers to work at their fullest capacity and to be effective. Why? If we fast, the Holy Spirit has more room and control over our hearts and minds. Faith becomes more powerful and we can ask *with authority* for His will to be done. Only then do we learn how to obey God and ask for things after His will.

"Then Jesus told His disciples a parable to show them that they should always pray and not give up." (Luke 18:1, NIV)

Let us take, for example, someone who prays for something specific, and he is certain that it is God's will. If God's response is late, and that person stops believing and praying, then he allows doubt, lack of faith, confusion, and disappointment to take root in his life. That will suffocate his prayers.

We must understand a principle, which is neglected by others. When you are certain that what you ask is in accordance to His will, you have the authority to ask and obtain it. I encourage you to persevere and believe because surely your answer will come. His promises are "Yes" and "Amen"! Do not fix your eyes on your problems, mountains or obstacles any longer, but believe in the power and faithfulness of the One who promised that He would listen to you.

Fasting will help you in such a critical situation, it will empower you not to give up. It will empower you to persevere by faith in prayers, until you receive what you asked for. Your eyes will shift from your problems and mountains that seem impossible to be moved to the Almighty God who is full of grace, mercy and love. His promises are "Yes" and "Amen". He gives you the right to righteousness and He responds to His children in love. He is your Healer, Jehova-Rapha. Jesus, your Saviour, healed a multitude of sick people and He has the power to heal you as well.

> *"He said, If you listen carefully to the Lord your God and do what is right in His eyes, if you pay attention to his commands and keep all his decrees, I will not bring on you any of the diseases I brought on the Egyptians, for I am the Lord, who heals you." (Exodus 15:26, NIV)*

> *"But He was pierced for our transgressions, He was crushed for our iniquities; the punishment that brought us peace was on Him, and by His wounds we are healed." (Isaiah 53:5, NIV)*

If you still did not receive an answer to your prayer, search your heart to see if there is any sin you did not confess. You must destroy every obstacle and every sin that binds you. With humility and repentance, turn from that sin. Then, by the Word of faith, declare and proclaim His promises for your life. Following the fast, you will receive light, revelation, faith and perseverance in prayer.

> *"And will not God bring about justice for His chosen ones, who cry out to him day and night? Will He keep putting*

them off? I tell you, He will see that they get justice, and quickly. However, when the Son of Man comes, will He find faith on the earth?" (Luke 18:7-8, NIV)

Perseverance in prayer is pleasing to the Lord because you show that you do not back down as you rely on His power and love. God is faithful and He fulfills His Word. Do not doubt, because if you relent it will be difficult to raise the problem before the Lord again. Your mind will remind you of your defeat and when you pray for something, you will face doubt and have a lack of faith. Give your burden to the Lord and continue to rely on Him because He has His own timing and way of responding to your need.

Christians must move on and fight because their reward will be great. If we do not give up, but persevere day and night in fasting and prayer, we will experience the victory of faith over Satan and his minions. We obtain a new measure of His power and we become fearless. The next mountain we face will seem small and we will easily surmount it. A victory will lead to another and the battle will become easier and easier to face. Once we are in the territory of faith, and are fully persuaded by His goodness and faithfulness, we become confident and aware of His promises.

Our understanding of God grows in every aspect:

- We know God is fighting for us;
- We know He provides for our every need;
- We know He is always by our side;
- We know in Whom we trust;
- We know God is faithful;
- We know He will never leave because He loves us deeply;
- We know that by His stripes we are healed;
- We know we are seated with Christ in heavenly places;
- We know that Satan is under our feet;
- We know that all things work together for our good;
- We know that Jesus is the Way, the Truth and the Life;
- We know that He desires to give everything in abundance;
- We know our fasting and prayers will receive an answer;

- We know that no weapon formed against us will prosper;
- We know and believe in the power of His Word, which is alive and working;
- We know who we are in Christ;
- We know who our Father and our God is.

Fasting, Nutrition, And The Human Body

There are millions of cells in our body. When these cells work, they interact through the electric stimuli that they transmit. They radiate life and act together as a powerful battery, charging our life and bringing health to our body. The food we eat maintains these wonderful cells so that they are always ready for new activities. However, when we eat too much, the cells are overcharged and choked and can become ineffective.

When the body is over-loaded, those cells can no longer keep up with the workload. The body becomes clogged with toxins and the immune system - and even organs - begins to crash. As a result, we get sick.

> FASTING AND PRAYER ARE THE EASIEST WAYS TO CLEANSE AND HEAL BOTH THE BODY AND THE SOUL.

The same happens on a spiritual level. When we allow worldly desires to take control, our spirit suffers, faith weakens and we no longer desire God's work. All that we desire is to fulfill our own lusts. When temptation, sin, problems and stress come, we fall because the inner man was not strengthened in the spirit with spiritual food. We become obsessed with feeding our flesh and we remain spiritually weak.

Without even knowing, many end up worshiping food.

> *"You say, 'Food for the stomach and the stomach for food,' and God will destroy them both." (1 Corinthians 6:13, NIV)*

Fasting is beneficial because during a fast the body relieves itself from unhealthy toxics that are detrimental to the body.

225

Fasting brings about detoxification. Even if the cells no longer receive nutrition, they keep on working for weeks, helping the detoxification process and eliminating the poison from our bodies. The stomach gets a break.

Fasting and prayer are the easiest ways to cleanse and heal both the body and the soul. God wants us to rid ourselves of the "old self", which can be associated with a filthy, stinky, old carpet, on which many people have stepped. Now, the carpet is brought to the Cleaner and can be placed in your house again.

At first, when we choose to fast for 10 days or more, it is not easy at all. You are under the impression that you are dying. Your old self is struggling and shrieking because it hates the process of transformation. Sometimes you might start feeling alone, as if everything is dark and it seems as if the Lord has forgotten you and is far away from you.

The first few days are the worst, especially the first day, because you get out of your routine and comfort zone of eating three times a day. If you are used to drinking coffee, you will have terrible headaches and you will feel as if your whole body is crying out. You will feel an intense battle within you, and you will become more agitated, irritated, angry and impatient during that time. The enemy knows the value of fasting. He knows that people who fast receive power and authority from Jesus.

> "I have given you authority to trample on snakes and scorpions and to overcome all the power of the enemy; nothing will harm you." (Luke 10:19, NIV)

Fasting and prayer are needed for His promises to become a reality in our lives. However, the enemy will do everything he can to stop you because he knows the effects that fasting has on him! He will try to disturb you through your family members or the people around you. You will be tempted to take a bite and then give up. You will feel nauseous, weak and weary. You might want to throw up or faint, telling yourself that you cannot fast any longer. This is the enemy's lie - do not accept it. Declare this: *I can do all things through Christ who strengthens me* (Phil 4:13). Fight, because only people who fight win the prize of glory.

Sometimes when you decide to fast, you may receive an invitation to a birthday or to lunch with friends that you love and who cook delicious food. They may tell you that they will bake your favourite cookies and your mouth may drool from just imagining the taste.

You should not forget that all these temptations and thoughts are your body's attempts to fight because you are crucifying it. The enemy is using these thoughts to stop you from fasting. Many people are heavily attacked before beginning a fast, and others are tempted and stop on their first or second day.

I tell you from my own experience that everything is possible for those who believe and for those who fight. I wholeheartedly believe that you can do everything in Christ if you rely on Him and if you discover the power of fasting.

The Preparation Before The Fast

Physical and spiritual preparation is essential before and at the beginning of a short-term or long-term fast.

1. **Know the power of fasting.** When you know the Word of God, the truth, the effects, the rewards and the power of fasting, this understanding will give you courage, faith, joy and perseverance. In this manner, you will know that something is working in your life and in the lives of the people you pray for, and that the fast is worth it.

2. **Have a vision.** You must have a vision, calling, motivation and passion for the will of God. This motivation will give you strength and make you fast irrespective of the obstacles you encounter.

3. **Be determined.** Declare that you will complete this fast by faith and write in your spiritual journal: *"Starting this day, I will fast for this long."* It is as if you are setting your mind and body to understand this firm decision and that they should not negotiate with you. You are determined not to listen to their complaints.

4. **Tell some close friends and family**. It is important to tell godly friends and family members that you are fasting. This is not the same thing as boasting. They will pray for you and at the same time hold you accountable. This commitment will help you carry on with your fast.

5. **Take it one day at a time.** Ask God for grace to finish everything well each day. It is important to focus on God every day of the fast. Do not constantly think to yourself: *"Lord, there are so many days left, how am I going to do this?"* If you only focus on this, discouragement is coming.

6. **Believe that you will complete the fast.** Declare that you will be able to finish the fast and that you will see the results and benefits.

7. **Spend time with the Lord.** Make as much time as possible to spend with the Lord in solitude, in His Word, in praise, worship and prayer. Steer clear from distractions. In the period of fasting, try to spend more time with the Lord than with the rest of your family, friends, internet or television.

8. **Drink as much water as possible**. It can be distilled, boiled or lukewarm. If possible, drink two to four liters a day. Do not try to taste anything because your whole body will scream after more and then it will be impossible to resist the urge. Still, if you do take a bite or more, do not give up and break the fast. Repent and hold the fast for one more day. Fight knowing the Lord is with you. Do not be fooled by the enemy who is trying to deceive you saying that your fasting is useless because you ate. He wants you to give up as easily as possible. When you feel hungry drink warm water.

9. **Prepare your mind and body**. At least a week beforehand, begin to eat less. Gradually remove the sweets and coffee. Eat more fruit and vegetables and drink plenty of water. This way it will be easier for you to start fasting. When you start fasting all at once, it is a natural reaction of the body to ache because there is a sudden change of diet and the body is not accustomed to it. It can help to prepare the body gradually the week before. However all the aches are still normal because the detoxification process is uncomfortable. However, the purpose and rewards of fasting are greater than momentary aches.

10. **Do not be afraid of anything**. Do not allow fearful thinking to stand in your way of fasting. It is not easy, but be sure that you won't die! Believe that the Lord is with you and you will finish well.

Do you want to see real results? Then be firm, disciplined and wise. You will overcome any obstacle because He who is in you is stronger than the enemy. If more Christians understood and practiced prolonged fasting only with water, a few times a year, they would certainly not be ordinary, worldly, lukewarm Christians with little passion. Only those who dare to enter new territories can understand the difference and will receive a new light and revelation regarding the fullness of Christ's life in them.

When we fast, we hang our flesh on the cross. In its complexity, the human nature controls us to its liking, and we do not even realize it. We can have our hearts filled with sin and not even recognize it: pride, envy, jealousy, anger, lust, gluttony and arguments. When we fast for a long period and meditate on God's Word, the flesh loses its power and grip over us and we allow the Holy Spirit to fill and lead our lives. Usually, our selfish nature is sitting on the throne of our lives, and its desire to be in control. It wants us to fulfill every lust and pleasure. However, fasting and prayer, together with His Word, wither the roots of the flesh and our very thoughts and actions will be transformed.

Fasting exposes whatever is old and ugly inside us. That is why the light of the Holy Spirit will penetrate the darkest depths of our heart. Then, there will be a profound cleansing. You will see things differently, both in your behavior and in your attitudes. You will be disgusted by your sinful nature, which you defended and protected, and which only hurt you and those around you. We must be totally surrendered and lie at the feet of Jesus, acknowledging that nothing good can come from us and from our wicked flesh.

Jesus has been waiting so long for these moments. He wants you to see and acknowledge your state. He wants to cleanse you and fill you with His light, love and humility. Humility is the key to elevation. Only through the cross we can be free from our sin.

Maybe you ask, *"Didn't Jesus' sacrifice at the Cross set me free?"* Of course, we are saved and forgiven by His blood, but we are still living in a sinful world. Until we receive our new glorified bodies, our present bodies are tainted by sin and we will be constantly fighting with the flesh. It is our responsibilities to take up the cross daily, crucify the flesh, and follow Him. The flesh is battling with us constantly. We have the key. The Lord did His part, now it's our turn to do ours.

Some Physical Reactions While Fasting

These physical reactions do not apply to everyone. If you encounter any of these problems, do not give up because they are only temporary and are normal. They are reactions to the fight for the detoxification of both body and soul.

VOMITING

Your stomach is rejecting the poison and the filth that was deposited, especially if your liver is not healthy. The vomit could be due to the spleen, which is jammed, allowing the toxins to reach for the stomach instead of the intestines. You should drink as much warm water as possible, which will cleanse your stomach.

Go outside, get some fresh air and inhale and exhale deeply. You can drink water mixed with a little lemon and honey (if you are nauseous). You can eat ice cubes and allow them to melt in your mouth. If symptoms persist, you can stop fasting, asking God for guidance to know when you can start another fast. In any case, do not forget to eat little and healthy!

INSOMNIA

When you fast, you can barely sleep the entire night, but you can see this as His blessing because He is keeping you awake to pray incessantly. Fasting must go hand in hand with prayer; they are like a flower bouquet. You will start losing around 400 grams of body weight a day, starting with the useless fat. The blood lost from the fat is absorbed to other parts of the body. A part of it goes to the head, so it gets warmer and causes insomnia. You lose only a small percentage of blood during the fast. Blood can now fight diseases, because it is no longer busy with the food we eat. In the meantime, the blood is cleansed.

URINATION DIFFICULTIES

These are rare. If your body has many toxins and poison in the kidneys, they will be cleansed. As a side effect, you may feel certain burning and itchiness. It is necessary to:

- Drink as much boiled or distilled water as possible.
- Take hot baths, sitting in the tub with warm water.
- Rest as much as possible (even take two short naps a day.) It's important to store and focus energy towards prayer.

HEART RATE

If you are an agitated person, your heart rate might be higher and you may experience an increased heart rate. Take a cold bath and your heart rate will drop down to normal. If it is actually lower, take a warm bath.

STOMACH ACHES

I have heard of many people who complained about stomachaches during the fast. Some have gastritis or other diseases and it might be difficult to fast. If you are in this situation, it is advisable to drink orange juice that has been diluted with (boiled) water as much and as often as possible. If you do not feel well after drinking citrus, do not drink it. Make yourself a hot tea with a spoonful of honey and lemon and go for a walk. Inhale deeply and call upon His Name. Focus on Him, your healer, and not on your pain.

I thank God that I hardly ever have stomachaches during a fast. When I was in pain, I stood up in faith and I declared to my stomach, *"Man shall not live on bread alone, but on every word that comes from the mouth of God" (Matthew 4:4, NIV)*. I would then start "eating", meaning I would read the Word aloud. God's Word is the freshest, tastiest and most nurturing Bread of life.

Many times during a fast, when I felt my stomach rumbling, I said, *"I command you stomach to be still in Jesus' name! I command all the pain to go away!"* And, to my surprise, the noise and the pain often disappear and I begin to feed myself with the word of God. I tell you this because sometimes the enemy increases the symptoms to make you stop fasting.

CONSTIPATION

If you feel constipated, it is advisable to drink water with salt to eliminate the residue in your body. For a 250 ml cup, add a teaspoon of sea salt. After you drink this, you will be thirsty, so you can drink as much water as you want. You will surely see good results in a short while. You must take this mix only in the first two or three days. If you decide to drink this, stay at home or nearby a toilet! Moreover, cabbage juice and plum nectar are good for constipation. When you finish fasting, you have to eat produce that is healthy for your body (more details on this later).

CRAMPS

Sometimes you may have stomach cramps. It is not advisable to drink cold water. You should drink room luke-warm water. You can add some lemon and honey. Walk and slowly massage your abs from right to left. Again, don't focus on the pain. Command the pain to leave and feed yourself in the Word of God.

Diarrhea

Do not worry if you have diarrhea because it is a part of the cleansing process. It is good and necessary. Diarrhea is only the beginning, especially if you drink water with sea salt. Do not leave home if you drink water with sea salt. If you only drink water, there is no chance you will have diarrhea. Usually, when you start eating again, you might get diarrhea, but if you eat rice and drink mint tea, you should be fine.

Bad breath and body stench

During the fast, your mouth and body reek. It is a sign that the body is detoxifying itself. It is highly recommended to brush your teeth, tongue and mouth frequently. Many do not fast when they go to work because of their bad breath. It is quite uncomfortable, but this should not hinder you from talking with God. Parsley leaves are advisable against bad breath. All you have to do is chew them, even if you are fasting. You could chew some mints as well. Chewing gum is not advisable because it could give you stomachaches and hunger. Gargling with aerated salt is good against bad breath.

Among the much-needed sacrifices demanded by fasting, bad breath is one of them. If this is the reason why you do not fast, then you are losing all its benefits.

Fatigue and weakness

It is only natural to feel weak, but it will go away when the body is cleansed of toxins. When you feel fatigued, rest a little, get some fresh air and pray with power. Usually, most people who fast are so weak that they cannot even pray. Fight the good fight of faith! Sometimes you may feel like you are about to faint. This happens to me after three or five days of fasting only with water. If I get up quickly from bed, I feel drained. If this is the case, it's good to continue to rest for another one or two hours.

If something like this is happening to you, do not panic. It is normal. After seven days, I am usually full of energy until the 40th day. If you think about it, it would be only natural to feel worse day after day, but the body is cleansing itself and it is adapting. Many people feel tired and without energy because they do not fast. The body consumes a lot of energy for digestion. When we fast, all the energy that was used for digestion is free to treat your body and give it the strength that it needs spiritually and physically. After your body is cleansed, you feel as young and as light as a healthy, cheerful child. Fatigue is natural because the muscles shrink and no longer have power. This is where God's grace intervenes by giving us strength.

Once when I fasted for 40-days, I felt fatigued for the first two weeks. I tried to pray, but I felt that I was powerless, that heaven was closed and that my words were in vain. I struggled and I kept asking the Lord for grace, but it was still hard for me to pray.

Soon after God allowed a certain situation with my children to crush me, I felt like my spirit was being suffocated. I was exhausted and sad before Him but God used that pain to break me. In that moment when I cried out for help, I sensed a mighty breakthrough. The clouds scattered and there was light again. Heaven opened and the angels carried my prayers to the heavenly Father. There was a tunnel between heaven and earth. I could pray in freedom, with passion and zeal. I was free, heaven was open and I could see my Father smiling at me. I had victory in my battle. The Holy Spirit urged me to carry on praying, interceding, pleading and praising God. Since then, I have been praying incessantly. My prayers flowed. I was in a continual state of prayer, wherever I was. The Holy Spirit interceded for the Father's causes, which were in His heart. At night, when I could not sleep, the Spirit would pray inside of me. When I slept, the Lord would give me prophetic dreams, of warning and notice. When I got up, the Spirit sang. I opened my mouth and I had to sing whatever song was inside of me.

After every prayer of petition, intercession or thanksgiving, the Lord would guide me to that deep state of passion for my God. My heart's prayer was and still is the following:

What I desire most is You, Lord. Yes, and I pray and ask to show me Your manifested power, that the blind will see, the lame walk, the lepers healed, the dead resurrected and the demons cast out! Yes, I desire all these for Your glory and for the good of Your creation. But more than that, my body, soul and spirit long for You and You alone. I want to know You, love You and see Your glory and beauty and to tell You how much I love You.

I want to see Your glory - like Moses did - to look into Your sweet and tender eyes because I know what radical transformation You will bring about in my life. I desire to live together with You every second and to never forget that You are in me and with me at every step I take. I want to live only in Your presence.

"Whom have I in heaven but you? And earth has nothing I desire besides you. But as for me, it is good to be near God. I have made the Sovereign Lord my refuge." (Psalm 73:25, 28, NIV)

Fasting makes you experience extraordinary moments, which edify you, enlighten you and help you grow spiritually in a place of hunger and desperation for God.

Should I take medicine while fasting?

Today's society is called a "consumer society". We consume a lot of expensive, excessive food, beverages, and medicine. If only we listened to God's commandments, and understood how we are supposed to eat, we would not be so ill. Extended water fasts, practiced every once in a while, is the best medicine.

If you want to fast and take medicine at the same time, this is your decision, based on your faith. Most medicines do not necessarily heal your body, it simply alleviates pain. If we can put our trust in medicine to feel well, why don't we put our trust in God, our true Healer?

Medicine carries toxic, chemical ingredients that might affect your body later. Antibiotics can destroy the germs for a while, but they affect our bodies in different ways by destroying the immune system. If by fasting, we detoxify ourselves of toxins and other poisons, I don't advise you to take medicine while fasting. Yet, if you really want to fast and you take medicine, choose a partial fast.

Blessed be the Lord! The last time I took medicine was 20 years ago. Since I started fasting and eating healthier, with wisdom, I have not needed medication. If I feel unwell, maybe because of food, I fast and pray because I understand the cleansing process.

Why did God command the Israelites to let the land rest on the seventh year? Why did God say to rest on the seventh day? God knew the power of resting and recovering. If even computers or cars need a break to recharge, how much more does our stomach or liver need one! Fasting gives our bodies a break. For example, if you feel unwell because you ate something too greasy or too spicy, the best remedy is to fast the following day by only drinking water. This is the easiest and safest restoration process for your stomach. After that, eat primarily fruit and vegetables or other life foods.

It is scientifically proven that most diseases are due to unhealthy dietary habits. Countless people passed away because they could not abstain from eating certain foods. We eat too much greasy and fried food, with no vitamins or minerals. We are bombarded with all kinds of tasty food. How can you fast when there is an abundance of food everywhere? If you can abstain from eating, you prove that you have self-control and wisdom. If you know that those kinds of foods are bad for your body, then stop! Otherwise, you will suffer the consequences of your flesh.

Why does the Bible teach us to have self-control? God wants to spare us of many sufferings. By fasting we develop self-control, and we are no longer slaves to our stomach and appetite.

If we have control over food, which is necessary for our bodies, we will certainly have control over others lusts and desires. Through fasting and prayer, the Holy Spirit will have control over your body, soul and spirit and you will lead a victorious and fruitful life.

If you want a healthy body, in which the Holy Spirit could dwell with pleasure, eat healthy, and eat less. The best produce are: fruit, vegetables, eggs, milk and raw seeds of all kinds (not baked). Moreover, your body needs animal protein, so you should eat meat including beef and chicken. Pork is not recommended. Even the Scriptures mention that it is not healthy, even if it is tasty.

If you cannot give up the medication while you are fasting, I advise you to take a partial fast. You can drink fruit juice, and eat fruits, vegetables and seeds when you take medication. If you are sick and have certain infections and germs in your body, fasting helps cure you. If you do not feed the body, you starve the disease as well. Most diseases remain in our body because we feed them food and medicine. All our body members and organs need a resting period and fasting allows the body to rest and detoxify itself.

CAN I WORK AND FAST AT THE SAME TIME?

I know it is not easy to work and fast at the same time. If you fast only with water, drink plenty of it! If work involves physical labor, you need energy and it is advisable to drink fruit juice or to eat a small meal in the evening. Fasting with juice is easier than water, but remember that if you are drinking fruit juice or eating a small meal, there is a bigger risk of temptation to eat more. When you fast with only water, that hunger will go away.

For those of you whose labor is difficult, you should fast with water or juice and eat something light and healthy, especially fruits and vegetables if you fast 10-21 days.

Also, do not forget that you must abstain from useless words and meaningless chatting. Fasting must be joined with much prayer.

SHOULD WOMEN FAST EVEN DURING THEIR MENSTRUAL CYCLE?

I was shocked when someone asked me, *"How do you fast for 40 days when you menstruate?"* I replied, *"Why should I not fast? What does one have to do with the other?"* Her reply shocked me, *"Because you are unclean!"* Such deceit and a lack of knowledge.

Some women have told me they do not touch the Bible nor go to church because they are unclean during their menstruation. Lord, have mercy! How can someone, who as a Christian accepted Jesus' sacrifice on the Cross, actually believe such nonsense? Does the Law or our own righteousness (described as dirty rags) save us?

It is outrageous that some sects, churches or people believe something like that. If that theory were true, Jesus Christ died in vain. We are made righteous before Him, we are forgiven and cleansed by Jesus' blood and we have free entrance before the throne of God at any time by the blood of the Lamb, who He spilled for us sinners. (*Hebrews 10:14-20*)

Women, it does not matter if you menstruate during the fast. Do fast when the Lord guides you, because your fasting is well received and you will be rewarded. My beloved, the Lord does not reject you and He does not consider you filthy or unclean. He sanctified you, cleansed you, and you are righteous because of His blood.

SHOULD SPOUSES ABSTAIN FROM INTIMACY DURING THE FAST?

Another question concerns marital, intimate relationships during the fast. It is better for spouses to abstain from intercourse during the fast. Apostle Paul says:

> *"Do not deprive each other except perhaps by mutual consent and for a time, so that you may devote yourselves to prayer. Then come together again so that Satan will not tempt you because of your lack of self-control."*
> (*1 Corinthians 7:5, NIV*)

There has to be mutual consent. If the wife's husband does not believe in Christ, he will not be able to understand her. This does not have to be a reason not to fast or feel guilty because the husband would not understand. Christian men who understand the power of fasting and abstain from food will only benefit. I thank the Lord for my husband, who has been a true hero in resisting so many days. He took God's call and ministry for our life in seriousness and he has paid the price.

Do not forget that the more things you give up, the more powerful fasting is, and the more you are blessed. This is what crucifying the flesh means. The Spirit of the Lord will guide you and give you the will and power to fast. Don't forget that these sacrifices only last for the duration of the fast, and God rejoices in our fasting.

What happens if I break the fast earlier than I decided?

Maybe you choose to fast for 10 days, but on the seventh day you feel that you cannot do it anymore. I advise you not to be affected by your feelings. Declare God's promises, and withstand the enemy, and he will flee from you. Remember that while fasting we are facing a battle. The fight will bring great victory but Satan will try his best to hinder that.

> IF YOU BREAK THE FAST EARLY, DO NOT ALLOW THE SPIRIT OF CONDEMNATION TO STEAL YOUR JOY.

If you do break the fast, ask for grace to finish next time. For example, if you decide to fast for 21 days, but begin to feel weak on the 10th day and break the fast, the enemy will condemn you and will try to make you give up altogether. If you do eat something, I advise you not to give up, and continue the fast. Finish the fast. If you started the fast by only drinking water and you feel weak and break the fast, continue on but consider switching to juice. Don't allow guilt to settle in your heart.

If you break the fast early, do not allow the spirit of condemnation to steal your joy. Try again, don't give up! Pray to God to give you grace. Fasting is a great fight against your body, soul and even demons, so we must be aware of that. My advice is to set time apart for prayer and worship in times of weakness.

If you want to fast a certain day, think about it beforehand, talk to your spouse, and pick a time when you are not stressed, busy or ill. Seek to fast when you have free time because you need to spend a lot of time in prayer. Be careful because there are times when we are so busy that you cannot set time apart to fast. Choose your fasting days and be firm, do not look back, run the race like a true athlete, fight and know that God will reward you.

NOBODY DIES FROM FASTING

If we fast with wisdom and we are disciplined, we will not encounter any extreme problems, because life is in the blood and we do not lose blood while we fast. On the contrary, the blood is cleansed and helps heal other diseases.

However, there are some physical diseases that people have that can prohibit fasting.

Still, I know a brother whose cancer began to spread, and he was about the die. The doctors sent him home. However, because the Lord had a plan for him, He told him to fast 40 days only with water. The Lord performed a miracle. After he finished his fast, he was completely cured! Then, God started using him in evangelism and for a healing ministry in China and other countries. Last time I spoke to him in 2010, he was 102 years old! How great is our God!

But pay attention. There are certain diseases or conditions that can forbid fasting. In any of these cases, please see a doctor first:

- **Cancer**. The first stages of cancer forbid fasting. But, remember we do live by faith. If the Lord has told you to fast, and many others have confirmed it by His Word, trust in Him. Many have been healed of cancer through fasting, according to their faith.
- **Anemia**. I was an anemic person, so I started with short-term fasts for 3-7 days. I was cured and the Lord gave me the grace to fast up to 40 days.

- **Pregnancy**. Fasting is certainly not recommended during pregnancy, but know that before delivery it is better to fast in order to have a smooth delivery.
- **Children with different diseases.** Some diseases will pass due to fasting. It is advisable for the child to fast only water for a day or two if he picks up a virus. This treatment is good especially if the child has contracted fever, mumps, diarrhea, headaches, sore throat, scalds, rheumatism, colds, stomach flu etc. Not taking medicine and not eating eliminate the toxins. If we are sick and we keep on eating, it will build resistance. However, when we starve ourselves, we starve the disease and it will eventually die off.

My children used to often contract the stomach flu. They would vomit the food I fed them. After I learned this lesson, I would not give them anything to eat (I would not eat as well) and in two days they would be fully recovered. I used to tell them, *"You have a little bug in your tummy; if we feed it, it will grow stronger, but if we starve it, it will die in one or two days and you are rid of it."* This is the truth about germs and viruses that we contract from the outside environment. They must be starved; only then, we will see the difference. If you are a parent, this is your choice.

Body And
Soul Detoxification

When we begin our fast, and by that I refer to the 10 to 40-day water fast, the blood and energy used for digestion begin a process of assimilation and start to purify our bodies, which are the Temple of the Holy Spirit. The blood can become unrefined, thick and scarlet-coloured for a couple of days, but it is in the process of detoxification.

When you feel weakness during the fast, this is mainly because the cleansing process is working. After a couple of days, the blood gets thinner and cleaner. It will flush all your veins. After the body is clean, weakness disappears. You and those around you will wonder about how great you are feeling!

Again, I can speak from my own experience, for God's glory alone. The first week is the most difficult, but afterwards, the hunger and weakness disappear and you feel normal. I worked, I cleaned the house, I went shopping for groceries, did house chores, I cooked daily and we had guests almost weekly. My life was no different. I did my job as a mother, just like before the fast. When I climbed the stairs, I felt a little fatigued and I felt powerless. In the morning, when I woke up I felt rested, cheerful and clear-headed, but I had to sit up in bed and get up slowly to not to get dizzy, and then I went to the bathroom. After that, I continued my routine. It is highly recommended to rest at least twice a day. From my experience, the body tells you when you need to rest. You have to know your symptoms.

The most important thing for me was that I felt a passionate desire for spending more time with the Lord in prayer. In every spare moment that I had, I felt the urge to talk to God. The spirit of prayer and intercession was always present, whenever the Lord called me.

I have a special place in the living room where I spend time with God. Even when I sat down in that place, my heart would feel Him and the prayers would overflow. I would worship and praise Him, I wept after His presence and I felt the urge to intercede for others. It was so wonderful!

You cannot enjoy certain earthly pleasures during the fast (food, marital intimacy, coffee), but you can certainly delight much more in the Lord because you are sitting at the table with Him and you desire nothing else but Him. This means that you have stepped into a heavenly, divine territory and you no longer desire to go down to the worldly territory.

One time when I was praying during a fast, I was saddened because I had to bear this "cross", while others enjoyed themselves and ate to their heart's desire. Then, the Lord told me, *"You cannot always enjoy worldly pleasures, but You can rejoice that you are with Me at My royal table. What I offer you is much more powerful and desirable than food and momentary pleasures. Your delight should be in Me and with Me. I am right beside you to protect you; I am fighting alongside you. You are not alone, even if you do not see Me or feel My presence. Now you are in a spiritual war, but do not forget that the victory is sure because you will receive the revelations and depths of My love, which other people cannot receive or comprehend. My grace is enough! I am with you, do not fear anything!"*

> TODAY I CAN DECLARE THAT EVERYTHING IS POSSIBLE FOR THOSE WHO BELIEVE!

Many friends and even doctors were concerned about my state and tried to persuade me to stop fasting. They looked at the situation from a human point of view and they could not believe something like this was possible. They could not understand my experience. Today I can declare that everything is possible for those who believe!

I did not accept for one second that something could go wrong with my body while I was fasting. After I read Franklin Hall's book, *"The Fasting Prayer,"* in which he wrote about regular people who dared to believe and fast for 21-40 days, I received courage, desire and faith necessary to fast.

How To Properly End The Fast

For me, ending my 40-day fast is one of the most difficult aspects of the fast. The hunger often returns between 35-40 days – just before the fast is complete. I start craving food again, remembering its taste and enjoyment. I make myself an orange juice diluted with water and drink it in the evening, preparing my body to start eating light food after I finish fasting. It is very dangerous for the body to start eating food all at once after you have fasted for more than 21 days. Our stomachs have straitened, and have become sensitive like a baby's. Therefore, it is important to consider how to properly finish a fast and transition your body.

This advice is for your own good.

I address those who fast for many days with only water. It is very important to end the fast with a glass of diluted juice, three to four times a day. This regime is important and must be kept for at least a week. Every day you must add vegetable juice (tomatoes, carrots, spinach, celery, beats, cabbage, etc) to your diet. Add fresh lettuce and vegetable soup to your diet for a couple more days.

Afterwards, eat fresh fruit and vegetables, milk and chicken soup, cereals, seeds, eggs, wheat, oats or other foods with cereals for the next few days. But add all these slowly, so that you don't get an upset stomach. When you consider that your stomach is ready for other food, add roasted meat. But do not forget to keep on drinking plenty of water and juice, also eat fruit, vegetable and salads. You will feel very well, both physically and spiritually.

> I NOTICED THAT AFTER FASTING, THE BODY REJECTS WHAT HARMS IT.

Do not rush the process!

It is very dangerous to start eating everything all at once. Do not eat meat and other products. It is true that the mouth begs for every craving, but the Lord gave us wisdom not to destroy what we built with such efforts. Bread and roasted meat should be added to your menu only after two weeks (if you fasted for 21-40 days). The healthiest food consists of fresh, uncooked food, full of the vitamins and minerals we need. Cooked, fried and prepared food will do your body harm. Avoid them! I noticed that after fasting, the body rejects what harms it. For example, I drink coffee every day. During the fast, I do not drink coffee. When I finish my fasting, I start drinking it again but my body rejects it. There are certain kinds of food I try to avoid, even though I enjoy them very much. They cause stomach pain.

After I fasted 21-days for the first time, only with water, I could not wait to eat bread for I craved and longed for bread. The first day after the fast, I toasted a slice of organic bread and put some cheese on it with two tomatoes. After I ate this small meal, I went to pick up my children. After 20 minutes, I started feeling so unwell that I could barely drive the car and I was stuck in traffic on a long bridge. I called my husband to pray for me. My whole body ached, I was powerless and my stomach hurt so badly. I repented and cried out to God and I got better. What had happened?

For 21 days, my body did not receive food. But when I began to eat my stomach and liver started to function properly again, and all of a sudden my body felt weak and full of discomfort. It was like a machine being rebooted and starting to function again.

When you finish a prolonged fast, if you do not comply with the body's necessities and you indulge in eating everything, your body and especially your feet will swell up. My advice is that you should not eat heavy food and you should steer clear from salty food because you will only suffer. If you already did that, stop eating anything and do not drink water. Take a hot bath, rest and relax as much as possible. If you can, fast for another two to three days. After you stop feeling bloated, drink plenty of water, fruit and vegetable juice, vegetables and light food.

During the fast, you lose around 1lb of body weight per day as the body uses the deposited fat. When we start eating again, if we do not eat in moderation, we will gain all of the fat again. We do not fast to get slim, but this is a convenient bonus, especially to us women.

We do not fast in order to impress or brag about it. In many of the places where I went to speak, some people judged me when I said that God called me to a lifestyle of fasting and prayer for the nation. They thought I was bragging or belittling others. However, this was clearly not my intention. If I ever let that impression form, please forgive me.

God knows the heart's motivation. I went to Romania and many other countries and I told the people about God's urge. I went to encourage people to fast and pray for revival. The Lord expected this from me, to see and understand its value and power so that I could be an encouragement for other people. I am sharing this for God's glory alone. I left a legacy of followers because many people were encouraged and fasted for many days, even 40 days. They experienced a breakthrough and great moments with God. Had it not been for God's grace, we would not have been able to do anything. Therefore, we must give Him glory and challenge one another to good deeds and a life of victory in this world.

Lastly, after a fast, expect even more revelation from the Lord! It is during the fast where we enter a battle with the flesh, but it is after the fast that we receive anointing, blessing and answers to our prayers from the Lord.

Different Types Of Fasts

1. **One-day absolute fast.** Fasting for 24 hours without eating food or drinking any liquid, including water. It is recommended to begin from 6pm until 6pm the next evening.

2. **One-day water fast.** Fasting for 24 hours without eating any food, and drinking only water. It is recommended to drink at least 2 liters of water during that 24-hour period.

3. **Esther fast.** Fasting for 3 days and 3 nights, with no food or water.

4. **Multiple-day water fast.** Fasting for many days without eating food, and only drinking water – and lots of it. It is recommended to fast for 3, 5, 7, 10, 21 or even 40 days, drinking water only. Another name for this fast is *"The Consecration Fast."*

5. **Multiple-day juice fast**. Fasting for many days without eating food, and only drinking fruit juice, vegetable juice, and water. It is recommended to fast longer than 7 days. It is important to note that certain fruit juices contain a lot of acid, and should be diluted with water. It is suggested to drink 2 glasses of juice, and 2 liters of distilled or boiled water per day. You can drink a fruit juice in the morning and a vegetable juice at night (apples, carrots, beets, celery, etc).

6. **Daniel fast (partial fast).** Fasting for 21 days and only eating fruits and vegetables, and drinking water.

7. **Extended fast.** Fasting from 3 to 40 days without eating any food during the day, but eating a small meal after 6pm in the evening. During the day, it is recommended to only drink

water, but some people choose not to drink water during the day. It is your choice. In the evening, it is important to drink lots of water before you eat the small meal. The meal should be healthy and fresh, and can include fruit, vegetables, raw seeds, salad, soup or lean meat. Avoid heavy, fried, and fatty foods. Some people extend this fast beyond 40 days, usually with their churches or together with other believers.

When you are feeling weak, you can drink some herbal tea or lemon with honey.

> ...FASTING ONLY WITH WATER, IRRESPECTIVE OF THE NUMBER OF DAYS, IS THE HEALTHIEST AND MOST POWERFUL.

What about coffee? God receives all kinds of fasting, but there are different kinds of results. We don't recommend drinking coffee during any fast. But, certain people really want to fast yet feel that they cannot give up coffee. I encourage them to begin their fast, and if needed, drink a coffee in the morning. With that boost of energy, pray. Have the goal to eventually give up drinking coffee during the fast. I know this is difficult, but I believe that giving up coffee is a very important part of fasting. This requires self-control for something that controls you.

All these types of fasting are well received, but I can tell you that fasting only with water, irrespective of the number of days, is the healthiest and most powerful.

By definition, fasting means abstaining from food. When you fast, it is also recommended to abstain from things like watching television, spending too much time on the internet, or even shopping, in order to spend as much time with the Lord as possible.

Dieing To Our Flesh

O ur flesh serves the enemy a lot. Therefore, it is not always easy to serve God.

"Very truly I tell you, unless a kernel of wheat falls to the ground and dies, it remains only a single seed. But if it dies, it produces many seeds." (John 12:24, NIV)

Fasting is a road less taken, but those who dare to take it have had wonderful experiences. Fasting helps edify and purify the Temple of the Holy Spirit. The greatest enemy that is difficult to overcome is the old self, the flesh. The food we feed our bodies day by day maintains this lust of worldly pleasure and our spiritual part is weak and weary. The habit of constantly eating, without fasting, weakens the faith and the power of our spirit.

> OUR FLESH SERVES THE ENEMY A LOT.

"The acts of the flesh are obvious: sexual immorality, impurity and debauchery; idolatry and witchcraft; hatred, discord, jealousy, fits of rage, selfish ambition, dissensions, factions and envy; drunkenness, orgies, and the like. I warn you, as I did before, that those who live like this will not inherit the kingdom of God." (Galatians 5:19-21, NIV)

Fasting is like a door's key. We must stretch our hand, grab the key and open the door in order to rejoice in the benefits and blessings behind the door. God put something of Himself in us: the fruit of the Spirit. If we collaborate with the Holy Spirit, we will be like Christ. Everything is possible with Him. You must know your identity in Christ and not allow fear, intimidation or rejection to put you down. You stay the same, the way God created you. You will bear much fruit if you mortify your flesh. During the fast, Christ's life takes root and regardless of what happens, you have peace, joy and trust in Him. You must be ready to enter this process, even if it hurts. Your worldly flesh is struggling and roaring, but if you love the Lord, you will obey Him. If you are selfish and want to control everything, to manipulate and to judge, then you will never be victorious.

Ask the Lord with sincerity to show you what your problem is and then apply the Biblical truths. If you allow Christ's life to manifest in you, if you die to yourself and to your ego, you will be a great blessing to other people. If you are a worldly man, guided by your desires, thoughts and feelings, it means that you are living only for your body and soul, and not for your spirit. If you become angry quickly and you know your flesh leads you, you need deliverance. If you are a spiritual man it means you are guided, counseled and directed by the Holy Spirit. Therefore, I advise you to fast longer, so that you may rid yourself of the flesh. It will not control you, but you will have power over it because you are filling yourself with Christ. His presence is within you.

> *"Then Jesus said to His disciples, Whoever wants to be My disciple must deny themselves and take up their cross and follow Me." (Matthew 16:24, NIV)*

Dying to yourself and carrying your cross is a daily process. You have to say no to temptation. Jesus did not care about having a certain reputation. He did not care about what the world would say about Him, but He desired profoundly to do the will of the Father. If you are still worldly, you care about other people's opinions of you, and as such you will not be able to do God's perfected will. Many have a neutral point of view in order to be accepted by people. In this case, they change or give up on what they decided upon to please others.

> *"Am I now trying to win the approval of human beings, or of God? Or am I trying to please people? If I were still trying to please people, I would not be a servant of Christ." (Galatians 1:10, NIV)*

A manipulative or controlling person is not truly your friend. When he sees he does not have control over you, he will back away. This is quite sad. However, be a perseverant person who does not give up, but moves forward. God will reward the ones who wholeheartedly seek Him. Surrender to His plan and timing. Surrender yourself in His arm and let go of the steering wheel!

> *"And He died for all, that those who live should no longer live for themselves but for Him who died for them and was raised again" (2 Corinthians 5:15)*

Jesus' death and resurrection made us new beings.

Sometimes, God allows a period of crushing to bring us to full surrender. If we run after Him, in complete surrender, He will give us His peace and we will feel His healing oil. No matter how terrible the night is, we must stay as close as possible to Him.

In that darkness, we must put our trust in God, in the invisible, to be pleasing to Him.

> *"And without faith it is impossible to please God, because anyone who comes to Him must believe that he exists and that He rewards those who earnestly seek Him."* (Hebrews 11:6, NIV)

During a fast, the old self is crucified. It screams and gets irritated; it tries every trick because it does not want to be hung on a cross. It wants to dominate you. It is an intense fight between body and spirit, but do not forget that the key is in your hands. Who will you allow to sit on the throne? The flesh is the greatest hindrance against the Holy Spirit. If the old self is not subdued to God's authority, we lose many blessings and answers to prayer.

FASTING IS THE WAY TO BE SET FREE OF EARTHLY PLEASURES THAT YOU WERE BORN WITH OR YOU INHERITED.

Apostle Paul says in 2 Corinthians 11:27, "*I have labored and toiled and have often gone without sleep; I have known hunger and thirst and have often gone without food; I have been cold and naked.*" Here you can notice the distinct difference between fasting and starvation/thirst. It is one thing to fast, and another not to have food to eat. Paul reminds us that we must be harsh with our bodies. He discovered the secret; he knew that the flesh has control and power.

> *"Put to death, therefore, whatever belongs to your earthly nature: sexual immorality, impurity, lust, evil desires and greed, which is idolatry." (Colossians 3:5, NIV)*

Fasting is the way to be set free of earthly pleasures that you were born with or you inherited. Fasting strikes back at your earthly nature and the flesh loses its power and control. During this time the Holy Spirit takes control and starts guiding your life. You will experience what it is like to have your new self desiring Jesus, who delights in doing good deeds, who intercedes for his enemies and who seeks first the Kingdom of God, who spends everything he has to help others, and who brings glory and thanks to God.

> *"You were taught, with regard to your former way of life, to put off your old self, which is being corrupted by its deceitful desires; to be made new in the attitude of your minds; and to put on the new self, created to be like God in true righteousness and holiness." (Ephesians 4:22-24, NIV)*

THE FLESH IS SUBDUED

The more we discipline ourselves, the more the flesh will be subdued. People who neglect these virtues are controlled by their lust and desire for food, sex, money, etc. When we fast, our desires are not directed towards us because we no longer fight to be fulfilled or to find pleasure in the world. We are hungry and thirsty after spiritual matters, after God and His Kingdom. We want the expansion of His Kingdom, we want lost souls to turn to Jesus, we want servants to work together with God.

I remember my first 40-day fast in 2007. What great moments I experienced! They follow me even today. Momentary joy and pleasures did not attract me any longer, I did not even like to talk about them anymore. The Lord's Spirit was upon me and I felt His anguish for the lost, the hopeless and the hurt. I wept for hours daily in my long prayers. I was in a spiritual labor. Every type of suffering on earth saddened me. I was burdened (and it still hurts) for the lost, for the poor, the orphans, the desperate ones, the lonely ones and the dying ones. I wanted to help them. The sufferings were from God because He put them in my heart, so that I might intercede and surrender them to Him. Only then did I feel relieved.

DELIVERANCE AND BEING SET FREE

Being set apart for God means to separate the worldly from the heavenly. What does it mean to be *"made new in the attitude of your mind?"* This is our subconscious mind. Throughout our lives, we have gathered millions of thoughts, words and actions. Science tells us that our subconscious state is at least one million times more powerful than the conscious mind. The subconscious mind records our every thought, word and feeling. The more we repeat something, the more our subconscious mind expects that things to be fulfilled. Therefore, a total detoxification of our negative thoughts and words is needed. Here, the principle of sowing and reaping applies. What we sow - our thoughts and words - we will reap. We inherit many bad habits from our parents through their sinful nature. In our subconscious mind there are many hidden habits or childhood traumas that we do not know about. When least expect it, we re-live those painful, bitter experiences with an inability to forgive. We find ourselves blind, hopeless, weak, wounded and attacked. What should we do in these situations?

Jesus' blood has power to wash and purify us from every impurity and sin (*1 John 1:7-9*). Even though Jesus has complete power to cleanse us, sometimes people still need to go through a process of deliverance.

First, we must confess all our sins and forgive those who wronged us. Here is a practical method: on a piece of paper write down all the people who wronged you or hurt you since childhood until now.

Then, pray to Jesus to help you to forgive them. Sometimes it will be difficult because you will re-live some experiences. When that happens, remember Jesus' love and Him standing right beside you, lifting your burden, setting you free and holding you in His Almighty arm. Say aloud, *"Lord Jesus, I choose to forgive all these people with all my heart! I bless them and I surrender them in Your hands."* Then rip the piece of paper and throw it into the fire. Ask God to forgive all your bitter feelings and the hatred you nurtured in your heart for years, which has tormented you. Your deliverance will be stronger if you apologize in person and ask for forgiveness from the people who hurt you. You can ask for forgiveness from those against whom you did nothing wrong as well.

You must forgive yourself because you allowed a spirit of condemnation to come upon you due to your past.

Then, by faith you have to break every chain of sin in your life, in Jesus' Name, asking God for a complete and perfect restoration. At the same time, you must radically change your thinking and speaking. Take God's Word and declare Jesus' words upon every negative state or bad habit every day. God's Word is alive and working, transforming hearts and circumstances. If you know good Christian counselors, I recommend seeking their help. You will be free *only if* you persevere and abide in the Word and prayer.

There have been books on spiritual healing written in this respect. Some of these can be useful:

- *"Healing through Deliverance"* by Peter Horrobin
- *"I Give You Authority: Practicing the Authority Jesus Gave Us,"* by Charles Kraft
- Books written by Neil Anderson and many others

By believing in Jesus' sacrifice and His blood and Name, you will be set free. If you still have problems with it, you must consider fasting and prayer, along with deliverance and spiritual counsel.

The Benefits Of Fasting

After we practice fasting and prayer, we can see many spiritual benefits as a result.

PRAYER IS INCREASED

Fasting becomes prayer. During times of fasting, I was in continuous prayer. This kind of prayer is fervent, perseverant and passionate, filled with compassion and with Jesus' tears (not tears of self-pity). Many times, I lost track of time. Hours had passed without realizing it; I thought they were minutes. Many times, I woke up hearing in my spirit how the Holy Spirit interceded. Blessed be the Lord who allowed me to partake in these sweet sufferings! I keep the 40-day fast every year. Blessed be the Lord because He gave me the grace of fasting for many days allowing me to taste and experience the beauty of such sacrifice. My life is not mine anymore. It is a pleasure for me to sacrifice my life for Jesus and His kingdom because I love and obey Him, and I know that He loves me. (John 14:15, 21, 23)

Many people do not understand my radical passion for God and for the lost, why I am so adamant in this fasting lifestyle. I owe it to Him and Him alone, He who searches my heart and fills me in every moment. Once you taste and see how good the Lord is, there is no turning back. I learned the secret of victory: lying at the feet of Jesus in fasting and prayer, in His Word and worship.

My beloved reader, maybe you desire a deeper relationship with the Lord and you do not know how to form one. You must pay the price: spend more time with Him and sacrifice the desires of your flesh and eyes. I wrote this book as an encouragement and a testimony for you.

Why did Apostle Paul say that he often fasted without food or drink *(2 Corinthians 11:27, NIV)*? He was aware of the fact that inside us there is a battle between the flesh and the spirit and he knew that the key to success is fasting and praying:

> *"No, I strike a blow to my body and make it my slave so that after I have preached to others, I myself will not be disqualified for the prize." (1 Corinthians 9:27, NIV)*

By fasting, Paul had control over his flesh and desires. He knew the fight was worth it and that it had a reward. The Lord rewards His children who fast on earth.

When we start to fast and pray more, our limited and incapable thoughts and minds will begin to understand and contain the Unknown. The worldly man cannot comprehend the invisible. Fasting and prayer attract God to touch us and to reveal Himself to us.

The Israelites could not worship an invisible God, so they created an idol. Faith means trusting the unseen, something that cannot be felt or heard. Faith means to believe before smelling or tasting. The reward of faith is that of seeing what you believed beforehand. The consecrated fast (21-40 days) will bring about faith that will move mountains.

Satan deceived Eve by tempting her to eat the forbidden fruit. It stole her authority and life she was given. Jesus came to bring life, not just physical bread, but spiritual Bread, His Word. Eternal life abides in us as long as Christ dwells in us.

When we surrender everything to God in fasting and prayer, the flesh and its lust lose their powers. This is the easiest method of bearing spiritual fruit. By fasting, God's glory descends and we enter into a profound reverence before Him. Then, our spiritual abilities open up and reveal more about God. We cannot have true faith until we see Him, until we taste the "Bread of Life."

By fasting and prayer, we understand the revelation of intimacy with Christ sooner. If we are aware of His presence in us, the victory is ours. We must declare Calvary's victory at all times. By confessing it, our faith grows and remains immovable. This is the position from which we beat the opposing forces.

May God make us confident in the victory He won at Calvary. If we are certain that Jesus won the battle against Satan, we can walk in freedom. We can rest assured, owing to His promises. The mystery of faith is incredible! He who finds it and lives it is free, triumphant and joyful. It is declared:

> *"I have told you these things, so that in Me you may have peace. In this world you will have trouble. But take heart! I have overcome the world." (John 16:33, NIV)*

Prayer full of faith must transcend the natural into the spiritual. In this process, we become vessels wholly surrendered in His hand. He will pour whatever is pleasant in us and through us. The flesh must be crucified in order to love and sacrifice ourselves for others. These are accomplished by faith, which works through love.

> *"For in Christ Jesus neither circumcision nor uncircumcision has any value. The only thing that counts is faith expressing itself through love." (Galatians 5:6, NIV)*

What does this verse refer to? From the moment we get to know God and to believe that He loves us and cares about us, our faith is strengthened and can clearly witness His love. At the same time, His love, which has been poured in our hearts, allows us to ask for the things we need because we know that we ask according to His will and love. If you focus only on yourself, you will never have victory in this life. The triumphant faith seeks God's glory, waiting for Him to manifest. Fasting and prayer motivate us to seek God's glory and steers our attention towards other people's needs. This is the powerful, tight bond between love and faith. The triumphant faith is like a light shining in the darkness.

> *"We also have the prophetic message as something completely reliable, and you will do well to pay attention to it, as to a light shining in a dark place, until the day dawns and the morning star rises in your hearts." (2 Peter 1:19, NIV)*

If you have such faith can see God's light in the darkness, and you trust the Lord, and if you believe God's Word, His words will be fulfilled in your life.

The Lord brings a solution in His right time. Fasting is sometimes misunderstood because the results come on God's appointed time and not ours. Be careful about doubt and lack of faith. You must believe that fasting works in reality and that you will receive your answer, sooner or later. People will understand its value only after they fasted for at least 7-10 days.

REVELATION FROM GOD'S WORD IS INCREASED

Another great blessing following the long fasts of 21-40 days is receiving new revelations from God's Word. I can testify to His glory, that following the fast I received a clearer understanding of His Word. I have read His Word since I was a child, but after I fasted the veil over my eyes was torn. God's Word became clearer, more alive and relevant in every aspect of my life. Every time I open my Bible, the Lord speaks to me personally and I cannot get enough of His Word.

Fasting gives us the grace of correct interpretation of the Scriptures. There are many wrong interpretations of the Bible and many fall victim to a spirit of religiosity and hatred against those who study the Bible in sincerity. Love for God, humility and hunger in fasting and praying allow us to understand the correct revelations and enable us to grow spiritually. We need the revelation of the Holy Spirit to understand the depths of His Word. The ones who contend and bring contention and division in the Church are in great need of fasting and prayer, so that they can receive the correct revelations from the heavenly Father.

Moreover, prophets need to fast for days to interpret the words they have received.

Fasting and prayer both empower us to renew our mind when we study the Word. We have to focus on renewing our minds and spirit (Ephesians 4:23). If we nurture something, it will grow and if we starve something, it will weaken and cease to exist. Therefore, let us starve the old nature by fasting! Even if we are allowed to eat and drink, to enjoy everything, our body is in conflict with the spirit. That is the reason why we are left with the strategy of fasting, so that we could subdue our flesh to the Holy Spirit.

After renewing the mind, there comes spiritual revival - sinners repent and there is miraculous healing. In his book, Franklin Hall confesses how in Indianapolis, in 1947, four people fasted with only water and prayed for 21 days. They urged others to fast for 14-21 days, without eating supper. This urge gathered 50 people. After 30 days, they had a meeting for evangelism and there were 11,000 attendees, even though there was only room for 10,000. Almost 600 people repented and many were instantly healed. The people who fasted were encouraged and urged other churches to join their plea of long-term fasting and praying. They confessed that the Lord would listen to their every prayer and increasingly more people were saved, delivered and healed.

Another occurrence was when people fasted: some for 3, some for 7, some for 21 and others for 40 days. Their prayers were so fervent and full of joy and faith because they knew God would work. There was a miracle: 1,000 souls were added to His Kingdom in a year in their city! Can you see the fruit of long-term fasting and fervent prayers in unity?

The Church should be called to commit to fasting and prayer. I know that even today some Christians fast for 21-40 days. I also know that many do Daniel fasts, but it is considered more of a diet than a fast. I personally don't believe it has the same power as a water fast. True and powerful fasting, which brings great results, is the one that entails courage and sacrifice, meaning one should not eat any kind of produce.

Maybe I have discouraged you, but my intention was to challenge you to do more. Do not tell me that you cannot do it, that you will get sick or nauseous, you are afraid to do it, or that you do not have reason to fast. If you are reading this book closely, you will find plenty of reasons and understand that a blessing follows every sacrifice, here and in heaven. You will understand this the moment you experience its power.

FAITH IS INCREASED

One of the greatest benefits of fasting is that it increases our faith. The enemy wants to steal our faith because he knows that all things are possible to those who believe (*Mark 9:23*). His tireless mission is to bring certain opposing circumstances by which he can sow the seed of doubt and disbelief. Faith was given to each and every one of us, with the same measure. It is our duty to plant the mustard seed in good soil, give it heat and water, and expect it to grow

Looking back, I cannot believe how many things were accomplished by faith. I had no money, but I stepped in faith and bought plane tickets, I rented a car, I arranged meetings and conferences. God, in His faithfulness, took care of every detail and need. Blessed be His Name!

Where does faith come from? We know that it comes from hearing the Word. We have to trust the Author of the Scriptures. Fasting and prayer helps us know God, through the Holy Spirit, and due to His profound relationship we establish a greater trust in Him.

From the first pages of Scripture, we see that the enemy sowed seeds of doubt in Eve's heart. He told her, *"Did God really say...?"* (*Genesis 3:1*). When Satan tempted Jesus, he came to sow doubt: *"If you are the Son of God..." (Matthew 4:6)*. The enemy wins a lot of ground because of our doubt. When we are unsure whether God's words apply to us, we lack faith and we fall. Yet God, in His sovereignty, wrote the Scriptures so that we believe in Him. *"Consequently, faith comes from hearing the message, and the message is heard through the word about Christ" (Romans 10:17, NIV)*. If we do not know God's word, we cannot know Him and we cannot have faith in Him. The enemy seeks to make us doubt God's goodness and His Word.

Remember everything that contradicts the Truth and God's Word comes from the enemy. Stand your ground, rooted in the truth of His promises. Sometimes it is difficult to believe, but we must fight in the spirit against doubt. It is easy for the enemy to attack and tempt us, if we walk by sight and not by faith. But the Word clearly says, *"For we live by faith, not by sight" (2 Corinthians 5:7, NIV)*.

A challenge for all Christians is to abide in the Word. Jesus says:

"If you abide in Me, and My words abide in you, you will ask what you desire, and it shall be done for you." (John 15:7, NKJV)

What a desirable and mighty promise! A prayer is answered only because of Him and His Word. The Word says:

"Every word of God is tested and purified; He is a shield to those who trust and take refuge in Him. (Proverbs 30:5)

Why does it say that His Word is *"tested"*? We do not understand how the spiritual realm works. Therefore, the Lord calls us to read His Word, to meditate on it, to declare it until it is deeply rooted in our hearts and subconscious mind. Meanwhile, the enemy will come with his attacks and will whisper the opposite of the words we declare, pointing to the contradicting reality. He is trying to steal our faith.

What do we do when we are faced with a storm or test? Do we continue believing and trusting what God promised us? We must overcome with the Word of God, trusting in His promises.

> WE MUST TAKE THE SHIELD OF FAITH TO EXTINGUISH THE ENEMY'S FIERY ARROWS.

The winner is the one who has more ground in us. If our relationship with God is rooted in the Word and is powerful, undoubtedly the Holy Spirit will strengthen and help us. We must take the shield of faith to extinguish the enemy's fiery arrows. Victory is on our side. However, if we do not have a close relationship with God based on love and we do not read the Word, the flesh and the enemy will attack us with fear, doubt, lack of faith, skepticism and disappointment. Therefore, extended fasting is necessary. It purifies us of all the impurities of the flesh and it helps us have passionate faith.

Hebrews 11:1 says, *"Faith is the firm assurance of things we hope for, and a strong conviction of the things unseen."*

If you see things through eyes of faith and trust in Christ, nothing can move you. Nothing is impossible. Through fasting, our faith increases.

TRUSTING GOD THROUGH THE FLAMES

Faith is activated when we ask and receive. However, if we do not receive, our faith is tried. Since we have a strong relationship with God, irrespective of the answer, we still believe and trust in His faithfulness and love. Our intimacy and fellowship with Him will lead us to complete surrender and trust in Him.

Therefore, we do not complain or murmur when we go through different trials because we know who He is, how much He loves us, and we know He is sovereign and in control. We are certain that all things work together for the good of those who love God.

Let us remember the three Jews who were thrown in the fiery furnace: Shadrach, Meshach and Abednego (*Daniel 3*). We do not know the details about their relationship with God, but from their behavior we understand that they knew God very well, to the extent that they risked their lives. They had a firm assurance in their hearts:

> *"If we are thrown into the blazing furnace, the God we serve is able to deliver us from it, and he will deliver us from Your Majesty's hand"* (Daniel 3:17, NIV)

They mention that God is able to deliver them. *"He will deliver us from Your Majesty's hand"* (v. 17). They had assurance in the unseen things, in God's character and might. We notice that the word was declared with faith, *"He will deliver us!"* They understood the power of declaring the promises of God by faith and that words have power. Confident in the Lord, they were realistic, admitting God's supreme right and will, *"But even if He does not, we want you to know, Your Majesty, that we will not serve your gods or worship the image of gold you have set up"* (verse 18). Why did they say that? Was that doubt in their hearts? They risked being burnt alive because of their loyalty to God, as not to worship other gods and idols. They had the courage to confront one of the most powerful and affluent kings of the time and by doing so they trusted God completely.

God had a plan, to be glorified by all nations. The king himself blessed God's Name, acknowledging Him as the only Almighty God. Whenever you find yourself in a trial, do not forget that God has a mighty plan. If He does not answer, it is because He has His reasons. If He had delivered them before entering the fiery furnace, how would they have glorified Him? Maybe a few would give Him praise. But even when they trusted in him, the Lord allowed them to be cast in the furnace and He showed up there for His glory.

I always wondered how the king knew how *"a son of the gods"* looked like. I believe Jesus' beauty is unmistakable and indescribable, so that everyone knew He was the Son of God. Interestingly, how did the king see Him? Did God open the eyes of this heathen king to see?

If God allowed a blazing furnace in your life, would people see Jesus with you in the furnace? How do we react to such a furnace? Do we complain and grumble? Are we scared, panicked or disappointed?

When we go through certain furnaces in life, it is obvious when we trust God or not. If we trust in Him, those around us will feel the peace and rest. We are living testimonies, showing people that God is real, that He cares about us, that He loves us and is with us even in the blazing furnace.

The fire burned their bindings (*verses 24-25*) and they were free. The fire of your furnace has the purpose of burning the chains of your past, generational sin, ungodliness and impurities. This fire can be associated with fasting and prayer, when you place yourself on God's altar to be cleansed. After a long period of time, you will come out clean and free and the Lord will receive glory from you and from others.

Testimony:
Great Victory After Fasting

In our lives as Christians we encounter many tests. I like to call them tests and not attacks from the enemy. When you say, "*test*," you think of an examination with the expectation of passing. When you say "*attack*," you think of a battle or Satan and can be worried and afraid.

During the early years of my fasting, I went through many tests. Some I have failed, but I learned my lesson. Some I passed by the grace of God, even though they were difficult. Today I praise the Lord for all of this because through every test I have grown closer to God.

When we got back from our missions trip in 2011, we faced a great test. Now, that I am writing about it, it does not seem so difficult. The Lord allowed me to learn some valuable lessons because He wanted to elevate me to a higher level.

After almost three months in the mission trip in which we served daily, we got back tired, but joyful of what God had done. Since we were away, my husband did not work. We spent the money we had and we did not have any left. This is the life of a worker of God. After a great spiritual victory, the enemy attacked us because he wanted to steal our joy and wanted to make us doubt God's goodness, so that we give up the ministry and calling.

When I saw that we did not even have money for groceries for the children, I started weeping bitter tears and I took offence. I then told God, *"How did you allow this, Lord? Why did you allow this? You are the One who sent us there. You provided for everything while we were on the mission's trip and now... you allow this situation? Where are you Lord? What did I do wrong? What do you want to teach me?"* All these questions tormented me. I was spiritually and physically exhausted, I did not have power left to apply His Word in my trouble to give me peace and trust on God, like I did before the mission's trip.

We must be careful because the enemy cannot wait to find us in a state of spiritual exhaustion or unpreparedness. He knows when we are weak and he can tear us down, hurt us and bring turmoil into our families. That is why we need to go back to the source and feed ourselves in His Word.

This is what happened to us. My husband was looking for work, but the companies he worked for before had hired other workers and he could not get his job back. He was frustrated and irritated that he could not get a job and the bills kept piling up. I was sad, worried, ungrateful and angry to everyone. We felt that hell was against us. We cried out to the Lord, but the heaven seemed like it was made of lead. The children were about to start school and we had no money to buy their necessary supplies.

> I THOUGHT ABOUT GIVING UP ON FASTING, PRAYER, COUNSELING AND EVER DOING MISSIONS TRIPS AGAIN.

Everything was dark and hopeless. Then, I felt I had to fast for 10 days, only with water. I cannot express in words the kind of attacks I received! Moreover, I felt sick. I fasted for 40 days many times, but never before did I feel so sick like then. My bones and joints hurt. I could not sleep. When I went to bed, the torture would start. I cried out to the Lord desperately, but felt left without answer.

The atmosphere grew tenser day by day and the disappointment grew even higher. Then, the enemy took his opportunity and attacked me head on. He told me, *"Look at you and the state you are in! Where is your God? If God loves you, why does He allow this situation? You sacrificed everything for Him and He does not even care about you."* In those moments I got really mad at God and myself and I said, *"Yes, Lord! He is right! Why will you not help me?"* Then I felt a great burden and disappointment leading me to one thing: to give up to the ministry God called us to do. I thought about giving up on fasting, prayer, counseling and ever doing missions trips again. I sensed a force to push me to think like that.

However, when I understood Satan's strategy I cried out to God, *"Lord, is this what You want? It is so much easier for me to stay in my comfort zone like other Christians and go on holiday trips to Hawaii, sit at home with my children and to be comfortable and rich!"* We gave up our vacations and all the money we had. We gave it all to the Lord's ministry, fulfilling His Word:

> *"Anyone who loves their father or mother more than me is not worthy of me; anyone who loves their son or daughter more than me is not worthy of me. Whoever does not take up their cross and follow me is not worthy of me."* (Matthew 10:37-38, NIV)

I was praying with desperation and I felt as if my soul was black, and in pitch darkness. I was torn not because I did not have any money, but because I felt like God relented and stopped intervening in my life. *My God, my God, why have you forsaken me?* The greatest torture for a Christian who has tasted God's beautiful touch is the feeling of being neglected and abandoned by God himself, and being attacked by demons. I want to emphasize that it is a *feeling* because Jesus promised that He would never forsake us. This was my test of faith. I had to rely on His promises, which are all "Yes" and "Amen" in Him.

We are tempted through different trials of life to make the mistake of focusing on the problem and not on God's infinite goodness. The enemy is waiting for the exact moment we stop looking at God and start focusing on our problems. The enemy wants to attack us, destroy our faith, steal our peace and make us doubt God's goodness. Consequently, spirits of fear, worry, doubt, frustration, ungratefulness, etc. come upon us. These lead to disappointment, depression, scandal, divorce or even death.

Why do all these things happen? It is because we let our guard down, because we forget about God and because we get stuck in our own pain.

We are in spiritual warfare, and if we are not aware of how the enemy works, we will be destroyed. We must remember that Jesus came to give us abundant life, a victorious life. In order to grow spiritually, He allows certain difficult situations and circumstances, but we should not lose our hope and continue to trust in Him.

In those terrible moments, I remembered God's promises for me, but they seemed to be powerless and lifeless. I knew I was going through the darkest night of my soul. I asked the Lord for help because I did not want to disappoint God and allow the enemy to rejoice.

God's beauty was manifesting wonderfully because throughout the trial, a spirit of intercession was upon me. I prayed for others with passion, tears and suffering. The Lord crushed me, to make me soft clay in His hands for His will. God works wonderfully and mysteriously!

The only solution to this situation is the battle of having faith and abiding in His promises. It is a difficult fight because reality checks in and you do not want to listen to its testimony. Focus only on God's promises and strengthen your thoughts through His Word.

On the 9th day of the fast, I fell facedown crying out because of my inner turmoil and attacks of the mind. I had lost peace and hope which is really serious for a child of God. This makes it clear that you are under a demonic attack.

I felt a fire burning inside of me again, for the Lord, for the lost and for the hurt. My spirit cried out *"No, I don't give up!"* After I heard again God's voice saying the exact words He told me in 2007, *"Whom shall I send?"* I fell facedown and I replied, *"Here I am, Lord, send me! I want to do Your will, God!"*

In those moments of crisis, I had the feeling that I could see God up there, looking at me without intervening. I could see Him full of peace and assurance saying, *"You will win, you will have victory, I chose this trial*

A SIMPLE TOUCH FROM THE LORD CAN CHANGE EVERYTHING!

to glorify My Name through you. I put value and power in you, which will surmount every obstacle. Even if it seems like I abandoned you, put your trust in Me."

Suddenly I shrieked so loud that I thought I would break the windows. The loud cry was from within me. I cried out *"Father! Father! Jesus! Jesus!"* And immediately I saw the wall that the enemy built around me cracked. A bolt of light came towards me from the Heavenly Father. I saw fire from above that tore the walls and entered my heart, similar to the time when I had my first encounter with Jesus.

In a fraction of a second, my pain, burden, disappointment and depression were gone. I do not know if you can imagine: I was in agony and desperation, close to death, but after I cried out to God,

I became another person in a moment. A simple touch from the Lord can change everything!

Then I understood the great victory of Jericho, when God's children shouted until the walls were destroyed. There is a great mystery here. I was reminded that God Himself shouted when He revealed Himself to Moses (*Exodus 34:6*). Many times, the Lord urges us through David to shout for joy (*Psalm 66:1*). In the Bible there are plenty of verses talking about how God responded to the poor and lost because they shouted out to Him.

I felt like I woke up from a nightmare yet I was a completely new creature. Not only was I delivered, but I was also filled with a divine power, with peace and gladness. I did not feel any worry or burden any more. My mind and heart were renewed and I had one desire, that of focusing on God's greatness.

I stood up and I told the Lord:

> *"Lord, what is happening to me? Why do I keep focusing on shortcomings and lack? Nothing and nobody has value except You. It is not worth worrying and being consumed with anything because I have You. Nothing is more important in this life! Forgive me, Lord, for I allowed myself to be attacked by the enemy and I focused on my problems and not on You. Please, forgive me, beloved Father! You deserve all praise, thanks and glory! Only You are worthy of being exalted! Forgive me for exalting my problems instead of You! Forgive me for making an idol out of my worry and frustration because that is all I thought about and talked about, losing sight of You.*

> *Lord, it does not matter what I'm going through, what I have or do not have. It does not matter how much it hurts, how much You crush me. I will still praise You and proclaim Your Name. I love You from the bottom of My heart, My Lord, My strength! Nothing can separate me from You: not even my troubles, hardship, sickness, famine, persecution etc (Romans 8:35). I thank You for allowing me to pass through trials in order to receive Your revelations and life-changing*

touch. Why did I get angry at You, Lover and Saviour? How did I manage to get fooled by the enemy, believing that You abandoned me? You gave me such divine peace and sweet comfort, Father! I praise You and I thank You! It does not matter what I'm going through. All things shall pass, but You remain. I want to remain with You!"

I could not stop praising Him and thanking Him. The more I praised Him, the more real I felt His presence sweeter and more powerful in me and around me. I started crying, but this time out of joy. What a great difference!

Then, the Spirit of the Lord used this opportunity to remind me of many verses and promises. I praised His Name and sang joyfully:

"With your help I can advance against a troop; with my God I can scale a wall." (Psalm 18:29, NIV)

"Blessed are those whose strength is in You, whose hearts are set on pilgrimage. As they pass through the Valley of Baka, they make it a place of springs; the autumn rains also cover it with pools. They go from strength to strength, till each appears before God in Zion." (Psalm 84:5-7, NIV)

Instead of coming before the Most High God with lamentation and mourning (which prove doubt and lack of faith), come before Him with songs of praise and with tears of joy, even if your problems are still present. They have no hold against you.

I was on my knees, facedown, hands outstretched towards heaven. I was in a divine Presence that cannot be expressed through words. The Saviour's true love manifested itself. I was in Him and He was in me. I experienced the reality of His love, perfected grace and divine peace. I told the Lord again how much I loved Him and about my desire to do His will.

...COME BEFORE HIM WITH SONGS OF PRAISE AND WITH TEARS OF JOY, EVEN IF YOUR PROBLEMS ARE STILL PRESENT.

After two hours of thanksgiving and fight, something supernatural happened. How great is our God! I felt His touch, I heard His voice and He told me wonders concerning me. His words are full of life, love and sweetness that I melted before Him. With my hands raised, I saw how the Lord put the terrestrial globe in my left hand and told me to intercede. He then put some money in my right hand telling me not to worry because He will provide.

Then, I saw in the spirit how I went beyond a backdrop. The Spirit carried me in His presence. I kneeled and asked Him to cleanse me and fill me with His love. I felt like *Yahweh* Himself breathed upon me. A Power entered inside of me, from head to toe. I do not have words to explain what I experienced. Then, the Lord spoke to me:

> *"Regardless of what you go through, My daughter, remember that I, the Lord, have called you. I love you and I chose you for great works here on earth. Even if you want to give up, I will not let you because what I started, I will bring to an end. Everything that I gave you will multiply. Many souls will be touched and changed. Proclaim the power of My love and the immovable assurance in Me. I desire a pure bride who is in love with Me, a bride who knows how to fight and one who praises Me incessantly."*

When I heard His words, I started worshiping Him and praising Him with more zeal. Then, a spirit of intercession came upon me and I prayed for all people. I prayed for leaders, pastors, women, men, youth and children. I tell you this only for His glory. I could not believe I prayed for six hours; it felt like 30 minutes. Then, I told the Lord, *"Lord, the trials and sufferings were worth it in order to enjoy such divine riches! Lord, I do not deserve such revelations from You, but I praise You and I thank You for Your unmerited grace!"*

The following day was the 10th and final day of the fast. It was so different! When I kneeled, the Lord told me not to make any plans or schedule anything for that day. He wanted me to pray and praise Him. Again, 5 hours felt like 5 minutes.

On the 10th day, my husband received phone calls from three different companies that were hiring! Also there was also a 24-hour prayer service at church and I went there to pray from 9pm- 2am. When I got back in the middle of the night, my husband showed me an e-mail, and somebody sent us $5,000! The Lord provides! How can I praise you Lord? How can I thank you? The money came from a dear family from Romania that we did not know for long. I was so in love with the Lord that I completely forgot about our bills and debts. The Lord had shifted my attention and energy to Him alone.

In this period, I learned a secret: irrespective of your situations and difficult circumstances, we have to live above them. Abiding in Christ means that the circumstances no longer control us. True relationship with God and true faith give us the power to laugh at tough situations. Can we rejoice when we are in so much trouble? Yes, because true joy starts from within and we prove that we completely trust in God's promises no matter the problem. This way we honor God.

Peace and joy come by faith in God, who can do everything, who is faithful and who loves us. This joy is rooted in God's character.

The manifested joy in us has another important benefit. It opens the heavens and our help will come, because where there is the joy of the Spirit, doubt and disbelief have no room. You rejoice in advance that you already received what you desired. Your answer will truly come (*Mark 11:23-24*). Peace, joy and praise strengthen faith and hasten His answer.

I thanked the Lord for the money, but my true joy came abiding in God's presence. I was joyful that God took away of all the suffering and burdens in my heart. He had taken away my worry before the money came – and that was the real miracle. I was so happy that I acted as if I were the richest woman on earth.

It is such an amazing grace to always be in God's presence! There is no burden, no problems, and no attacks. In reality they still exist, but the joy abides in the revelation that you no longer carry them. You have a different mission, that of praising God and thanking Him. It is not easy, but the Lord can work the same in your life.

> …PRAISE MAKES THE MIRACLE POSSIBLE.

The next day, I would talk to the Lord and reading His Word became more and more fresh, interesting, powerful and timely. Such great blessings stemmed from suffering, fasting and prayer! Then, I asked the Lord:

"Why didn't we receive the money earlier? Why did I have to suffer for almost a month?" The Lord answered me in a wonderful manner: *"As soon as you learned the lesson of praising Me in the midst of trouble and sufferings of all kinds, you allowed My miracles to take place in your lives."* In other words, praise makes the miracle possible.

Since then, even if other problems came up, I reminded myself of His words and this experience. I want God to search your hearts as you read these lines, irrespective of your storm, remember to shout to the Lord and praise Him because the answer is on the way.

Psalm 107 helped me better understand God's desire to be sought and praised for His wonders.

> *"They were hungry and thirsty, and their lives ebbed away. Then they cried out to the Lord in their trouble, and He delivered them from their distress." (Psalm 107:5-6, NIV)*

In verses 8, 15, 21 and 31, we notice how much the Lord desires our praises:

> *"Let them give thanks to the Lord for His unfailing love and His wonderful deeds for mankind!"*

Let us begin a life of praise and worship for the Lord and we will see Him at work. When we praise Him, we prove that we have faith and confidence in His Almighty powers. Faith and praise go hand in hand. When you trust that God will help you, you start praising Him and thanking Him joyfully, as if you already received what you asked for. Moreover, praise increases faith. The more you thank Him and praise Him, the more your faith increases. And then the miracle is on the way. If only we understood the beauty of praise and thanksgiving! It would spare us from suffering, trouble and pain.

> *"It is good to praise the Lord and make music to your name, O Most High, proclaiming Your love in the morning and your faithfulness at night." (Psalm 92:1-2, NIV)*

274

The Miracle
Of The 3 Doves

After this experience, the trials did not stop, but neither did my praises and thanksgiving to the Lord. By His urge, I entered a 21-day fast, interceding for Romania and other causes. Like I mentioned before, the aim of the fast is to draw you closer to God by a renewal of the mind and detoxification of your heart's impurities.

During this fasting period and as I was praying, I received a phone call in the morning from my children's school. They reminded me that I did not pay for some of their fees, about $1000. I completely forgot about the fees and I did not have money saved up. I felt the spirit of grief, burden and tribulation come again. I started praying and weeping, but the Lord used my broken heart to intercede for those suffering from other reasons. I interceded for two hours. I received peace and I praised the Lord, thanking Him yet again. I repeated David's words:

> *"Hear my prayer, Lord; let my cry for help come to You. Do not hide Your face from me when I am in distress. Turn your ear to me; when I call, answer me quickly."*
> *(Psalm 102:1-2, NIV)*

After that, I received an e-mail from a dear friend from Timisoara, Romania. She told me, *"As I was praying, the Lord told me, "Pray for Marian and Rodica Volintiru because they need $1,000." I started praying and the Lord showed me a vision of a dove with some banknotes in its beak. Not too far away there was another dove with banknotes in its beak and a third dove was close to the second. I understood from the Lord that money would come through three persons shortly, one after another."*

When I read the e-mail, I was glad, but I cannot tell you that I was excited. My lack of trust made me wonder why I was not happy. I had to search my heart and I found out that I was ungrateful. I thought that it was not fair that the Lord permits this state when He knows that we need money. *"Oh, woe is me! Who will deliver me from this body of death? Nothing good dwells in me..."* When I realized what state I was in I quickly repented, saying, *"Forgive me, Lord and help my disbelief. Help me take Your Word seriously. Forgive me because impatience, disappointment and doubt overcame me. Let Your light and truth cover me; I want to trust in You and act by faith."*

Three weeks passed and I almost forgot about what the Lord told me through Fely, my friend from Timisoara. It was Sunday and we were invited to dine with some close friends. When we got there, they told us that they received from the Lord to bless us with $300. We could not believe it because they were suffering financially themselves. We thank the Lord and we blessed the family.

After a few days, some brethren invited us to a prayer night at a church, to pray for a family who faced some problems. It was a wonderful night. As I was going to my car, the sister I interceded with put $200 in my pocket. I refused, because I knew they also were not wealthy. But she insisted, saying that the Lord told her to give me the money!

I thanked her, blessed her family and went home. At about 1 a.m. I could not sleep. Suddenly, I was enlightened and I shouted out, *"Lord, are these two families the two doves?"* Suddenly I took God's words seriously. I told God, *"Lord, if these two are the two doves, it means there is a third dove on the way. But the third one must bring no more and no less than $500 because this is what You told my friend; it must add up to $1,000. Please, Lord, make it in such way that the person blessing us does not know about our situation."*

That happened on Friday night. On Sunday morning, before praise and worship, a sister gave us an envelope with a congratulations card. When I saw the envelope, my feet started shaking in reverence for the Lord. I did not open the envelope because I was too nervous. My thoughts were turning about, *"Lord, is this true? What if it is just a Christmas card? What if there is only $50? But what if it is a $500* cheque?" I could not wait any longer and I opened the envelope. To my surprise and joy, there was a $500 cheque. I almost fainted! I was ecstatic and joyful. When you see how God works in such a wonderful and mysterious way, you are speechless and reverent before the God you serve. He is more real than anything else, He is so close that you can touch Him and fall facedown due to amazement, love and holy reverence. I wanted to say, *"Lord, turn from me because I do not deserve these blessings!"*

When the service ended, I impatiently asked the sister why she gave me the money. She said, *"Yesterday when I was praying, the Holy Spirit guided me to pray for you and to give you $500."* When I told her about the vision about the doves, she was thrilled because she obeyed the Lord's voice. God's word was fulfilled exactly as He said. How faithful and holy is God!

> THEREFORE, ASK BY FAITH, EXPECT JOYFULLY AND THANK ME BEFORE YOU RECEIVE IT.

It is important that people are at God's disposal, to hear His voice and then obey it. Did you know that there are many works and ministries that do not happen because we do not listen and obey what God tells us?

I was now curious about the details in which God worked in my situation. I called the sister who gave me $200 and I asked her why she gave me the money. She said, *"While you were speaking at church, I heard the words '200 dollars,' but I did not have the money on me. In that moment, my husband unknowingly whispered to my ear, 'I have $200 on me and I feel that we should give it to her.'"*

This was the confirmation that what the Holy Spirit said was at work. How great is our God! When I got home, I prayed and asked God, *"Lord, what should I understand of all this? What do You want to tell me? Why was Fely from Timisoara involved in conveying the message?"*

Then, the Lord spoke to me with clarity:

> *"I want you to take My Word seriously and never doubt. To receive it and be aware of the fact that it is straight from Me. Believe it and thank Me.*

I want you to see My faithfulness. Even though you did not expect it and you doubted it, I was faithful owing to My Word.

Even if you prayed, you were in a state of frustration, grief and ungratefulness. Therefore, I needed someone else to pray for you, to believe for you so that you may be blessed. I am seeking for faith so that I can fulfill My plans.

I am the God of detail. I wanted you to understand and believe that I am the Author of any good deed that comes through people. I am the one orchestrating everything towards achievement.

I use people at My disposal.

I wanted to show you the beauty of the supernatural, what happens in the spiritual realm and how it manifests in the natural.

I wanted to show you how much I care about you, how much I love you and how I use other people to bless you.

You will see great and mighty works; I have prepared such things for you and for all the people who love Me and keep Me in their hearts.

Seek Me, trust Me, be at My disposal and do not be afraid for I am in control.

I want to you share My wonders with others, so that they praise Me and give Me thanks. I want them to believe that I am real, that I am near them, watching over them and responding to them.

Therefore, ask by faith, expect joyfully and thank Me before you receive it.

Trust in Me, irrespective of the trial and bring Me glory and honor, for I am faithful in My Word.

All those who sowed in your life will in turn be blessed."

God bless those families for their obedience!

I understood from this experience how faith, prayer and expectation work together. I prayed, but the Lord saw my weak faith and He sought someone else to hear His voice and activate faith.

The most difficult test in a Christian's life is praising the Lord in every circumstance. The Bible tells us about a sacrifice of praise (*Psalm 50:17*) that the Lord expects from us. It is easy to thank God when all things are well and prosperous, but what do you do when everything seems upside down and you are sick and in trouble? When we seek the Lord and thank Him for what He brings in our life, our offering is received and we are protected by His glory. When we get sad and worried we are like a minefield, we risk falling prey to the enemies of frustration and malice.

Ungratefulness is offensive to the Lord. It is as if you are saying, *"I do not like God right now because He does not answer me when I am most desperate."* With such an attitude, we open the door to the enemy and he brings doubt and confusion in. God's love is difficult to comprehend because of these negative thoughts.

Therefore, fasting and prayer, together with the Word and worship must be our inseparable friends in life. Fasting was invaluable to me in these experiences. God is so good and faithful that He rewards every sacrifice. God promises that He will reward everyone after his or her actions and deeds. Fasting and prayer by faith open up the heavens and bring provisions to His children, provisions that hell tries so hard to keep away from us.

Overcoming Fear

Fear can be overcome through fasting, prayer and the Word of God. In this chapter you will be equipped with the tools to fight fear every day because many people are controlled by the spirit of fear.

Fear could be the work of an evil spirit or a sin you committed in your life. It could be a continuation of worries or childhood traumas. Other people who have scared you could cause it; or it could be birthed from the enemy's lies. The Word of God associates the evil spirit's work with fear:

> *"For the Spirit God gave us does not make us timid, but gives us power, love and self-discipline." (2 Timothy 1:7)*

> *"There is no fear in love. But perfect love drives out fear, because fear has to do with punishment. The one who fears is not made perfect in love." (1 John 4:18)*

Once you confess your fear before God, don't pay anymore attention to it.

Once it is confessed, it only exists in your mind. It's just a lie of the enemy. The enemy operates by fear and lies. As soon as you open those doors, they take control and power. In other words, fear blocks God's power in our lives. But when we walk in love, fear is powerless. Speak the word of faith, not the word of fear!

- Fear is an enemy, an evil spirit.
- Fear is faith in the lies of the enemy or other people.
- Fear immobilizes you, pulls you from the tracks and affects your physical strength.
- Fear blocks your faith and makes your prayers inefficient.
- Fear is a lack of faith.

- Fear destroys and paralyzes us.
- Fear and pride are the worst strongholds, holding the children of God captive in sufferings.
- Fear separates us from God.
- Fear is the spring of many evils; it opens the door to immorality, lying, corruption, crimes and worries.
- Fear makes us believe that our obstacles and problems are insurmountable; it eliminates God from our life, leaving us alone in frustration and pain.

The weapon, which destroys fear, is the Word of God. It is our shield of faith. With it, we can extinguish the enemy's fiery arrows. Instead of fear, confess what God has given to you: love, strength, power and a sound mind. If you don't confess it, fear will haunt and torture you, bringing punishment.

> ONCE YOU CONFESS YOUR FEAR BEFORE GOD, DON'T PAY ANYMORE ATTENTION TO IT.

> "In addition to all this, take up the shield of faith, with which you can extinguish all the flaming arrows of the evil one." (Ephesians 6:16, NIV)

Fear destroys the peace and trust in Jesus' victory. The antidote to fear is faith paired with the Word of God.

> "The weapons we fight with are not the weapons of the world. On the contrary, they have divine power to demolish strongholds. We demolish arguments and every pretension that sets itself up against the knowledge of God, and we take captive every thought to make it obedient to Christ." (2 Corinthians 10:4-5, NIV)

Because we find answer in the Word of God for every fear attack, please read these Bible verses out loud and see how God wants you to respond to the enemy:

- Are you afraid of being considered incapable? Declare:

  "I can do all this through him who gives me strength."
  (Philippians 4:13, NIV)

- Are you afraid of being weak and not knowing what to do? Declare:

  "The Lord is my light and my salvation— whom shall I fear? The Lord is the stronghold of my life— of whom shall I be afraid?" (Psalm 27:1, NIV)

  "... Do not grieve, for the joy of the Lord is your strength."
  (Nehemiah 8:10, NIV)

- Are you afraid of not having safety, money or a job? Declare:

  "And my God will meet all your needs according to the riches of his glory in Christ Jesus." (Philippians 4:19, NIV)

- Are you afraid of getting sick? Declare:

  "But He was pierced for our transgressions, He was crushed for our iniquities; the punishment that brought us peace was on Him, and by His wounds we are healed." (Isaiah 53:5, NIV)

  "He said, 'If you listen carefully to the Lord your God and do what is right in His eyes, if you pay attention to his commands and keep all his decrees, I will not bring on you any of the diseases I brought on the Egyptians, for I am the Lord, who heals you.'" (Exodus 15:26, NIV)

  "Who forgives all your sins and heals all your diseases..."
  (Psalm 103:3, NIV)

- Are you afraid of people? Declare:

"Never will I leave you; never will I forsake you. So we say with confidence, 'The Lord is my helper; I will not be afraid. What can mere mortals do to me?'" (Hebrews 13:5-6, NIV)

"I, even I, am he who comforts you. Who are you that you fear mere mortals, human beings who are but grass, that you forget the Lord your Maker, who stretches out the heavens and who lays the foundations of the earth, that you live in constant terror every day because of the wrath of the oppressor, who is bent on destruction? For where is the wrath of the oppressor?" (Isaiah 51:12-13, NIV)

• Are you afraid of death? Declare:

"Since the children have flesh and blood, He too shared in their humanity so that by His death He might break the power of Him who holds the power of death—that is, the devil— and free those who all their lives were held in slavery by their fear of death." (Hebrews 2:14-15, NIV)

• Are you afraid of the enemy? Declare:

"You will not fear the terror of night, nor the arrow that flies by day, nor the pestilence that stalks in the darkness, nor the plague that destroys at midday. A thousand may fall at your side, ten thousand at your right hand, but it will not come near you." (Psalm 91:5-7, NIV)

"I have given you authority to trample on snakes and scorpions and to overcome all the power of the enemy; nothing will harm you." (Luke 10:19, NIV)

"They triumphed over him by the blood of the Lamb and by the word of their testimony; they did not love their lives so much as to shrink from death." (Revelations 12:11, NIV)

"Even though I walk through the darkest valley, I will fear no evil, for You are with me; Your rod and Your staff, they comfort me." (Psalm 23:4, NIV)

"You, dear children, are from God and have overcome them, because the one who is in you is greater than the one who is in the world." (1 John 4:4, NIV)

"I sought the Lord, and he answered me; He delivered me from all my fears." (Psalm 34:4, NIV)

Don't forget! Fear comes from the devil. Don't accept it; it's a lie. Accept God's truth and peace. Be free in the Name of the Lord Jesus! The enemy uses the spirit of fear disguised as:

Doubt: Should I go there where the Lord guided me? What if anything happens? Did God really say it was His will? What if I don't get healed? What if the Lord doesn't answer my prayers? Is this exhortation really from the Lord?

Worries: Why is my child running late from school? What if someone assaulted him? What if he got into an accident? I'm afraid he might have got into trouble. What do I do? I don't have food to feed my children. I don't have money to pay the bills!

By worrying we forget what the Lord tell us:

"Therefore I tell you, do not worry… and your heavenly Father knows that you need them." (Matthew 6:25-32, NIV)

"Do not be anxious about anything, but in every situation, by prayer and petition, with thanksgiving, present your requests to God." (Philippians 4:6, NIV)

"Cast all your anxiety on Him because He cares for you." (1 Peter 5:7, NIV)

Hesitation and uncertainty: I don't know what to do. I don't want to go there because I'm afraid. I don't know what to do. Is it God's will or not? I promised my brother I would go, but now I changed my mind. Do you really think God would help me? What if something bad happens to me?

Fear will only grow if we fuel it, like a tiny worm becoming an enormous monster. The more we allow these thoughts to torture and agitate us, the more powerful they get. Satan desires to control us through these thoughts. Why are children afraid of monsters at night? Fear paralyzes them and they can no longer tell truth from fiction. Every shadow seems like a monster to them. Fear is the result of imagination fueled by the enemy.

Thoughts have great power, all the more reason to pay attention to our thinking. Thoughts can destroy us, or lower us to great depths of disbelief. It has been stated that you can negatively affect someone only by thinking negatively about him or her. It has been said that negative thinking can damage our entire bodies and bring mental

> FEAR IS THE RESULT OF IMAGINATION FUELED BY THE ENEMY.

and physical sickness. The Lord said in Matthew that He *"knew the thoughts" (Matthew 12:25),* and in Genesis that *"every inclination of the thoughts of the human heart was only evil all the time" (Genesis 6:5; see 8:21).*

> *"When anxiety was great within me, your consolation brought me joy." (Psalm 94:19, NIV)*

> *"For I know their works and their thoughts. And the time is coming when I will gather all nations and tongues, and they will come and see My glory." (Isaiah 66:18, AMP)*

> *"Hear, you earth: I am bringing disaster on this people, the fruit of their schemes, because they have not listened to My words and have rejected My law." (Jeremiah 6:19)*

We see in all these verses how our thoughts can bring about the wrath of God. Everything starts with a thought. Once the unclean thought is sown in our minds, it will affect us with its lie. The more we fuel it and worry about it, the more it will grow. In other words, by thinking about those thoughts, we say them out loud and share them with others. Once we talk about them, we start believing them. Then they take root, grow and manifest. We take action and put them in practice. In this manner we end up doing something we never intended to do in the first place.

Remember, everything starts with a thought.

> *"Take captive every thought to make it obedient to Christ."*
> *(2 Corinthians 10:5, NIV).*

> *"The Word of God judges the thoughts and attitudes of the heart" (Hebrews 4:12, NIV).*

> *"We have the mind of Christ." (1 Corinthians 2:16, NIV)*

> *"Set your minds on things above, not on earthly things"*
> *(Colossians 3:2, NIV).*

> *"For out of the heart come evil thoughts..."*
> *(Matthew 15:19, NIV).*

I mentioned only several Bible verses through which God shows the importance of our thoughts, their severity, and how essential it is to make them obedient to Christ.

So I conclude with this:

> *"So I tell you this, and insist on it in the Lord, that you must no longer live as the Gentiles do, in the futility of their thinking. They are darkened in their understanding and separated from the life of God because of the ignorance that is in them due to the hardening of their hearts"*
> *(Ephesians 4:17-18, NIV).*

CONDEMNATION

Read and declare all the verses below when you are in those specific situations.

The spirit of condemnation destroyed many souls, especially women's souls. They keep many sins hidden and the enemy rejoices because he has the legal right to torture them due to those hidden sins.

If you find yourself in this situation, find someone trustworthy and confess your sin, otherwise you won't be free of condemnation. Believe Jesus' promise which says that He forgives you; He threw your sins in the sea of forgetfulness. Only the enemy can remind you of those, in case you don't know the *truth* declared in the Word of God:

> *"Therefore, there is now no condemnation for those who are in Christ Jesus." (Romans 8:1, NIV)*

INFERIORITY

> *"For he chose us in Him before the creation of the world to be holy and blameless in his sight. In love He predestined us for adoption to sonship through Jesus Christ, in accordance with His pleasure and will— to the praise of His glorious grace, which He has freely given us in the One he loves. In Him we have redemption through His blood, the forgiveness of sins, in accordance with the riches of God's grace that He lavished on us. With all wisdom and understanding, He made known to us the mystery of his will according to His good pleasure, which He purposed in Christ, to be put into effect when the times reach their fulfillment—to bring unity to all things in heaven and on earth under Christ. In Him we were also chosen, having been predestined according to the plan of Him who works out everything in conformity with the purpose of his will, in order that we, who were the first to put our hope in Christ, might be for the praise of his glory." (Ephesians 1:4-11, NIV)*

DOUBT

"Truly I tell you, if anyone says to this mountain, 'Go, throw yourself into the sea,' and does not doubt in their heart but believes that what they say will happen, it will be done for them. Therefore I tell you, whatever you ask for in prayer, believe that you have received it, and it will be yours." (Mark 11:23-24, NIV)

"But when you ask, you must believe and not doubt, because the one who doubts is like a wave of the sea, blown and tossed by the wind. That person should not expect to receive anything from the Lord." (James 1:6-7, NIV)

BITTERNESS

"If I had cherished sin in my heart, the Lord would not have listened;" (Psalm 66:18, NIV)

"Get rid of all bitterness, rage and anger, brawling and slander, along with every form of malice." (Ephesians 4:31)

UNFORGIVENESS

"And when you stand praying, if you hold anything against anyone, forgive them, so that your Father in heaven may forgive you your sins." (Mark 11:25, NIV)

"'If your brother or sister sins, go and point out their fault, just between the two of you. If they listen to you, you have won them over.' Then Peter came to Jesus and asked, 'Lord, how many times shall I forgive my brother or sister who sins against me? Up to seven times?' Jesus answered,

'I tell you, not seven times, but seventy-seven times'."
(Matthew 18:15, 21, 22, NIV)

"In your anger do not sin: Do not let the sun go down while you are still angry, and do not give the devil a foothold." (Ephesians 4:26-27, NIV)

IDOLATRY

"I hate those who cling to worthless idols; as for me, I trust in the Lord." (Psalm 31:6, NIV)

"Love the Lord your God with all your heart and with all your soul and with all your strength." (Deuteronomy 6:5, NIV)

GREED

"Whoever shuts their ears to the cry of the poor will also cry out and not be answered." (Proverbs 21:13, NIV)

"A generous person will prosper; whoever refreshes others will be refreshed." (Proverbs 11:25, NIV)

"The generous will themselves be blessed, for they share their food with the poor." (Proverbs 22:9, NIV)

"Bring the whole tithe into the storehouse, that there may be food in my house. Test me in this," says the Lord Almighty, "and see if I will not throw open the floodgates of heaven and pour out so much blessing that there will not be room enough to store it." (Malachi 3:10, NIV)

"Give, and it will be given to you. A good measure, pressed down, shaken together and running over, will be poured into your lap. For with the measure you use, it will be measured to you." (Luke 6:38, NIV)

The Mystery Of Love

We were invited to Ponoara, a mountainous locality in western Romania where thousands of Christians of all denominations meet yearly. People from all over the country gather to fast and pray for 5 days. The Lord allowed me to speak there many times, but it angered many men because I am a female preacher. They reacted as if I had killed someone. I suffered to see the hatred the children of God have against women. I got in our car with my husband, I cried and prayed for them. The next day I was supposed to speak again and I felt as if hell was up against me. I was shivering due to the cold and because I was nervous. Then, God in His goodness spoke to me:

"Look at this crowd. Do you love these people?" There were about 5,000 people. With teary eyes I replied, *"Yes, Lord!" You know how much I love them. Did I not cry and fast for days for them? Did I not sacrifice everything for them, regardless of their religion?*

Then, the Lord revealed a great mystery and it made me wonder for a long time:

> *"Only in love, and filled by My love, can you stand before this crowd without stage fright, without fearing this crowd's opposition because "There is no fear in love" (1 John 4:18). Nobody has the right to preach, speak, evangelize, sing and prophesy if they were not filled with My love beforehand, before being touched by the flames of My love. There are plenty of works done, but because they lack My love and because they lack fervent prayer made in love, they bear no fruit.*

> *My Spirit works only through love and it is the only way to search their hearts and change the hearts of the people. My plan and desire is that every servant I use has filled with My love, because My love can be felt by others, and it bears fruit.*

The world is thirsty after My love. My love touches hearts, it does not judge, criticize, complain, suffer and sob.

You sacrificed yourself for those people and your words will carry a special anointing, born out of divine love. Their state of heart, sins and suffering pains you, and you speak to them with a broken heart that understands suffering from sin, the hurt of disappointment, loneliness, desperation, and unrest. My Spirit is free and it will flow through you and heal others, give them hope, strengthen and edify them, and prepare them for the next level.

Indeed, you love them, but you were aggrieved and you allowed fear to come into your life because you fixed your eyes on the opposition and on your weakness. You did not fix your eyes upon Me.

But the time will come, My daughter, when the fear of men will have no effect on you, when you will not be intimidated. You will be adamant in standing your ground. You will give Me the freedom to work exactly how I want through you to help other people. Believe, pray and wait patiently because these days are coming. I will fulfill everything at My set time. Abide in Me!"

When I heard God's words, I received absolute peace. Although I was scheduled to speak, I chose to cancel so that I would protect the leaders who called me to preach, that the crowds wouldn't go against them. I had to *"die to myself."* I felt a profound crush, but I decided to pray all night long. We drove to the motel where we checked in and started a long and powerful spiritual battle. I wept bitter tears, but full of love for the Romanian people. I was in agony and in spiritual labor. I interceded intensely, asking God's glory to manifest itself.

I was glad that after a whole week of rainy days, it was sunny for the last session. In this last session, many people were saved, others were baptized and healed. I thanked the Lord for crushing me, so that I could be soft clay in His hands. He used me to intercede for this event and His people even though I didn't speak.

The enemy sought to destroy me, to stop me from speaking, but the Lord turned this trial into something wonderful and much more powerful. When the Lord calls us to minister, there is no room for our ego, desires or personal opinions. There is room only for the plan and the will of the Master.

The Lord told me, *"Walk before Me and do not seek the approval of men. Do everything with Me and for Me, for My glory. You will have peace and victory if you fix your eyes on Me and My purpose. The enemy cannot intimidate you because you abide in Me, in the centre of My plan and will because you do not seek your own benefits. Do not look at your shortcomings and lack, but look at Me with total confidence because I am at work and I am fulfilling My plan through you, My daughter."*

Maybe you, my dear reader, have gone through or will go through something similar. Remember that if you are completely surrendered to God and to His cause, You must not be sad, angry, captive to your flesh or proud of anything. You are a worker in His vineyard and you must be on the same page with the Holy Spirit. Be careful and pay attention to His every move. It is not about who you are - your rank or ability - but it is about who He is. You have to see past opposition, trials and yourself. Moreover, when you understand the mystery of the Body of Christ, you will have peace and divine rest and you will desire to be at the right place, time and ministry the Lord calls you to.

PART III

PERSONAL REVELATIONS FROM GOD

"The words I have spoken to you – they are full of the Spirit and life."
John 6:63

"For the word of God is alive and active. Sharper than any double-edged sword, it penetrates even to dividing soul and spirit, joints and marrow; it judges the thoughts and attitudes of the heart."
Hebrews 4:12

"Your word is a light for my feet and a light for my path"
Psalm 119:105

Revelation From God's Word

In this section of the book, I want to explain more revelations that I received from the Lord during my times of fasting and prayer.

REVELATION OF THE SEED

The Word of God has life in it because it is God. The Word of God is like an imperishable seed (1 Peter 1:23). But what allows this seed to germinate, grow, and come out of the darkness? The soil, sunlight and water are all necessary for the germination process. If all these are adequate, the life in that seed can grow. Some plants grow even on a concrete wall. Seeds need photosynthesis and were made to bear fruit.

God's Word is like a seed in which life never drains out. We need to sow it, plant it on good soil, and then add water, heat and time. Only then we will see the growth, fruit and blessing of the seed.

> *"As the rain and the snow come down from heaven, and do not return to it without watering the earth and making it bud and flourish, so that it yields seed for the sower and bread for the eater, so is My word that goes out from My mouth: It will not return to Me empty, but will accomplish what I desire and achieve the purpose for which I sent it."*
> *(Isaiah 55:10-11, NIV)*

Why do we not take advantage of this powerful and valuable seed of the Word of God? Why don't we enjoy its fruit? What are our obstacles? Our greatest obstacles can be:

- Lack of knowledge
- Disbelief
- Doubt
- An Unforgiving heart
- Fear
- Ignorance
- Indifference
- Unrepented sin
- A Busy schedule
- A religious spirit
- Legalism

If you do not know that there is life in a seed, then you will either throw it away or put it in a jar. Therefore, you will waste plenty of blessings and a great harvest. Unbelievers do not understand the truth of the Word and they ignore the Scriptures. But even some Christians do not wholly believe in the power of God's Word. They are doubters. They live by sight and not by faith. Consequently, they live a life dominated by panic and suffering because they do not believe in the transforming power of God's Word. Because they do not meditate day and night on the living Word, they cannot become as a tree that bears fruit.

> *"That person is like a tree planted by streams of water, which yields its fruit in season and whose leaf does not wither— whatever they do prospers." (Psalm 1:3, NIV)*

> *"But blessed is the one who trusts in the Lord, whose confidence is in Him. They will be like a tree planted by the water that sends out its roots by the stream. It does not fear when heat comes; its leaves are always green. It has no worries in a year of drought and never fails to bear fruit." (Jeremiah 17:7-8, NIV)*

If we allow sin to dwell in our lives, we stop the manifesting power of the seed's life and we will not have the desire to pray. We must stop and be still, search our hearts, repent and ask for God's power in our lives. If we do not apply these steps, the enemy rejoices about the veil that is put on our eyes and he whispers his lies in our ears, which we freely and wholeheartedly accept. We feed on them and we no longer believe the truth. The seed of the Word of God is lands on dark, lightless, dry and barren soil. The seed's life can no longer confront its opposition and is no longer able to bear fruit. This is the reason why we need a real cleansing and washing in the Word, and the living water of the Holy Spirit.

We are so blessed to have God's wonderful Word because we can encounter God: Father, Son and Holy Spirit. Whatever we need in our lives, be it financial, spiritual or personal, we find it in abundance in His Word. We must search for the treasure is hidden in Him, which are the His truth and His life giving words concerning our situations. The Holy Spirit brings enlightening upon us.

Many times God's Word is bound because of our lack of faith, so it cannot take action.

The Lord once told me:

> *"Rodica, I want you to speak about My Word because it is neglected, ignored, misunderstood and they do not believe in it. People must be taught about its truth and then it has to be applied. Never separate Me from the Word, because I am the Word. Those who do not believe it or neglect it do not discover its power. The Word without Me in it is nothing but shallow words, therefore it indeed brings death to some people. There are so many people using the Word without Me to attack each other, seeking their own righteousness and justice. This is the reason why there is division among Christians. My Word is a mystery: with no revelation and intimacy with Me, you cannot understand the Scriptures. You need Me to open your eyes to understand My word. I give life to the Word.*
>
> *Pray that the Lord prepares workers in His vineyard, workers who know Me and know how to use the Word as a seed, fire and sword. Soon you will see and experience how the Word*

works together with Me and your faith. Abide in Me, in My Word. Meditate because I will reveal mysteries unknown to you, which will aid you and My people. Revelations will multiply. I am the Word and I dwell in the Word.

A REVELATION ABOUT LOVE

One time I was at a prayer meeting at church. The Lord spoke to me again, telling me that we must be ready for the great wonders that will unfold on earth: some good, some bad. These are God's words that I received then:

> *"I want all of you to be like a pen in My hand, in complete surrender, so that I can use you with My power. I want you to be a living testimony of My love because it is the strongest weapon, which creates, lifts us, encourages, forgives and shuts the mouth of the enemy."*

In the vision I received, I saw written on our chests the word "*LOVE*". Those were not merely letters, but a word that had life, divine brilliancy, consumed by a continual fire. I saw the beauty of God's character and love through every letter.

In that moment, this is how I perceived God's *LOVE* in my heart:

L means I am:
- Love
- Light
- Life

O means I am:
- Omega
- Omnipresent
- Omniscient
- Omnipotent

V means I am:
- Victorious
- Vine

• Valuable

E means I am:
  • Emmanuel
  • Eternal
  • Everlasting

I understood the beauty and depth of the word "*LOVE*," which is the foundation of God's Word because God is love. I saw beyond every letter, as if I saw God's heart through a window. The Lord said:

> *"My children, I desire you to penetrate My heart, so that you truly understand My love, tears and pain for humanity. When will you understand and know My love, the world will see beyond you and it will be attracted to Me as My love dwells in your hearts. Are you ready to leave everything for Me? Are you ready to pay the price of knowing and loving Me? Are you ready to stand in the gap for the lost? Are you ready to face your Goliath? Are you ready to forgive everyone and humble yourselves? You WILL be ready once you encounter My divine Love. Make a decision and answer the call today! I am with you to fulfill the plan I have for you, says the Holy One. I am that I am!"*

REVELATION CONCERNING SPIRITUAL WARFARE

These words made me aware of the power that works in each and every one of us. The Lord continued speaking to me and He showed me that we had entered a new season. Now, He demands of us to change our thinking, our way of praying and worshiping, our behavior, our attitudes and our hearts' intentions. He wants us to break free from tradition and religiosity, and to walk in His light and truth. For a time like this, fasting and prayer are important.

Let us pray that the Lord gives us a Spirit of revelation to know Him deeply and to understand the enemy's plans against us.

For example, if you are in the midst of a fight and you do not understand who you are in Christ or if you do not know whom your enemy is, you will only lose. It is critical for us to know who we are in Christ, and be actively aware of the enemies' schemes. Satan takes advantage of the fact that we do not properly know our identity in Christ and His riches, privileges, power and authority available in Jesus. We sometimes are like the beggars who have millions deposited in the bank but never withdraw the money. God invested His power in us, He put His Spirit in us, we have everything in Him, we are children of the King of Kings, and we are priests, holy, righteous, chosen and beloved. Yet, Satan still takes advantage of our ignorance and weakness and he mocks us, pulling us back. Let us rise to the calling God has for us! We must walk boldly in the blessings we have in Christ because God wants to give us new hope, new power, new anointing, new clothing, new vision and new opportunities.

He wants to multiply His blessings after the measure of His goodness. Let us pray with all our hearts that the Lord opens His doors for the nations, so that the King of glory and honor enters the place.

"Lift up your heads, you gates; be lifted up, you ancient doors, that the King of glory may come in." (Psalm 24:7, NIV)

It is time the Lord entered the gates. Before He comes again, He will reveal His glory and honor on earth. Let us pray that watchmen rise up and stand by the doors of every fortress and use the power and authority they were given to destroy and eliminate every demonic strategy and power.

It is time for the Church of Christ to rise in unity, and to open the gates of their nation for the King of glory. Let us pray that God's glory falls upon our countries how the Lord promised. We will witness miracles, signs, wonders and crowds turning to God. If you truly understand God's greatness, then you will see His glory and you will receive according to your faith. What you speak with your mouth, you will have it, be it positive or negative. How much you ask, you will receive.

Therefore, the Holy Spirit urges us today not to limit God. Certain thinking patterns and prejudices must be eliminated. Let us allow Him to lead everything, to manifest His glory and power! Doubt, disbelief and tradition stop God from manifesting. Be free and open for great and new miracles that the Lord wants to perform in your nation. Today, He is seeking men and women, children and elders who do not limit Him, but who walk by faith and take action according to His Word.

REVELATION DESCRIBING "I AM THE WORD"

"For the word of God is alive and active. Sharper than any double-edged sword, it penetrates even to dividing soul and spirit, joints and marrow; it judges the thoughts and attitudes of the heart." (Hebrews 4:12, NIV)

On New Year's night, the Lord spoke to me, *"I want to tell you something more powerful than I ever told you before. Take the Bible in your hand. Now, every time you take this Book in your hand, you are taking Me, for I am the Word. It is not Moses, Paul, Peter or the others who is speaking, but Me, Jesus."*

> *I am the Word.*
> *I am the Way, the Truth and the Life.*
> *I am the Resurrection and the Life.*
> *I am Alpha and Omega, the Beginning and the End.*
> *I am Peace, Joy and Wisdom.*
> *I am the Redeemer and Saviour.*
> *I am everything; I am the Life Source.*
> *I am Jesus, the One who died and resurrected, the Shepherd, the Teacher.*
> *I am the Healer and Deliverer*
> *I am the King of Kings, Lord of Lords.*
> *I am the Gate for the sheep, Light of the world*
> *I am the Prince of Peace, the Knowledge and the Wisdom.*
> *I am the Lamb of God, the Bright Morning Star.*
> *I am the beloved Bridegroom*
> *I am that I am.*

Only then, I understood for the first time *who* Jesus really is, the Word who became the flesh and lived among us full of grace and truth (*John 1:14*). I never heard someone explain the power that is in God's Word. I understood the importance of praying with Bible verses and I understand His promises, if we have faith, they will manifest in our lives.

In John 1, the Lord said, *"And the Word became flesh and made His dwelling among us. We have seen His glory, the glory of the one and only Son, who came from the Father, full of grace and truth."*

Ever since then I understood the importance of His Word and why we are urged in Psalm 1:2-3 to meditate night and day on His Word - so that we may become a tree that bears fruit, which is deeply rooted in Christ. In this manner, *"I have hidden Your word in my heart that I might not sin against You" (Psalm 119:11, NIV)*. Meditating on His Word, we start to "see" life and the power hidden in Him.

It is as if the Lord said, *"In order to find Me - the Life, Power, Patience, Light, Wisdom - seek Me and meditate on My Word day and night."*

The Lord showed me how His Word is like an orange. You must peel it first, and then you can enjoy the pulp and its juice. His Word is also like a seashell. You must break it open first to find the pearl inside. His Word is light and truth, but most of the time we cannot understand without revelation from above. Thus, Paul said,

> *"For I always pray to the God of our Lord Jesus Christ, the Father of glory, that He may grant you a spirit of wisdom and revelation of insight into mysteries and secrets in the deep and intimate knowledge of Him."* (Ephesians 1:17, AMP)

We need to understand the Word and pass beyond the written words, so that we may find God, the true richness, life, delight and revelation - everything that is in Christ.

> *"But blessed is the one who trusts in the Lord, whose confidence is in Him. They will be like a tree planted by the water that sends out its roots by the stream. It does not fear when heat comes; its leaves are always green. It has no*

worries in a year of drought and never fails to bear fruit."
(Jeremiah 17:7-8, NIV)

This tree sends its roots by the stream and bears fruit every month. The tree's spring is Jesus Christ and it does not seek anything else. When you find Him in the Word, you receive revelations. You will see how many barriers you have been fighting with and worldly teachings will wither and fall. Through the Spirit of revelation you will truly start to know God and fall in love with Him. You will fight to cling onto Him and He will use you mightily. God desires each and every one of us to be like this.

One day I was waiting for God's providence so that we could set out for a mission. I told you before that the Lord wants us to depend on Him. We walk by faith so that He is glorified and so that we will not have reasons to brag about our own powers. The Lord gave me a couple of verses, which I declared on a daily basis. I trusted in Him and I was waiting for His power to manifest. He showed me an image: we were on a hill and there was a valley before us. We had to reach the other side. *"How do we get there, Lord?"* I asked Him. He replied, *"You must build a bridge from My Word so that you can cross to the other side. You must walk on water, meaning you have to trust on My Word."*

After, I started declaring daily:

> *"And my God will meet all your needs according to the riches of His glory in Christ Jesus."(Philippians 4:19, NIV)*

> *"The Lord is my shepherd, I lack nothing."*
> *(Psalm 23:1, NIV)*

> *"Never will I leave you; never will I forsake you."*
> *(Hebrews 13:5, NIV)*

> *"So do not fear, for I am with you; do not be dismayed, for I am your God. I will strengthen you and help you; I will uphold you with my righteous right hand."*
> *(Isaiah 41:10, NIV)*

I declared these verses and others alike. With my eyes of faith, I could see how the bridge was forming day by day, and I would walk on it. I would feel "dizzy" because I made the mistake of looking down to my shortcomings and not on Him. Nevertheless, I persevered in faith and I declared His promises daily. I fought doubt and other attacks only through His Word, I declared who He was and I spoke about His character and faithfulness. Moreover, I praised Him and thanked Him for the victory that was about to come.

When I finished "building the bridge" by His Word of faith, I reached the other side and then received a miracle of provision. We went on a mission, rejoicing and praising the Almighty God for His grace, goodness and faithfulness, for the power I clearly witnessed through His Word.

The Lord says:

> *"Truly I tell you, if anyone says to this mountain, 'Go, throw yourself into the sea,' and does not doubt in their heart but believes that what they say will happen, it will be done for them. Therefore I tell you, whatever you ask for in prayer, believe that you have received it, and it will be yours."* (Mark 11:23-24, NIV)

Here is the mystery of faith: *to already see* something that you asked for and to rejoice, as if you received it already. In this process you are involving your mind, heart, feelings and subconscious. The Spirit of the Lord fulfills what we ask; believe and declare daily.

Unfortunately, the problem is that we are infected with negativity and doubt of all kinds, which are holding us back from receiving what we asked for. The more we know God, the more powerful we are in His Word, and we can fight. We are fighting against our senses, which are focused only to the visible world.

Faith does not rely on visible reality, but on the realm that cannot be seen with physical eyes. Faith is confidence and assurance about what we hope and desire, about something that your physical eye cannot see. In order to see some results, we have to repent of all the impurities we gathered along the way. They are the result of long-term frustration, dissatisfaction, lack of knowledge or lack of truth.

The process of renewing your mind will start by declaring His Word and by constant meditation on His Word.

Prayer Journal Entries

I am in my 23rd day of fasting and prayer. I thank the Lord that I feel well both spiritually and physically. (It is difficult to fast for long periods, but at the same time is so wonderful because I no longer think about food and focus all my energy on God). I long more and more after the Lord, after His perfection and after a deeper collaboration and fellowship with the Holy Spirit. How I wish to be together with Him and with Him alone, to talk to Him, to praise Him and to intercede after His will. I prayed that heaven would invade the earth with everything that is heavenly. May God's glory and goodness fill the earth!

At that time, the Lord told me, *"I want all My children to know, understand and believe in the power of My Word. My Word is:*

- *True food for the hungry*
- *Living water for the thirsty*
- *Honey for the bitter*
- *Health for the sick*
- *Strength for the weak*
- *Light for those in the dark*
- *Freedom for the captive*
- *Comfort for the afflicted*
- *Salvation for the lost*
- *Guidance for the confused*
- *Wisdom for the ignorant*
- *Shelter for the homeless*
- *Friend for the loners*
- *Shepherd for the lost*
- *Joy for the afflicted*
- *Peace for the upset*
- *Faith for the doubters*
- *Love for the haters*

- *Hope for the disappointed*
- *Wealth for the poor*
- *Justice for the wronged*
- *Medicine for the hurt*

Through my Word, you can know Me and commune with Me. This is a living Word - it is not dead."

Lord, reveal Your truth, this limitless power, overflowing and bringing transformation, life, healing and freedom!

During another period of fasting, the Lord reminded me of His Word again:

"If you would believe in Me with deep passion and sincerity, you would see and recognize My face, My presence and My perfume. They are always with you. How different would your life be if you only believed! If you knew that I looked after you, you would have peace, joy, safety and reverence. You would be protected against sin. You would control your emotions. You would do what is right, pure and holy. I have My eyes fixed upon you, so be careful of what you say or do. I want to be pleased by My children who are aware of My presence and who choose to give Me glory.

Bring Me offerings of thanksgiving wherever you are and I will come and bless you. I act according to the principles and laws that I arranged. I do not act like you do, according to frustration, dissatisfaction, misunderstandings or unholy desires.

When you pray, do not come before Me with your dissatisfaction or disappointment from the past years. Come based on faith, your trust in Me and in the power of My love, which takes action all the time.

Ask for wisdom and revelation of My mysteries, because only then will you see with clarity. "Go, wash yourself seven times" - that water is My Word. My Word is like clean water that washes filth, dirt, leprosy and any veil over your eyes.

Dig deep into My Word. Do not give up, the more you dig, the more treasures you will find there. Do not stop after only a few scoops because the adventure has barely started. Gold has to be dug out and it will shine as bright as the sun. It will be processed and used as jewelry. The same is with My Word: it is hidden and if nobody searches or digs, it will not be of any help. The unfolding of My Words gives light (Psalm 119:130). You must seek My Word in order to find its depth. Those who will dig deep will be happy and rich because they will feast upon the riches of My Word and will experience its blessings.

There are people who say that they are rich and lack nothing. They rely on their tradition, but do not realize that the things they rely on are a hindrance in understanding the true values and riches of My Word. Their values are false. They need ailment for the eyes in order to see their nakedness. This ailment is My Word, which enlightens. My Word will be spoken by a wise mouth, anointed by Me, which will speak only the truth. I want to prepare you, to give sight to the blind, so that they may see my truth clearly. I want them to turn from their wicked ways to be saved and set free."

REVELATION ABOUT THE POWER OF JESUS' NAME

One time when I was in a 10-day fast, I dreamt that an older man kidnapped a woman and a child, and later he killed the woman. When I saw him carrying his prey like an enraged tiger, I realized that evil spirits possessed him. Suddenly, he tried to catch my sister and I. While he was busy, we fled to the woods, but the trees were too spread out.

We ran in panic and climbed a tree, thinking he would not notice us, but he was already by the trunk trying to climb after us. We wanted to jump to another tree, but the branches were withered and dried and I knew they would break. When he got near me, he tried to pull me down. In that moment, the Spirit of the Lord came upon me and I commanded, *"Get out! Leave, in Jesus' Name!"* In an instant, the evil, fierce man became as meek as a lamb.

Then, the background changed: I was standing in a room with other people. The police came and took the man in and he seemed rather normal. I asked him, *"Why did you come for us?"* He replied, *"Because I saw that you had peace, joy and safety. I wanted to harm you for that. But, the moment you shouted the name of Jesus something came out of me and I saw things with clarity I was free and I wanted to know everything about this Name. Even if I will go to jail, I want to tell other about this name Jesus."*

I woke up and I meditated on the power of His Name. I understood that we must believe that we have power and authority through Christ over the power of the enemy and we must rely on the Name in which all power lies. We have to use it when it is needed.

REVELATION OF THE HOLINESS OF GOD

One Saturday night, during a 40-day fast, we gathered together with many believers to pray. Heaven opened and we felt the supernatural touch of the Holy Spirit while we were singing, *"Let us be a generation marked by Your Love, a generation purified and set apart..."* The Spirit filled me with power and to everyone's surprise I started praying aloud and shouting:

"Holy, Holy, Holy is the Lord God Almighty!"

I felt a powerful divine presence covering me so I fell facedown. I felt yet again the power and fire of God's holiness, which was overwhelming.

In those moments I realized how holy, pure and almighty God is. Our being cannot resist this power. It is indescribable. I wanted to open the floor to hide because I felt that I was melting from His consuming fire. It was the kind of power that penetrated every fiber of my body, soul and spirit. I realized how sinful I am in comparison to His holiness and purity. I realized how much I depended on Jesus' blood. To some extent, I experienced what Isaiah experienced, and I prayed, *"Lord, I am such sinful flesh and my lips are filthy! Please, touch me with Your blood, cover me with Your wings, because I cannot stand bare before You."*

I started shouting. My flesh and body were in a process of melting, but my spirit was quiet. However, I was not afraid that God would destroy me, punish me or that I would die. It was a divine reverence, only experienced when God reveals His holiness. In that state, I wanted to cover myself. I sought a blanket or something to put on me. The Lord allowed me to experience such encounters at least five times. Once, I took the carpet and covered myself, facedown. Other times I took a blanket. These experiences brought an abundance of joy, peace and blessings to my life.

Each time I experienced it, I reached another level of faith, love, revelation, power in prayer and ministry. Each time God reveals Himself to us, He prepares a new ministry, work, and power to overcome new tests in our lives.

God is so faithful! He is a tender and loving Father. He sometimes reveals Himself like a comforter, protector, friend or lover. Each feature is manifested in a different way. Many times, I experienced His love as Father and Saviour. How sweet and reassuring were those moments! However, when He comes in His holiness, we tremble, shake and fall facedown. Even if I thought I was on the right path in faith, I saw myself as dirty and I was terrified because He is so pure and holy, that my flesh, mind, heart and eyes could not even fathom His qualities.

Blessed be the Lord, that through Jesus's blood there is forgiveness. We are purified and we can stand in His presence. Therefore, whenever I experienced such moments, I tried to take cover and hide as I called Jesus' blood to be upon me. The Lord protected me with His hand, so that I would not be consumed.

When Isaiah witnessed God's glory, he felt guilty, even though he was one of the Bible's most remarkable prophets. He needed cleansing by a burning coal to stand before the Most High God. Why did his mouth need sanctification? The mouth, especially the tongue, is the filthiest body member because through the mouth it is easiest to sin against others and God.

Even though His presence would manifest like a consuming fire, I felt a magnetic attraction to His presence. The Lord started speaking:

"You do not know My holiness because no one can see it without dying. You speak so lightly about Me and My holiness. I want from you holiness, complete consecration, no compromises, doubts or dissatisfaction. It is time you changed - do not waver. Press on forward on the path I designed for you through My Word. The enemy has set a trap, but My children will not get lost as long as they know My way, the truth and the Word.

Also, be vigilant and watchful. Take precaution against the enemy that seeks to destroy you. I want to reveal Myself to all of you who are searching for Me.

You will see Me in every living matter, for I am Life. Any dead cell will receive life, because I will flow in every cell. I dwell in you if you abide in My Word.

Call My Name because I am Jehova-Rapha, I am Jehova-Jireh. Ask in faith and receive My gifts. They will be used for the edification of My Church."

I then understood how adamant the Lord is in His desire to bless us, help us, fulfill our needs and fulfill His plans and works. Then, God in His faithfulness gave us a confirmation from Isaiah 35. God wanted to awaken us and prepare us. Blessed be the Lord!

REVELATION ABOUT WORSHIP

At church, during praise and worship, the Lord reminded me, *"When you really engage in praise and worship, in spirit and in truth, where My heart is touched, expect new revelations."* He then told me, *"You will have great power, peace, joy and truth in abundance if you receive the revelation that is in My Word and in My Name. Some people speak My*

Name with words, with no faith or real connection to Me, so their words are powerless. The life and power of those words are hindered from showing their true power. When you worship me, you create an atmosphere for me to work on your behalf. During the worship, I create millions of acts. This is the atmosphere where I delight to dwell. Praise Me and worship Me!

I then asked Him, *"What should we do, Lord?"* He said:

> *"Ask My Spirit of revelation to come upon you. Abide in worship and adoration. The revelation of My Name will enlighten you and will reveal the nature of My love, so that your worship will be effective, full of life and anointing, reaching My heart. Then, I will open the eyes of your heart and you will understand who I am. You will love Me more, you will praise Me and be in awe."*

I responded, "Lord! Bring us to that level sooner! Bring us to Your Temple so that we can stand in awe of Your beauty!" The Lord kept speaking to me:

> *Each and every Word of Mine is full of life, power, glory, strength and beauty.*
>
> *I am Wonderful and everything I say is wonderful.*
>
> *I am Good and everything I say is of infinite goodness, which touches and blesses.*
>
> *I am the Light and everything I say is pure, covered in My divine Light, which destroys the darkness.*
>
> *I am the Truth. My Word is true and wipes out deception and lying; it brings peace and joy.*
>
> *I am Faithful. My Word is holy and just. I impart to you My Word of Life, which brings faith. It will enable you to understand My dimensions, to see the way I am and to*

honor Me, "And without faith it is impossible to please God" (Hebrews 11:6)

I am Love. My words are spirit and life. They are full of love and can love even the loneliest and most sinful person.
I am your Protector. You see it written in My Word that I outstretch My wings to protect you. My children, I care about you, I find pleasure in you, I seek you, I feed you, I strengthen you by My loving hand.

Why won't you believe? Have your eyes fixed on Me, by faith, without which nobody can understand or believe My promises that are "Yes" and "Amen"!

Prophetic Word For Romania

One Sunday, during the praise and worship time at my church in Vancouver, the Holy Spirit spoke to me. I saw a white hand writing something. It was translucent white and it used a pen. It wrote, *"For the Romanian people."*

It caught my attention and I felt a deep feeling of reverence that I felt I needed to fall facedown. Then, God told me to grab a pen and write what He would tell me. When I started writing, it was as if the pen wrote without me even thinking. The Spirit would speak and my hand would write God's message. Some words may sound familiar, but I felt that the Lord wanted to emphasize them so that we take them seriously:

> *"For you, the Romanian nation, the trumpet is blowing and bursting today! Be ready because I want to come to you, touch you, speak to you like never before! Your prayers, fasting, tears and sacrifices and those of your ancestors are before Me. I am ready to respond to those who are waiting for Me, who love Me and who desire Me more than anything. Wake up, My people! Wake up, My Bride! Do not be dormant, do not sleep, for I, your Groom, am coming! I miss you, I love you and I want to show you My glory. I want you to rejoice in My blessings!*
>
> *Get ready, My people, for great wonders and works, which the eye had not seen, the ear has not heard and the heart has not experienced.*

Prepare the way for My glory, so that it may overflow through you. Do not look back, do not look to others or to yourselves, do not look at your problems and opposing circumstances! Do not abide in formalism and tradition, but set it aside and abide in love and power! Do not listen to the enemy's whispers, tempting you with earthly things. It is time, more than ever, to look at Me and only at Me. To seek My face, My love and I will respond. I will come and I will show Myself to all of you who love Me and await Me.

I will make a great difference between those who serve Me wholeheartedly and out of love and those who do not, between those who love Me and those who love tradition, law, formalism, their good deeds and their righteousness. I want to send My fire, so that it may consume the sacrifice on the altar, but what sacrifice are you offering Me? Is there something for Me to burn?

I desire your living sacrifice of praise and love. When the perfume of the sacrifice comes before Me, it will determine My power to unfold before you and throughout the earth.
I desire repentance and humility, a clean heart - open, determined and free - to be Mine and only Mine.

Stand firm on My Rock of salvation and shine bright like a lighthouse in the darkness! The darkness shall not reign for long because My light will come with great power and will reveal even the darkest and farthest places. I am the Light of the world; do not forget that you are a light for the world as well.

Be ready My people! Prepare My way by a deep thirst and hunger for Me. I will saturate you! I and only I will satisfy and quench your thirst. Then, you will be channels of blessing for the depressed, discouraged, lonely, stricken, crushed and for those who seek the truth.

Pray and be vigilant! At the same time, rejoice in your faith that you will see crowds of people, men, women and children running from darkness to light. The dead will be resurrected, spiritually and physically. Many sick people will be healed, many poor people will be enriched, many desperate people will be strengthened, many lost people will be found and the sinners will be saved.

Take heart and strengthen yourselves in My Word, in My promises, walking in love and humility. My power and authority are upon you. Use them with boldness and the enemy will flee from you. Be vigilant and pray, says the Lord!

These were the words that the Spirit urged me to write. Even if we already know these words, the Lord wants to stress them so that we do not fall from exhaustion into a lack of faith or disbelief.

Prophetic Word For The People Of God

"*Prepare yourself, get ready earth! I will come and judge. Your iniquity has reached Me. Your prayers are few in My cup, therefore I will send trials upon the earth. I will make it so that every sinner and hardened heart prays and cries out to Me.*

Focus only on Me, seek My face always. Difficult days will come, but abide in Me. If you live by faith and by My Word, I will multiply the oil and flour. Start now, bless the bottle of oil, sack of flour and your fridge so that they will not run out. In order to see My miracles, you must have faith!

"For, In just a little while, He who is coming will come and will not delay." (Hebrews 10:37, NIV)

The righteous will stand in faith. I will send physical and spiritual fire because I want the fire of My love to consume you for Me and for the lost. How much do you care about the wounds of My people? How much do you care about those who cannot distinguish good from evil? How much do you care about those who go to hell? About the hopeless? Who will come before My throne for them? Who will pray for them? Who will preach the Truth? Why do you fight amongst yourselves, when the world is dying and the enemy rejoices?

Wake up My children! There is no time for triviality! Why did you put down your weapons? Can't you see the enemy is attacking you? Wake up, wake up, equip yourselves and charge and attack for I am with you. It pains me that you are so dormant, bound, indifferent, and above all, you are great accusers, critics and are very ungrateful. That is the reason why you fell victim to the enemy. I called you, but you ignored Me.

Your prayers are without substance; they have little spiritual weight. They float and eventually fall. They are lifeless and faithless.

Behold, the fire of My wrath, it is coming. Those who are clean will stand untouched and the fire will not consume them, owing to their love for Me. Those who are built on My Word will be triumphant in every trial. My fire purges and burns everything which is not of Me. Blessed are those who understand the message of My divine fire! I will baptize them with the Holy Spirit and fire

Therefore, I will send fire so that your prayers are clean, fervent, filled with essence, power and faith. I will open the heavens and the forces of darkness will back down. My children, you who know My Name, I will tell you again: fear not, for I am with you and together we will do greater, mightier works, even in those days of trouble. Rejoice and bless My Name always, for I am good and My mercy and faithfulness endure forever. Regardless of the challenge, praise My Name and bring Me honor. By praising and thanking Me, heaven will open and I will come to your help, for I dwell in the midst of the praises of My children."

PRAYER FROM THE BOTTOM OF MY HEART

I was in a fasting period of 21 days. I wept a lot.

The Lord woke me up at 5am, and I was guided to pray and worship. From 8am-11am, I wept. I was desperate and thirsty after God. This thirst was burning in me continuously, even until today. I miss Him and His love; I want to gaze at the beauty of the Lord and on His might. He is the One who motivates me to pray and intercede for the causes of the earth and for humanity's greatest need: that of seeking and knowing Christ, of seeing His beauty and glory.

Lord, how are we supposed to gaze on Your beauty? It is impossible to do that if You do not pull us up, cut every foreign bond that might hinder us from knowing You, if you do not reveal Yourself to us. Jesus, You said in the Word that You abide in the Father and He abides in You. You said we could only meet the Father if You revealed Him to us, so please reveal Him!

As I was praying, I was reminded of Moses, who said to the Lord, *"Show me Your glory!"* The Lord allowed His outstanding beauty to pass before Moses.

I heard the Lord say to me, *"If you meditate on My Word, My character and My Name, I will be merciful to you. Read My Word and you will understand My love, goodness and plan for each of you. All these things will amaze you and draw you closer to Me, you will praise Me and thank Me even more."*

I said to God, *"Lord, please let Your Spirit of wisdom and revelation come upon us, so that we might understand and know Your will. We want to worship in spirit and in truth. Let this worship be a continuous flow of praise and thanksgiving.*

Lord, reveal Yourself to Your people once more. Show us Your goodness and faithfulness in a concrete way. I want to see Your hand at work, touching us and our suffering, dissatisfaction and short-comings. We make efforts yet we do not see the results we expected."

The Lord told me, *"You said it right: you make great efforts because you do not trust Me or rely on Me. Rely on My Name, My character, My goodness and My faithfulness. Rest in Me."*

I started declaring, singing and blessing the Name and character of God:

Lord, lift us higher in Your presence, to gaze at Your beauty. Jesus, You are much needed on earth! We beg you, come to Your chosen workers. We want You to manifest with power, Lord, so that the world might see Your glory, love, forgiveness and revelation. I want them to receive hope and turn to You with joy.

Lord, the vision and desire of my heart is that all people repent and that nobody perishes. I want You to transform them so that they might love You with all their hearts, praise You and bless Your Name because You alone are worthy!

Conclusion

As I mentioned in the beginning of the book, I want to exalt God and His beauty that has worked and transformed many lives through His goodness, through His Word, and through this book.

Everyday I receive messages from people who have read this book. God has revealed His light to many people, He has challenged them, changed them, and has provoked a deep hunger and thirst after Him. Almost every testimony reveals the same thing: a deep desire to know more of God, and a deeper desire to fast and pray. This has been a great joy and encouragement for my family and I because we see the fruits of our labor and sacrifice for God's kingdom.

Many people, including churches, are beginning to enter into extended fasts between 10 and 40 days. Some churches even fast 100 days continuously. Other churches pray, fast and worship for 100 hours continuously. God has rekindled the flame in the hearts of many people, in many churches and in many countries.

During the ministry, there have been many physical and spiritual storms, as well as great and painful trials, attacks, evil spirits, diseases, lack of money, gossip from people against the ministry, against women and against me. It was incredibly difficult! However, at the same time it was a powerful mission, with anointing and fruit for God's glory. The Lord guided use, protected us, and confirmed His works through us as His vessels. We saw the Holy Spirit working through us with power. Oh, how His presence fell upon His people! God prepared people and groups from Romania and abroad to pray for us. God is faithful!

These last seven years have been difficult for us. As a family we have paid a great price to follow Christ in this ministry, but after 7 years we can say that everything is worth it.

After 7 years, we are beginning to see all the seeds that have been sowed begin to grow for God's glory. The fruit that we see today fill my heart with joy because the Father is being glorified! We are glad because we have been obedient to Him and God has used us to play a small part in His wonderful kingdom.

I know, and I'm sure, that for anything good, someone must pay a price.

Now, you who are reading this book, I'm sure that the Holy Spirit is challenging you to enter into His calling and destiny. Do you want to be that person who stands in the gap for your family, your church, your community or your nation? God is still looking for someone who is filled with His love to do His will. God is waiting for you to come before Him, to fast and pray, to deny yourself without pretense and without a personal agenda in total surrender.

He is waiting for you to say, *"Here I am Lord, I have come to do your will."*

The more we seek His face, the more we see His beauty. The more we know Him, the more we fall in love with Him. Once we are connected with Him through His *agape* love, we are able to stand in the gap with fasting and prayer for nations saying, *"Here I am, send me."*

Lord Jesus,

I thank You and I praise You because only Your grace, goodness and Your great plan have helped me to write this book, with all the experiences, wonders and revelations from You and Your Word.

Now, Father God, I pray to bless every person who reads this book, to have new revelations about You, about Your word, about Your love and about Your beauty.

I pray for each one of them to have more passion, determination and desire to know You and to serve You.

I call on Your name and Your blood, Jesus, to protect and bless those who read this book, so that they will enter into their destiny and fulfill Your mighty purposes for their lives.

I declare by faith that no one will be the same! The power and the anointing of the Holy Spirit will touch, change and transform their lives.

I thank You Father for every person who will obey You and do Your will.

I thank you Jesus for the power of Your Name and Your blood that will save many lives.

I thank you Holy Spirit for helping them to discover God's beauty through fasting and prayer.

Amen!